Jesus: The Legacy of Christianity

Jesus:
The Legacy of Christianity

H. M. Kuitert

SCM PRESS

Translated by John Bowden from the Dutch *Jezus: nalatenschap van het Christendom. Schets voor een christologie*, published 1998 by Uitgeverij Ten Have b.v., Baarn, The Netherlands, fourth impression 1999.

0 334 02772 1

This edition first published 1999 by
SCM Press
9–17 St Albans Place London N1 0NX

SCM Press is a division of
SCM-Canterbury Press Ltd

Printed in Great Britain by
Biddles Ltd
Guildford and King's Lynn

Contents

Preface

'A sense of collective insecurity is a form of security'

(Herman de Coninck)

This book isn't a patient exposition of Jesus Christ to raise the spirit or titillate the ear. Nor does it set out to dismiss the many versions of Jesus which are flooding the religious market today, though I hope that those who read it will be somewhat better armed against them as a result. I hope that readers will also be better armed against the seductions of the church's Christ. He too is not the real Christ.

Before readers get the wrong idea, I am just as little concerned to try to extract the real, the absolutely real 'real' Jesus from the material of the tradition. We do not know the real Jesus; we only know what they have made of him.

That is what this book is about. Its theme is what people have made of Jesus from the first followers to the present day. Read it as a kind of reception history of the Gospels, and many of the tangles into which both the churches and the followers of Jesus outside the churches have got themselves will sort themselves out. So the first thing that readers may expect is enlightenment (and they may blame me if they don't get it).

I shall not leave readers in suspense; this book also has a standpoint, a commitment to a particular point of view which, I expect, will make it possible to leave the muddle of views behind, which will purge the religious aspirations to which Jesus has been subjected and which will even serve as a viable way of dealing with the Christian tradition of faith. That's also what readers may expect.

Whether they like all this isn't my affair. Those who don't want to know either how everything could develop as it did, or why Christianity got stuck in what helped it to get going, its christology, mustn't read this book. It will only disturb them, and people don't like being disturbed. Many people can't cope with it, above all over matters of faith. Surely these things are meant to reassure us? I don't agree. There is nothing wrong with a reassuring religion, provided that one's eyes are open to all the uncertainties in it. That's part of believing.

This book is about Jesus, Jesus as the God-man of the classic doctrine of the church and the Jesus of the imaginative works of today. I reject both, for different reasons, but from one and the same perspective: at the very least, Jesus of Nazareth must fit into every version of Jesus. What is a christology without him? So the question is not one of Christ figures as fantasizing about Jesus. Nor is it one of worshipping him as a second God, since he never claimed to be that. Jesus doesn't fill the God-shaped gap in our culture. As an instrument of God, he stands or falls with God.

So this book is more about doctrine. People don't like doctrine; they see it as arguing over the architecture of a castle in the air. Even church people are no longer stirred by it. Who or what God is, what we must think about Jesus – churches want to be successful, and doctrine doesn't help here. That's my view, too. But Jesus did once exist, the Christian church is named after him, and to investigate what has been made of him, and why, seems to me to be a meaningful way of being occupied with the Christian tradition.

I myself would go even further and regard being occupied with doctrine as a form of pastoral work: clarification, illumination if you like. That's the function of theology: it isn't there to *write* but to shed *light*. I'm trying to help both believers and non-believers to broaden their horizons. I know that that has to be done at the cost of a warm nest; that's one of the reasons why people are afraid of it. But the reward lies in a rather greater grasp of the development, in insight into what moves us and others, in the possibility of self-criticism.

Why have I written this book? I have already been preoccupied for a long time with the over-abundant, overflowing worship of Jesus in the Christian church. It's too much of a good thing, too much of an obligation, to make all Christian language Jesus language. Could it also be that we don't mean what we're saying? Add to that the ever expanding possible uses that Jesus, the God-man of the church's christology, seems to be able to offer to starving religious people, and the current jungle of views is complete.

Why does anyone write a book? I read somewhere that whatever has been formulated is no longer chaos. So first of all one writes to clarify one's thoughts, and not to prescribe to others what they must think. But those who write also want to be read, otherwise the manuscript might as well stay in the drawer. So it's clear that I assume that I can help others sort out their chaos.

Amstelveen, 15 March 1998

Introduction

The stripping away of the church's Christ

'Do you see these great buildings? There will not be left here one stone upon another, that will not be thrown down'

Jesus, in Mark 13.2

1. *A culture disappears*

The year was 1962, the place a bridge over a canal in Amsterdam. There for the first time I bought my children an ice-cream on a Sunday. The family was out for a midday walk; I was wearing a black suit (I had preached in the morning and had to preach again in the evening); no one was surprised and I thought nothing to it. The ice-cream man must have regarded us as customers like everyone else, but still for me it was quite a daring act! Later I felt that this tiny event belonged in a wider context, the disappearance of a culture as a way of life which people share with one another and recognize from one another.

For me, the culture was that of a church which is officially called 'The Reformed Churches in the Netherlands'; it had (has?) a very loyal potential membership, recognizable by a unity of behaviour which regulated every branch of life. One lived as a member of the church community which was a kind of central office, which stored energy and guidelines – both – for everyday life. Roman Catholics (and ex-Catholics) can tell similar stories. The Reformed church culture paled by comparison with the rich life of Rome. The minister kept out of the bedroom, the priest didn't.

This culture, life regulated by the church, is almost a thing of the past. Children no longer know what Sunday churchgoing is. They no longer thumb through the Bible and the prayer book if the sermon is too long. They don't even have the nostalgia of the middle generation, because their preoccupations are quite different from those of their parents.

Parents are somewhere in between: what is Christian is no longer fixed. Not only has the old uniformity of behaviour been lost (that was the ice cream on Sunday), but even teaching is up in the air. I grew up in years when people still talked about Abraham Kuyper and the other great names in Dutch theology. These names were respected everywhere. They didn't need radio or television to be known everywhere; they could do without that. They became topics of everyday conversation for ordinary people – even if such people didn't exercise themselves over the problems with which they were concerned – by a process through which these people took talk about their leaders to their workplaces and back home again. Today the names of these leading theologians are forgotten; theological students are no longer enthusiastic about them (*if* they still know anything about them) or choose them only as subjects for dissertations. The world of socialism hasn't fared much better. Marx is dead. A century ago workers still relished names like Engels or Trotsky; their work was studied and discussed. Today not a soul knows who we're talking about.

Sound doctrine – as sound doctrine – has gone adrift with this culture and so too has christology, which is the heart of it. This book is about christology, the church's teaching about Jesus Christ. That teaching might look like a block of reinforced concrete, but nevertheless it's shaking on its foundations. What Jesus prophesied about the temple seems almost applicable to the time-honoured teaching about Jesus: not one stone is left standing upon another.

2. *Jesus Christ is being stripped away*

Christianity takes its name from Jesus Christ, and as a distinctive religion among the religions it stands and falls with him. With christology we are touching on the sinews of its existence. No wonder that many Christians are following developments here, both inside and outside the churches, with bewilderment. For century upon century the teaching about Jesus hasn't changed. God from God, light from light, two natures united in one person; it didn't occur to anyone to meddle with it. Wherever else the knife was put in, it wasn't in christology. That was an unassailable tradition. And suddenly this unassailability is a thing of the past. Not suddenly, there I'm taking too big a step. The Enlightenment put a question mark against the historical trustworthiness of the Gospels; that seemed to be enough to set the wheel turning, but slowly. It turned slowly, or, to dispense with metaphor, few Christians bothered about historical criticism and all that it involves. Only in the second half of the twentieth century has the critical approach also been extending outside the circle of the professionals, and in the past few decades it has broken over the church's Christ like a tidal wave, both inside and outside the church.

The life of Jesus (or what passes for the life of Jesus) has become the subject of films; musicals have been composed about him, some with respect, as an honest attempt to paint a picture of him. But by the same token entertainers make jokes about his life (you have to stop at Muhammad, but you can joke about Jesus), and the respect has gone. I'm not imputing any malice here, but only indicating a shift; and I know from experience how believers can be disconcerted by it. Is nothing holy?

That's outside. Meanwhile, inside the churches the unity of the picture of Jesus has been lost. The conservative part of Christianity hears sermons on Sunday as they've always been given: Jesus and him crucified. The part that calls itself progressive experiments with the significance of Jesus, as the fancy takes it. Will Christianity survive this enrichment of the figure of Christ? Is Jesus Christ decompensating? I'm borrowing this term from medicine. Decompensation is a term for the disintegration of an organism: the equilibrium by which it remains what it is collapses. Is the church's Christ dying before our eyes at the hands of his doctors?

I'm describing a situation in shorthand and therefore incompletely. But I think that the description is convincing enough to indicate that believers of good will are finding themselves in a maze of views from which they cannot discover a way out. I can do something about that maze in this book, if only to show how it fits together.

3. Is Christian doctrine worn out?

In the following chapters I shall be describing the disintegration of the picture of Jesus as a process of the stripping away of the church's Christ, a process with roots which lie in the church's Christ himself. The gilding which the Christian church applied to Jesus of Nazareth doesn't come from above; it doesn't come from eternity and it isn't destined for eternity. People of a particular time and a particular culture clothed Jesus with two natures, and saw him as God on earth. But the human part slipped away; the teeth of time attacked it. So is Christianity worn out? Has the church's christology outlived itself, and is that why it is fanning out on all sides?

This question cannot be answered with a simple yes or no. The church's christology, the classical doctrine of the two natures, and all that it involves, has had its day. I dare to say that: in the course of this book I hope to make clear why that has happened, or, to put it more strongly, why it is unavoidable that we should bid it farewell. That's one side of the matter. At the same time, and with no less verve, Jesus is being covered with new plaster and stickers. That's the other side. Both developments are keeping pace with each other, they're two sides of the same coin. The more the church's Christ is being stripped off, the richer the gilding with which a new time is reclothing him, in an almost endless series of particular christologies. Jesus of Nazareth isn't disappearing from the religious scene. People are leaving the church, but they seem to be taking a bit of Jesus with them. He's clearly usable, indeed he's a sought-after figure; the world is teeming with Jesuses. Think only of the books which are appearing about him. Even if one can't (needn't) take them all seriously, the sheer number of them is an indicator. A boom in new images of Jesus is calling for recognition, if only under the title 'Who was Jesus really?'

Fine! However, what for one is anarchy, fantasy about Jesus run wild, sacrilege, is for another a creative contribution to religion. So we end up at doctrine again. Some criticism must be possible, there must be some criterion, if everything, absolutely everything, isn't to pass as Christian.

4. Interference with doctrine. Is it necessary?

Which christology is more justified and which less, and what authority decides? That's the main question to which this book is devoted, and it offers an answer. So as not to arouse any false expectations, let me say right at the beginning that I do end up somewhere. However, this isn't the restoration of the church's Christ; far less do I make this the criterion for christology.

Nor am I uncritical of the wild christologies (as they are called in this book) which we encounter outside the Christian churches. Not because they are imaginative creations (that once also applied to church doctrine); on the contrary, they deserve respect because of the creative impulse and the fantasy that they sometimes express. But that in itself is no reason for approving of them. So I am taking a stand in two directions: I am undertaking a critical evaluation of the wild christologies, but directing equally firm criticism at the church's Christ.

That goes along with one and the same concept of a christology. I am emphasizing a different point from the church's christology, namely Jesus as an adherent of the Jewish religion, and with the help of this emphasis I want to restore the church's worship of Jesus to appropriate proportions. This book contains a proposal for that; the proposal is in the form of a sketch, but nevertheless it is meant seriously.

That means interfering with church teaching, by simplifying it. That makes such interference look rather more attractive. Nevertheless, it is interference, and the question is: is it really necessary? An alternative would be to rummage around in christology but to leave everything as it is, arguing that in the end the issue is not one of magisterial responsibility but of the mystery of belief in God's presence in our world, which no reasoning, however subtle, can touch. I think that there is much to be said for that alternative. However, people who think like that needn't read my book: they won't enjoy it. The reason why I myself can't take that course is the impossibility of attaching such a version of christology to what we then call the historical Jesus. For me, that is a precondition of accepting any christology whatsoever. I don't mean it as a protest against mysteries of faith, but mysteries of faith shouldn't saddle us with inconsistencies; or rather, to elevate inconsistencies to the level of mysteries of faith too easily ends up in an evasion of intellectual honesty.

5. Jesus as the legacy of Christianity

The title of this book, *Jesus: The Legacy of Christianity*, calls for clarification. The Christian church has bequeathed more than Jesus to European culture. It's left it behind, as orange peel and cartons get left behind after a day out in the country. The church has left behind troubles, religious wars, damaged people, power-crazy hierarchs and so on. But also Jesus.

First, it should be noted that this Jesus is a creation of the Christian church; in other words, Jesus is the church's Christ. There are churches even in the smallest villages of Europe; the maps would show a forest of towers if you could mark them all. For centuries and centuries, the churches preached Jesus Christ in word and image, took morality into their hands, encouraged culture, and got a grip on life and all that there is in it. The church regulated sexual life (it couldn't have been otherwise) and violated it (that needn't have happened); tamed violence (thank God) and at the same time legitimated it (alas); taught the acceptance of suffering but also glorified it; attacked sins where there were no sins and overlooked them where they were unforgivable – and so I could go on. The church's Christ has become culture, Europe as a Christian part of the world. The church's Christ is first a creation of the church and finally – in terms of culture – its legacy.

Secondly, we should note the nature of legacies. If the Christian churches should vanish from Europe (which I neither believe nor argue for), there is still their legacy, and as we know, heirs are free to do what they want with legacies. That's even the point of what we call a legacy: the testator has got rid of it; it has fallen into the hands of the legatee.

In this book I shall begin from that picture of the situation. The church's christology isn't played out; it has fallen into other hands. Formerly there was just one Jesus, Jesus Christ. Defended for centuries by the Christian church with blood, sweat and tears, this one Jesus has been given up: the churches have to watch how others deal with him. The church's Christ has been parcelled out; a multitude of views about Jesus is going the rounds; there is a complete Jesus market.

Rather than hold back that process, I would first of all be in favour of rejoicing at it. Can the churches wish anything better than the church's Christ as material for the human religious quest? Only if this boldness is cherished for what it is can an evaluation begin. That is what I am undertaking in this book, and in it I shall sketch out both the church's Christ and the imaginative creations.

6. The plan of this book

I have said enough about what I'm going to do in this book. I am not concerned with a new version of the historical Jesus, the umpteenth 'authentic' one. Those who expect that will be disappointed. They will do better to read other books. I'm taking quite a different course. What have people made of Jesus in the course of the centuries, why did they do so and what lies behind the continuation of such a process? I already made a beginning on this in my *I Have my Doubts*.

Part I describes how the development began. It can be read as a piece of theological history, with the emphasis on 'what really happened': who began the questions (Reimarus), who saw the consequences (Lessing), who summed up the quest for the historical Jesus (Schweitzer), who said that it was not about history at all (Strauss), and who endorsed him (Bultmann). That sort of information. It provides sufficient explanation for us to be able to guess the consequences.

Part II then describes the turning point in the approach to the Gospels: they are text. Text consists of language, and language calls for exegesis. Hermeneutics becomes the signpost of theology; it lays bare (or at least attempts to lay bare) how Jesus came to be 'meaningful'. So do we still need a reference to the historical Jesus, to what 'really happened', or can we do without it? This part ends with what I have called 'christology as reception history': what have successive generations made of the Gospels? Of course I also include the doctrine of the two natures in the reception history.

Part III defines a standpoint, with as thorough a supporting argument as possible. A christology which seeks to be Christian needs to legitimate itself by Jesus as a historical figure of the past. Much of what is told about him isn't historically sound. That's a pity, but faith doesn't depend on it. One thing is certain: Jesus was an adherent of the Jewish religion. That cuts both ways. The Christian religion must at least be in tune with the 'religion of Christ', which means – to mention the most important point – that Christians cannot worship Jesus as God on earth: he didn't see himself in this way. Is the Christian church more enlightened about God than Jesus himself? It also settles the controversy with the Jews over where Jesus belongs. God's plan, to which the Christian church holds, doesn't change through Jesus (that is why the ritual of atonement has just as important a place in Christianity as it does in Judaism); all that changes is the scope of Jesus' God. He is also God-for-non-Jews: the Christian faith knows no ethnic limitations.

In Part IV I come to the tricky question of what we must then do with the past: the doctrine of two natures, the Creed, the Christian festivals of Jesus. And also Jesus piety, which creates a separate relationship with Jesus alongside the relationship with God. That's not on, as I shall say at that point. You can't pray to Jesus; that makes Jesus a second God, and even in terms of classical christology that's a serious heresy.

The last part (Part V) sums things up under the heading of 'legacy'. Jesus bequeathed the church (at least, that is what the churches think; whether it is the case is another matter), and the churches in turn bequeathed the church's Christ to Europe. We can do what we want with him. But this development has a perspective. I see Europe itself in turn as a legacy of the church's Christ, Christ transformed into cultural Christianity.

7. *No theology. The readers*

I also aim to write clearly in this book, having in view even people who think that religion needs to be an obscure matter. I shall not use technical jargon; there is no need for it. The readers I am looking for are those who find my theme interesting enough to make some effort to deal with it. So although I am not talking with theologians about theology, nor writing for specialists, I shall not just squat down to teach a kindergarten lesson. That is to overestimate the degree of difficulty in theology (everyone can do it with some patience) and to underestimate the reader's intelligence.

Theology brings clarification; that is why it is practised as a discipline. It doesn't judge, nor does it prescribe. I don't do that in this book either. It is meant as an aid to map-reading: which way do the roads go and how do I get out of my maze? I don't do more than that. Not to prescribe anything isn't to say that everything is equally good. That's a kind of self-destructing liberalism. This book is about doctrine, with reasoning and arguments. It's also about christology.

Christology isn't the whole of doctrine; it's only part of it, by no means the least part, but no more than a part. For an account of the Christian tradition of faith as a whole, for other topics than christology, for the rise of religion in human history, for the question why it isn't nonsensical to believe in God (to mention just a few topics), I would refer readers to other books of mine.

Doctrine isn't everything, not even the whole of doctrine. Life goes on, even if the truth cannot be established. Children are conceived, born, have families themselves, and die. Summer, winter and autumn go round as if there were no christology. This thought can keep us from having excessive expectations of religious truth or excessive fights over it.

I

A Stone in the Pool

The present tense

Your holy hearsay
is not evidence:
give me the good news
in the present tense.

What happened
nineteen centuries ago
may not have happened:
how am I to know?

The living truth
is what I long to see.
I cannot live upon
what used to be.

So shut the Bible up
and show me how
the Christ you talk about
is living now.

Sidney Carter

Nothing happened as described

1. *The evangelists perpetrated a deception. Reimarus*

No one had previously made out the evangelists to be deceivers. Of course, as long as the Christian church has existed there have been a great many views about the person of Jesus, but most of them have fitted within the framework of church dogma, or at least have seemed to. As long as the divinity of Jesus was beyond dispute, even what according to the rules should have been called heresy caused little or no commotion. Even the great dispute between Rome and the Reformation (Luther and Calvin) was not about the person of Jesus Christ, since all parties accepted the early church dogma of the two natures united in one person lock, stock and barrel. To put a question-mark after Jesus' divinity, if need be, was beyond the horizon of the time.

But that was precisely what happened in the eighteenth century, to the bewilderment of the church and theology. The starting point of this, and of the quest for the so-called historical Jesus which it set off, was a number of polemical writings by Reimarus (died 1768). Reimarus was not a theologian, and after his death these were published (anonymously) by Lessing (died 1781) under the title *Wolfenbüttel Fragments*. Reimarus didn't mince matters (moreover the whole of the church world of the time attacked him); in the fifth fragment he called the church's teaching about Jesus a fiction, and the evangelists outright deceivers. In his view we have to distinguish between the purpose of Jesus and the purpose of his disciples. What Jesus wanted (Reimarus thought that he was a kind of revolutionary; he saw Jesus as a zealot) failed. See his cry from the cross, 'My God, my God, why have you forsaken me?' Albert Schweitzer would later draw the same conclusion on the basis of the same statement: Jesus is a failed Messiah. However, the disciples, Reimarus went on, would not and could not give up their ideal, and the picture of Christ, resurrection and all, was their idea. In other words, the church's teaching about Christ is a cheat and not worth believing in.

That was precisely what Reimarus wanted to achieve with his historical approach: he deliberately wanted to launch an assault on the church's teaching about Jesus. In his view, the pale Christ of the church, in the wrappings of dogma, is an insult to honest people: a being exalted to supernatural stature, to whom all humanity is alien, cannot possibly be an object of worship.

We shall not be concerned further with the picture that Reimarus wants to put in its place. He is on the wrong track, as most historical critics today agree. The consequences of his polemic make it significant, and these consequences proved fatal for the peace of the church's Christ, which never recovered. With his *Fragments* Reimarus wrought havoc in a way which still determines the course of the discussion: for the first time the church's Christ and Jesus of Nazareth no longer coincide. The way to the investigation of the so-called historical Jesus lies open.

Reimarus himself did not get that far. For him, historical research was at the service of criticism, bringing down the church's Christ. Historical investigation led to exposure. Only years later – roughly speaking, in the age of Romanticism – was historical criticism given a positive function. It has to keep the authentic Jesus above water; the Jesus who remains when the clothes of the church's Christ have been stripped from him. I shall go on to talk about this in detail in a later chapter.

First I want to show that Reimarus' intervention was an attempt to get Jesus out of the deep freeze of church dogma, but that the result was the opposite: he became frozen, and the more time went, on the more frozen he became.

2. *The dispute over 'what really happened' flares up*

The Christian tradition of faith proclaims as good news that around the beginning of our era a boy was born of the virgin Mary, conceived of the Holy Spirit, that this boy was the Son of God and that through him, his cross and resurrection, God saved humankind from being lost, after which the Son returned to the Father in heaven. That's a short summary. That means that God's ultimate self-revelation has a historical character, has a place in history, consists of historical events.

This brief description makes it clear why people joined forces against Reimarus: he was tampering with an essential element of the Gospels, their character as event. If Jesus didn't really walk on the water, didn't really summon his friend Lazarus from the grave, and didn't rise from the dead and ascend to heaven; if all that is no longer historical truth but the fantasy of his disciples; if the real truth is different, the Christian message of salvation falls apart like a house of cards. Believing means believing that the gospel story really happened, truth as historical truth.

The 'what really happened' which is still argued about today is thus a point that was introduced into the church's reflection by Reimarus. The traditional doctrine of the church, orthodoxy (I use this term to describe the traditional standpoints) could set up a line of defence against Reimarus only by taking its stand, establishing itself, on 'what really happened'. It did this sometimes very reasonably, sometimes utterly obtusely, as a 'no it isn't – yes it is' game. But in fact it was by no means a game: the orthodox felt that the truth of Christian faith was at stake. Christians believe in 'saving facts', as they later came to be called; they believe that the cross and resurrection of Jesus 'really happened'. Indeed they were *saving* facts; they were facts with a significance, a far-reaching significance; but saving facts remain facts, said the conservative Christians: they must really have happened. If not, then faith is stripped of its content. So those who talk of 'saving facts' want to bring out two things. First of all the belief that in the historical person of Jesus, his actions and his faith, his suffering, cross and resurrection, God has performed his saving work for humankind and the world. But in that case everything must have 'really happened'. In other words, believing is once again believing in 'what really happened', otherwise the bottom has dropped out of Christian faith. Those who do not believe that saving facts are *facts* really do not believe anything; to use the language of the Athanasian Creed, they cannot be saved.

The idea that the dispute over 'what really happened' is the real dispute over Christian faith continues in conservative circles to the present day. That's a pity, because it is not only a tragic but (as I shall show later) also an unnecessary fight, which causes great confusion and – I think – dissuades people from faith rather than helping them to believe.

It isn't that there is a defect in the passion for what really happened and what didn't. On the contrary. But the way in which in the orthodox tradition people tried (and still try) to deal with the problem that arose is the stumbling block. I shall first discuss that problem, in the next section, and then steer round it.

3. Events call for historical investigation

Historical events are open to historical investigation: what has happened and what hasn't. In any tradition, Christian or non-Christian, we try to distinguish between the two. Long before the time of Reimarus, for example, investigations had made it clear that the Twelve Articles of faith (called the Apostles' Creed) did not come from the twelve apostles but from a Christian community in Rome, and so before Reimarus there were more examples of historical investigation which amounted to criticism of the tradition.

It is clear where the trouble lies for Christian faith. If historical events form the content of faith, then whether we like it or not, faith is exposed to historical, viz. scholarly investigation, which is now called on to judge its truth, in so far as this consists in what 'really happened'. That puts believers in a fix. Suppose that tomorrow it is suddenly proved that Jesus didn't walk on the water. All right, that isn't the end of the world, it's an innocent example which I have deliberately chosen; it won't turn faith upside down. But if tomorrow it should prove that Jesus was an ordinary man who led an ordinary human life, who married and had children (like so many rabbis from that time), what then?

A few years ago we had a good illustration in the Netherlands of the problem which arises. I'm referring to the Mary of Brunssum, the statue of the Blessed Virgin that in the middle of 1995 stood shedding tears of sorrow about the world. Were they real tears? Scholarly investigation has to establish that, and when the tears proved to be solder (or some other fixative which kept the eyes in the statue), that was the end of the miracle. Believers were an illusion the poorer, and credibility was punished in a tragic way.

I know that the parallel isn't complete, but it makes one think. To mention something that will only concern us later: what could the 'what really happened' at Brunssum have been good for? A miracle, indeed, a sign of life from the supernatural order, a manifestation of the heavenly Mary, or something more pedestrian: a crowd-puller for pilgrims. But would humankind really and truly have benefited from that? I shall return to the point, for of course there is a background to this fixation on 'what really happened'.

For the moment I have another concern. The character of Christian truth as event seems to be an extremely precarious one. Orthodoxy doesn't want to drop it, for then faith collapses: at a stroke it loses its content and its foundation. But the more it insists on it, the more it hands over faith to the scientists, exegetes, professionals who now judge historical events. So in the end once again the certainty of faith is at stake. Certainty about 'what really happened' is, in ordinary terms, certainty which depends on scientific investigation. But in the traditional view faith stands and falls with this certainty. In that case can we contract out a decision about what 'really happened' to scientific investigators?

4. Salvation history and ordinary history

I shall not weary readers excessively with the complicated arguments which were devised in the centuries after Reimarus to make saving facts facts and yet not ordinary facts. The orthodox theologians argued that the saving facts are the work of God in history and that God's work cannot be established by ordinary means. Thus a virtue was made of necessity: ordinary facts are accessible to everyone, but because of their special character saving facts are not. So we have a kind of double book-keeping: ordinary history and salvation history, historical events and superhistorical events (think of the parallel with natural and super-natural). 'Superhistorical' then means both outside the reach of histori-cal investigation yet 'what really happened'.

I don't wish to disparage this solution, but I don't find it acceptable. There is something tragic about the fixation on 'what really happened'. What the conservative wing of Christianity wanted – rightly – to dis-sociate itself from is the so-called positivistic understanding of history: the real facts are bare facts, facts without meaning. The meaning is so to speak stuck on later. That idea rests on a misunderstanding. Facts are always and only narrated facts: events, I would prefer to say. Events are facts with and in their meaning, and because of this meaning they con-tinue to be related, otherwise we would never have heard of them. The distinction between 'historical' (ordinary facts) and 'superhistorical' (facts with the significance of salvation history), which the orthodox seized on to preserve 'what really happened', loses sight of that, and involuntarily falls victim to the very evil that it wanted to combat: it leaves the positivistic belief in bare facts (to which historical research has access) to the scholars, and it rescues the saving facts, facts with the significance of salvation history, from the rubbish heap by bringing them into a storm-free zone which is inaccessible to scholarly investiga-tion.

That is not only to step into the trap that they wanted to avoid, believing respect for bare facts, but it also solves nothing. On what did orthodoxy base its certainty that the question was one of facts, albeit saving facts? On its doctrine of Holy Scripture as the trustworthy Word of God, also in the sense of a reliable historical source. What was written, happened. On the basis of the traditional view of the Bible, historical investigation (which now begins with doubt about 'what really happened') is superfluous, and not only that: since Reimarus there has also been something suspicious about it.

So the conservative side of the church (the majority) solved the problem of historical certainty with a dogmatic answer to a historical question. Or rather a good question ('What really happened?') is given a wrong answer ('That's already established'). This was a solution born out of necessity, certainly understandable on the premises of that time, but not a real answer to a very normal challenge. Anxiety at losing everything played (and still plays) the main role. This anxiety is responsible for orthodoxy not seeing the problem very clearly and giving too hasty an answer. It rooted the certainty about the past, about the saving facts as *facts*, in a theory, a theory about the Bible, so as to rescue it from the hands of learned investigators. Orthodoxy did not get to the question whether faith can rest on historical facts.

5. The quicksand of history: Lessing

Lessing had already seen this. According to him, Reimarus with his *Fragments* had put a healthy drop of venom into the church's opinion-forming. Healthy? Certainly, the content of the Christian faith was events, so it all fitted together; according to Lessing, God had his reasons for this. But, as Reimarus' work shows, a dependence on events would get the church stuck. Quicksand, said Lessing: my neighbour who allows his faith to rest on historical events is building on quicksand. Soon someone will come to argue it away, not with idle stories but with a thorough scientific investigation which makes it probable that something quite different happened, or perhaps nothing at all.

Thus according to Lessing the fixation on 'what really happened', on historical events as the foundation of faith, means leaving the certainty of Christian faith to historically trained scholars. That can prove only one thing: the principle is wrong, historical truths can never be the foundation of faith. His good advice is to desist and to look for the foundation somewhere else, in something that is secure and cannot be undermined by scientific investigation. The shaky historical truths (the truth which the evangelists relate) must be replaced by eternal truths, by the eternal truth of God's love for humankind. God is love. That is the essence of Christian faith, and Jesus is the illustration of it.

Whether Lessing was right that God's love of humankind is an eternal truth is still to be seen. I shall be returning to it when I touch on Kierkegaard's doubts about eternal truths. First I shall let Lessing score a second point. Even if you believe that everything really happened as the evangelists would have us believe, what advantage is that to you? Is that what we as Christians mean by 'believing'? Lessing indicates the shortcomings of historical faith in precisely the same way as orthodoxy past and present. More is needed to be a Christian than to believe that everything really happened as we are told in the Gospels. Are Lessing and, for example, the Reformed Alliance then in agreement on that?

6. From historical faith to saving faith. Orthodoxy

Those who do not believe that God has revealed himself in the events of Jesus' life are not Christians. But are you a Christian if you accept that everything 'really happened'? No, for the fathers of orthodoxy that was going too far. And rightly so. Just imagine that everything really happened as the evangelists relate it and that the interpretation of the Christian church fits in with this: Jesus is the Son of God, he came down from the heights of heaven, he sacrificed his life to God, he became the atonement for human guilt, rose on the third day and overcame death, then to go to God in heaven. There may be differences over the precise significance, but just imagine that to a large degree the question of 'what really happened' has been solved. What would it benefit a person to believe all that = believe that it really happened? Nothing.

Orthodoxy has had to concede this: to believe that the Gospels are telling us the historical truth was at least necessary for being a Christian, but it wasn't enough. Thus the term 'historical faith' came into vogue. That means that it isn't enough simply to believe that everything happened precisely as the church proclaims. Of course you must also believe that! Without that faith you are nowhere. However, a historical faith isn't yet a saving faith, and only when the latter has been formed in you may you say that you are a child of God.

What is a saving faith, and how does a person get from one to the other, from a historical to a saving faith? The somewhat old-fashioned-sounding terminology is that of orthodoxy, and I am using it here and following its argument here, because it will help me to show the great changes that the experience of faith has undergone over the last few centuries.

The classical tradition of faith as used by orthodoxy had no difficulty in leaving Jesus as a historical person quietly in the past. Certainly that caused problems. Every minister has felt that when he has had to preach from the Gospels. Jesus healed a paralysed man; does he heal like that today? He even raises the dead; does he still do that today? As a student I saw a film by Kai Munk which depicted this problem graphically: a preacher believed that Jesus could also bring the dead to life today, but came to grief on that belief – the dead remained dead – and lost his faith. But as I have said, orthodoxy didn't deal with that kind of question. Jesus today? For that, Jesus didn't need to be dragged from the past to the present, for after his ascension he had gone over as it were to another mode of existence: to put it somewhat inappropriately but clearly, a lesser Jesus came into being, more Jesus in the form of Word and Sacrament, by whom people in the church could comfort themselves as much and as often as they wished. Historical faith (with which everything has to begin) at some point developed into a saving faith under the breath of the Spirit, by which the sinner is brought to life. The view of the church – I would add in passing – was therefore also different: the church was the authorized distributor of Jesus, transformed into Word and Spirit or transubstantiated into sacrament.

7. *Historical faith and the person of Jesus*

Historical faith is not a saving faith. Lessing, too, holds this view, but he thinks rather differently from the usual Reformed theologians. That comes about – again – through Reimarus. In fact this removed another stone from the structure of orthodoxy. One may say that the historical investigation of the Gospels brings the historical Jesus to the fore; it makes him the focal point of Christian faith. But wasn't he that already? Certainly, but in a different way, as the church's Christ, formulated once and for all by the Council of Chalcedon (451). Doctrine about him was fixed for good, and accordingly, as I have said, dealing with him was regulated by word and sacrament.

Investigation into what 'really happened' almost automatically brings under review the ritual, in a sense impersonal, way of dealing with Jesus, and that meant in turn a shift in the concept of the Christian religion. The focus of faith shifts from the Christ of dogma to Christ as Jesus, as a person, in the terminology of the nineteenth century: 'the person of Jesus', or often 'the person of Christ'. That is already clear in the case of Schleiermacher (died 1834), who was also inspired by the Herrnhutters, and also for well-known theologians like Albert Ritschl and his pupil Wilhelm Herrmann, for whom everything turns on the 'person of Christ'. It can certainly be said that Karl Barth (who in turn sat at the feet of Wilhelm Herrmann) did not get his theology-as-christology from a stranger.

If the person of Jesus becomes the centre of Christian faith, then of course the characteristics of 'believing' are called into question.

Believing must consist in a living relationship to the 'person of Christ'. But how does one get a living relationship with someone from the past? Another problem crops up.

The past is the past. We ourselves weren't there. Jesus may have made an impression on the people who met him; they may even have seen him or felt him to be God on earth, but they were people living then. We weren't there; we are living now, and hear only what others say about him. How can their stories ever arouse the emotional reaction which the disciples' encounter with Jesus evoked at that time? Impossible, said Lessing. Moreover in his view a deep ditch divides the present (us now) from the past (Jesus then), and the more that believers put the emphasis on 'what really happened', on Jesus' historical actions, as a basis for faith, the more they will face that unbridgable gulf. A historical Jesus has no effect.

Thus for Lessing believing as believing in 'what really happened' is too little, above all because it does not produce a true religion: a demonstration of spirit and power, inward resurrection, rebirth, conversion, attaching oneself to God with all one's heart, to mention just a few phrases from his arsenal. At this point Lessing and the Reformed Fathers are utterly at one. They are even in agreement that as a historical figure, Jesus is a figure from the past and must remain so. But Lessing did not provide a different aspect of Jesus (Jesus fused into word and sacrament), as orthodoxy did. Thus for him the question becomes that of how the deep ditch between then and now, between Jesus and us who live today, can be bridged. Or rather, that is no longer a question, since in his view it is impossible. We are not contemporaries of Jesus, nor can we become so; we cannot get to him nor he to us.

What I mean is: for classical doctrine the question was not how we get to Jesus but how Jesus comes to us, becomes contemporaneous with us. It had an answer to this question. We can meanwhile see what a shift there is with the reversal (since Lessing): how we can come to the Jesus of that time; how can we become contemporaneous with him?

8. *Jesus as an illustration/demonstration of God's love*

God is love, and Jesus is an illustration or a demonstration (I use both words in the same sense) of God's love. For Lessing that was the way to leave Jesus in the past, as someone of that time, not fiddling with the gulf between then and now. And at the same time it gave Jesus a key role for faith. He sees the 'then' as a temporal expedient, pedagogy from God, for people who have to be brought up to the truth which is truth even without this pedagogy: God is love. Is that so odd? Jesus as a demonstration of the God who is love? Despite the scorn that Lessing drew down upon himself from orthodoxy, there are countless orthodox Christians to the present day who firmly agree with this position: to see Jesus as an illustration (or demonstration) of God's love is quite normal Christianity.

But Lessing got stuck. If we make Jesus' life and fate a pedagogical instrument, the teaching that through him we arrive at the insight who God is – Jesus is the revealer – there comes a moment when we know this, and no longer need the pedagogical instrument. Strictly speaking, to see God as the loving Father makes the role of Jesus obsolete. Had we not been such backward people, Jesus so to speak would not even have been necessary. The truth about God is not constituted by Jesus but only demonstrated by him. So how necessary is Jesus still as an illustration?

By way of a contrast, orthodoxy arrived at the opposite edge of the abyss, and sometimes toppled into it. Jesus' historical life and work is indispensable, because Jesus *makes* God love; God wasn't first love, but became love through Jesus' sacrifice. Therefore the history of Jesus as the Gospels present it is an indispensable history, and as such forms the content of preaching.

This is a theory which puts its finger on something which is overlooked by the idea of illustration: there must be an answer to the question why Jesus is so necessary, why his historical role, his cross, his resurrection was necessary, extremely necessary. Alas, orthodoxy located this need as a need of God himself. Only through Jesus' sacrifice does God begin to think differently about the sinner. Someone like Calvin found that a crude distortion of Christian faith. God didn't need to have his mind changed. God already was love, even if we had no awareness of this. But in that case why Jesus? I shall come back to this question later.

Back to the idea that Jesus is an illustration or demonstration of God's love for humankind: it is the idea that we can read the Gospels as the embodiment of a universal truth, a historical (as Lessing thought) or mythical embodiment. Of course the difference mustn't be overlooked: in the case of Lessing something happens in the history of Jesus which cannot be lost sight of for the education of the human race. If you go to read the Gospels as a mythical garb for a message, then nothing need have happened; the past is of no importance. In a later chapter I shall show how this notion, too, gained ground. We then get rid of the problem of how we can become the contemporary of someone from the past, but the price that has to be paid is high: he (Jesus) need not even have lived to be important.

9. *Contemporaneous with Jesus. Kierkegaard*

For a solution to Lessing's problem – we were never there, so how ever could we come under the impact of Jesus as a person? – we must go to the Danish philosopher Kierkegaard. What he has to say is a knock-on effect, one of the widest ripples from the stone which Reimarus threw into the Christian pool. Kierkegaard storms against the orthodoxy of his days: the figure of Christ, far from being made present through word and sacrament, has been made impersonal through the church, and thus sabotaged in his effect as the Christ. What you hear preached in the church, Kierkegaard said mockingly, are negotiations over the firm God and Son. But he was no less hostile to the liberals, the enlightened free thinkers and philosophers (above all Hegel) of his time. In his view they don't know what they're talking about because they don't know what religious truth is. Truth about God isn't a universal truth, however religious it is made out to be. There is no such thing as universal truth about God; people don't arrive at faith by reasoning and argument. If they do, then this is a bloodless faith, and according to Kierkegaard it isn't authentic faith. Religious truth is personal; I am the only one who knows it; for knowing means joining in, experiencing Jesus as saviour. I think that it was Wittgenstein who described the difference between Kierkegaard and the rest (as one may put it) with the help of a brief discussion between an atheist and a Kierkegaardian Christian. The atheist says, 'God doesn't exist.' The Christian shakes his head: 'How can you say that? He has saved me.'

According to Kierkegaard, one can certainly be confronted today with Jesus who lived yesterday, as though we were his contemporaries. Contemporaneity with Jesus, he said, is not bound up with time: to want to go back to former times to join with the great and the good is even a perverse desire. There was nothing to see! According to the Gospel, the essence of Jesus was that he had no presence or glory. And according to the apostles, this inconspicuous man is the Son of God. Those who stumble over this haven't understood what revelation is: God reveals himself by veiling himself. There was nothing to see and yet there was God: that is precisely the God whom we encounter there.

Kierkegaard calls that the paradox, so to speak the trade mark, of God's action. That is how it is to be recognized. And preaching which is authentic Christian preaching still does today what it did for people of that time; it confronts them with the decisive choice of their lives. It is preaching of the paradox that the infinite God makes himself present in the form of the finite, the exalted in the form of the humiliated, the wise in the form of what people who claim to be understanding can only find absurd. Moreover faith is something quite different from accepting that there is a God, something quite different from accepting that this God is the redeemer: believing is going down on one's knees, submitting to the impossibility that is nevertheless reality. Truth (God exists) and reality (he is my saviour) coincide in faith. Outside faith there is no religious truth; only the outpourings of clergy and professors in theology who think that they understand things and simply by talking evade faith.

So how is the gulf between then and now bridged? By preaching Jesus as a paradox, as an affront to our understanding, as an impossible possibility, which puts us back to square one. In this way, according to Kierkegaard, we engage in the same confrontation as the first disciples, the people of the first hour, the people who were there bodily. Bultmann, who was very much under the impact of Kierkegaard (as too was Barth when he still made a common front with Bultmann), was later to say that the preaching of Jesus Christ announces bankruptcy to a person, and that believing is accepting the bankruptcy.

I shall not go further into the repercussions which Kierkegaard had in his turn. His influence extended far wider than I have sketched here. The definition of truth in (later) existential philosophy was prepared for by Kierkegaard. Much theology in the middle of the twentieth century clung to him like convolvulus.

Nor shall I investigate belief as submitting to something which must seem absurd to a reasonable person. That needn't extend to the *Credo quia absurdum* (I believe because it is contradictory), although it seems to. But it's let go of again. Faith as a leap, if not a leap in the dark (which then immediately proves not to be dark), remains.

The question was how we can become contemporaneous with the Jesus of that time. Kierkegaard's solution doesn't need a 'what really happened'; 'what really happened' isn't the foundation of faith, and so historical investigation can do neither good nor harm. Yet according to Kierkegaard, the Jesus of the past can make an impact on the present, by making no impact. And to teach us to see that as God's way to human beings is the masterpiece of faith.

Is this a solution? Here are two remarks by way of a commentary. Certainly believing amounts to more than accepting that it 'really happened'. But that is rather different from there being no truths which can be related further; if that were the case, there would be no Christian proclamation left. The personal element of faith is preceded by the 'hearsay'. One must at least have heard the gospel of the Christian church, the story of Jesus, and made some sense of it, to join in that story. *Traditio quaerens fidem*, tradition precedes faith.

My second remark is that personal commitment, even personal faith, does not make anything a religious truth. Jesus was not truly born of a virgin because I believe that: people can believe in blatant untruths. Faith certainly makes something a subject of devotion and conviction for me. Faith needs conviction and dedication, a demonstration of the spirit and power, if it is to be worthy of the name faith; it must prove itself by that demonstration. But no demonstration of spirit and power is as yet a proof of faith, let alone of its truth.

10. 'The religion of Christ'

In the next part of this book I shall try to show that this fixation on 'what really happened', with all the effects that it has had, isn't necessary. It has made belief in God more difficult than it need have been, and thus betrays a background which I would call a wrong move rather than a foundation. Faith has no foundation; that is what faith is. Moreover once again to lay that foundation in 'what really happened' makes the train go completely off the rails.

It is quite appropriate for me to leave what did or did not happen in Jesus to the historian. The place which Jesus occupies in Christian faith is a key one; however, the certainty of the Christian faith does not depend on the outcome of historical investigation into Jesus but on the encounter with God which is marked out in the Christian quest for God. The uncertainty, the quicksand, in which Christian faith rightly finds itself if it cannot give up 'what truly happened' is a kind of punishment for sin. It could rescue itself from this by a dodgy manoeuvre: that's what it says in the Bible and that's what really happened. This manoeuvre is not only unnecessary; it perpetuates a disturbance in christology which I shall be discussing in the next chapter, the disturbance which makes Jesus an independent, second quest alongside the quest in which Jesus himself was engaged. And so Christians, as an extension of this, have to seek two certainties: one about God and one about Jesus as the historical person who is Son of God. That doesn't work at all. There is only one certainty, for there is only one quest, and this doesn't lie in the clarity of a universal religious truth, far less in a leap (as its opposite), but in the finding of the One was known to us by hearsay through the traditional quest.

To impose a second certainty on belief, namely historical certainty about 'what really happened', comes up against the insoluble problems that I have tried to describe in this chapter. It squares the circle, rejecting historical (viz. scientific) investigation and at the same time observing the requirement of historical certainty about Jesus' life.

Where does the train go off on the wrong line? According to Reimarus, the religion of Jesus, 'the religion of Christ', didn't coincide with 'the Christian religion'. He thought that the Christian religion was better, was authentic, and so we have to dissociate ourselves from the 'religion of Christ'. Since Reimarus, this question has constantly recurred, and although later generations think less in Enlightenment terms about Christianity and are less negative about Judaism, the standard answer remains that Christianity does not coincide with the 'religion of Christ'.

But that is a quite remarkable outcome. The result is that Christianity engages in a different quest for God from that of Jesus. That may well have been the case down the centuries: naively or deliberately, the 'religion of Christ' has not come up for consideration in the construction of the church's christology. The whole development of christology can be held accountable for that, with the result that one quest is made into two. But all that is still to come.

2

Who was Jesus really? Albert Schweitzer and historical criticism

1. Do the Gospels show us the real Jesus?

I have followed the dispute over 'what really happened' up till now in so far as it has become a dispute (to the present day) between orthodoxy and its adversaries. In this chapter I shall unwind another thread from the cluster of problems with which Reimarus saddled Christianity as a result of his *Fragments*: the historical investigation of the real Jesus. We shall soon see that this coped with only half of the problem. If the evangelists tell their story and the story doesn't fit, then there are two possibilities if one wants to go further. One can engage in historical investigation, and ask what really happened and what didn't. That came to be called historical criticism. But one can also follow the evangelists, the text as such, for if everything didn't really happen, there's also something wrong with the text of the Gospels. What kind of a writing is it which presents itself as a story yet doesn't prove to be historically reliable? This led to what later came to be called literary criticism. These are two approaches to the same question. Moreover Reimarus didn't just raise the historical question, what really happened, but also seized the evangelists by the collar, or rather by their texts. The evangelists draw a deceptive picture of Jesus: we don't encounter the authentic Jesus. Later investigators did not adopt his negative attitude towards the evangelists. Like him, they indeed thought that Jesus must necessarily be dragged out from the material of the church's Christ, but unlike him they thought that they could peel the authentic Jesus from the Gospels, provided that these were read properly. Historical investigation had to serve this good aim, and not break with Jesus.

This questioning already inevitably brings us to the character of the Gospel narratives. However, I shall only go into that later; in this chapter I shall limit myself to historical investigation. That also works on the Gospel narratives, but sees them through the eyes of the historian. These (the eyes) form the problem, as we shall see.

I shall use this first section of the chapter to set out at least the main ingredients of the investigation, which since Reimarus have remained fairly constant. They relate above all to the presuppositions with which the investigator operates. To begin with the main one: the investigation is undertaken in opposition to the church's Christ. Every investigator says that we can no longer begin with this nowadays. What must emerge is the authentic Jesus. That brings up the second ingredient: for the investigators, 'the authentic Jesus' is a Jesus of flesh and blood, Jesus who lived then. The dogmatic Christ of the church can never have been the authentic figure.

The 'authentic' figure is the so-called historical Jesus. This term is also an ingredient of the problem. I shall use it now and then, but it can be misleading, as will emerge (that is why it has become an ingredient). It suggests that the so-called historical Jesus is the fruit of unprejudiced scientific research into history: for the authentic Jesus we have to go to the researchers. Generally speaking, that is a mistake. Of course the opposite view, that for the authentic Jesus we have to go to the church, to the confessing believer, is just as a great a mistake. People seem to be able to confess anything. A statement does not become true by virtue of its character as a confession. But that aside, quite apart from the question how unprejudiced historical investigation can be, the investigators whom I describe here were in any case not like that. Their investigation was made in the service of one all-embracing publicly acknowledged interest: the 'authentic Jesus' must be brought from under the shine and glitter of the church's dogma, and to whom could the task be better entrusted than to those engaged in historical criticism?

2. *Historical criticism*

From the publication of the *Wolfenbüttel Fragments* on, all kinds of new investigations into the authentic Jesus began, with great zeal and just as great fantasy, in the firm belief that inquiries into the past could peel him from the embrace of fantasy and the depiction of dogma. Historical criticism cannot be dictated to by what the church says or does not say.

Those investigating the Gospels cannot begin immediately from 'what truly happened' – that's where the 'critical' element comes in. So specialists may not read the Gospels as texts of supernatural origin, which people must keep their hands off; they must be read in the ordinary way, like all texts: with eyes sharpened by historical criticism to see what they claim has 'really happened' but has not. Nowadays such an approach attracts no attention; every approach to any text, sacred or not, is historical-critical by nature. The term has lost its barb. But in the time when it was coined (and for a long time afterwards) it was a real battle-cry which resounded in the ears of conservative Christianity as a summons to close ranks.

It could hardly be otherwise. For the initial aim of historical investigation was ultimately to provide a rival picture of Jesus, however positively meant. The motive force or engine behind all this was to show Jesus' attractiveness to a new generation: the authentic Jesus is more attractive than the church's Jesus. Jesus' true greatness must be restored in its original splendour. That was the greatest task that the ranks of nineteenth-century theologians had set themselves.

I shall not weary readers with examples of this here. In the next section we shall meet a few of them. Sometimes their pathos is moving, and at other times they arouse one's wrath by their malice. But no matter what image of Jesus the researchers conjure up, only one conclusion is possible: they wasted their efforts on it. Not because there was nothing to find fault with in the image that the Christian church had developed of Jesus of Nazareth – the church's Christ, I shall call it (we shall see the contrary) – but because the investigation was doomed to failure in the form in which it was undertaken. The man who showed that irrefutably was Albert Schweitzer.

3. *Albert Schweitzer*

Albert Schweitzer (he died in 1965) wrote a book in which he examined the history of the historical investigation of Jesus' life. His study not only surveyed that investigation as it had been undertaken up to his day, but also put an end (a provisional end) to it. The book is a big one (more than 600 pages) and informative, with a wealth of facts about theologians and researchers from the eighteenth and nineteenth century, but above all magnificently written and unequalled in its illumination of predecessors and contemporaries. It is compulsory literature for (rising) theologians.

What does Schweitzer have to say? In short, historical research has not produced what people expected of it. The Jesus of Nazareth who is so dear to us, the Messiah, the Saviour of the world, who proclaimed the kingdom of God, indeed who thought that he was establishing it on earth and gave his life in belief in his divine calling – this Jesus never existed. The quest for him was begun joyfully: people went out in the conviction that they could give new life to the bloodless figure of the church's Christ, and indeed a human being came to meet the investigators. The rest of the passage is too splendid not to quote: 'however, he (= Jesus) did not stay, but went past our time and returned to his own'. By that Schweitzer means that the Jesus who finally appears from historical investigation is so different from us, so much someone from a past time, that we no longer know what to make of him. He represents a thought-world which has become alien to us. According to Schweitzer, Jesus saw himself as the eschatological bringer of salvation, the bringer of salvation in the end-time (in theological language *eschaton* means 'the end'), who proclaimed the end time, expected the end of the world during his lifetime and acted accordingly. In other words, Jesus is an apocalyptic figure, a kind of prophet as Dennis Potter has since depicted him in his film *The Son of Man*.

Apocalyptic is a technical term from the study of religions: it denotes a religious current (with a great following at the beginning of our era) which believes that it can uncover the secret of history ('apocalypse' = 'unveiling'). Spectacular events are about to occur; they are signs of the catastrophic end which has already begun (so 'apocalypse' can also stand for Armageddon), and will end with the destruction of the old world and the establishment of the new world, the world of the kingdom of God. The biblical book of Revelation is a typically apocalyptic book.

According to Schweitzer, Jesus also lived in this thought world; he believed that the end of the world was near, and sent out his disciples to prepare the world for the end (see Matthew 10). He saw himself as 'the Son of man' from the book of Daniel, that mysterious figure who will come on the clouds of heaven to judge the world. In short, he felt that he was the person who not only proclaimed the messianic kingdom but would also establish it on earth. He even wanted to force this end by offering himself as a sacrifice when the end did not come by itself.

Unfortunately Jesus had to see his messianic mission fail. The last we hear of him is, 'My God, my God, why have you forsaken me?' According to Schweitzer, that is where historical investigation takes us: not to the Christ of the scriptures (who never existed), but to a messiah of the end time. On this point Schweitzer endorses Reimarus: over a messiah who did not succeed.

In adopting this standpoint, Schweitzer differed from his contemporary William Wrede (he called the first edition of his book *From Reimarus to Wrede*), who shortly beforehand had written that not only the picture of Christ but also the *consciousness* of Christ did not come from Jesus but from his first worshippers. In Wrede's view, the whole of

New Testament christology is Jesus dressed in the clothes of Christ. On that point Schweitzer was less radical: Jesus certainly felt that he was the Messiah. Schweitzer wanted to maintain this as a historical fact (and thus secured some agreement from orthodoxy): there could be no Christianity without a Jesus of whom it was historically certain that he felt called as Messiah. But for the rest, the line I quoted above applied: 'he returned to his own time'. We have no use for this eschatological bringer of salvation. It is the thought world of the time; we think otherwise. We have grown out of apocalyptic.

That doesn't mean that Jesus has become unimportant. I shall return shortly to how Schweitzer thought he could continue. But first a short survey of one of the consequences of his view of Jesus (it is called 'thoroughgoing eschatology').

4. *Apocalyptic or not? The Son of man*

How does one deal with unwelcome results of historical research? After Schweitzer, a great controversy broke out over his results. Was Jesus an apocalyptic figure or not? Did he feel that he was the Son of man or did he mean someone else by it? This question is of only secondary importance for my argument, but I will go into it briefly, because the answer shows so splendidly that the problem with which Christianity – orthodox or liberal – is wrestling is not so much historical investigation as the question how we can fit our historical discoveries into what we have believed hitherto. Matthew 10, Mark 13, the coming of the Son of man on the clouds of heaven, the bystanders who will experience this coming during their lifetimes, as Jesus himself says (Matthew 10.23): is there room for these apocalyptic aspects of Jesus? I shall sketch out a few positions.

1. First, that of Schweitzer himself, who came to the conclusion that the apocalyptic element in Jesus comes from Jesus himself: Jesus felt that he was the Son of man who would come to establish the kingdom of God. That is the only thing that is certain – in the midst of everything that the Gospels say about Jesus.

2. Then that of William Wrede. He thought that he could establish that it was not Jesus but the evangelists – if you like, the preaching (Jewish) community – who introduced the apocalyptic element into the story. Jesus did not think himself the Son of man; the preaching community made him so. These two basic positions form an alternative: which do you choose and with which arguments? Simple as it seems, that becomes complicated. I shall list the possibilities.

3. We can, for example, agree with Schweitzer that Jesus saw himself as the eschatological bringer of salvation and thus was rooted in the apocalyptic world, but in expounding this go on 1. to weaken the apocalyptic element to some degree, and 2. at the same time expand its scope in some sense; it is also a feature of the Son of man that he must suffer and die. Jesus' death is thus not to be explained as a failure (as Schweitzer thought), but is part of the task of the Son of man.

4. We can also agree with Wrede that the apocalyptic colouring comes from the first (Jewish) followers and is not to be attributed to Jesus himself. He himself never spoke of the Son of man, but was *made* this eschatological figure after what is called his resurrection from the dead, for is not 'resurrection of the dead' (thus the first Jewish community) *the* sign that the end has dawned?

5. Intermediate positions are possible, for example that Jesus indicated that he was the Son of man but not in this apocalyptic colouring. This comes from the believing (Jewish) community.

6. Or yet another intermediate position: Jesus did speak about the Son of man, but meant someone else by this. It was the believing community which first identified him (Jesus) with the Son of man.

There is something to be said for all these positions, and arguments for them have been produced. I am not going to make a choice; I am not competent to do so. That is, if there is a choice to be made. For it is crystal clear that the choice between the different possibilities ultimately goes back to the question whether in their picture of Jesus the investigators and exegetes can make anything of the apocalyptic thought-world in which Jesus is said to be rooted.

5. A muddle. Clearing up apocalyptic

Another possible standpoint is to remain very close to Schweitzer (respect the apocalyptic) but not conclude from his position that *therefore* we cannot begin with Jesus. This in fact consists of a revaluation of what is called apocalyptic and goes as follows. Granted, it is a thought-world which teems with fantasies in which we can never share, since it presupposes a picture of the world which is outdated from A to Z, and cheerfully produces fables about history and its end. Jesus as the eschatological bringer of salvation, as the Messiah who comes at the end of times, the Son of man who plays a key role in the coming of the kingdom of God, must not be taken out of this context. He fits into it very well, and it even gives him his real weight.

Thus for example someone like Bultmann argues that Jesus must be accepted qualitatively as an eschatological figure; not as someone who will come at the end of time but as someone who is 'the end!'. All that the ancient world found to be of decisive significance is projected as a cosmic event on to the screen of history. It is for us to strip these images of their mythical content and to translate them back into what they mean for people of today. For the evangelists, Jesus' appearance was clearly a confrontation which was decisive for their lives; God awoke them in Jesus, and apocalyptic was the material in which they expressed that. So the apocalyptic comes from the community = the community understood the significance of Jesus well. Thus it is an obvious task to strip this preaching of its mythical character (which is called 'demythologizing').

That is an attractive solution to the problem. There is no need to fiddle around with historical investigation; the apocalyptic image formed around Jesus can be quietly left in place, since we need not use it. What made Jesus a figure with apocalyptic proportions for his first followers was the decisive word of God that they experienced in his appearance. That is how we must preach about Jesus today: not as a historical figure of any kind, but as the Word of God that is addressed to us.

The more conservative researchers found Schweitzer much more difficult. They wanted to hold on to the Gospels as a historical account, but if one maintains that consistently, how does one explain what we find in Matthew 10.23? If everything is historical, then so is this statement of Jesus! That is an insoluble problem for conservative theologians. Nevertheless, to the present day there is an innocent orthodoxy which understands the end of history as a historical event, according to the customary pattern that Jesus' coming on earth will be followed by a return on the clouds of heaven.

Has the curtain thus fallen for the 'end' in a historical sense? No. A theologian like Pannenberg, for example, does not want to sweep away the apocalyptic features of Schweitzer's Jesus or to reduce them to 'in him they were confronted with what concerned them', but wants to make the most of what Christians must do with history. Does apocalyptic imply the view that God is bringing history to an end, to a consummation? So for Christians it is not so odd to understand God's revelation as history, the events as ways of God which will unveil their meaning only at the end, when all is over. According to Pannenberg, that is the framework in which we must put the story of Jesus. We must see his resurrection (an apocalyptic event *par excellence*: it indicates the dawn of the end time) as a foretaste of the end of history, of its outcome. The Christian proclamation consists in an 'advance' knowledge of that end: through Jesus Christians know the destination of human beings and the world.

I shall not go into Pannenberg further; later he qualified his views, and moreover we would then have to look at his dogmatics. That is not my intention. In this section I wanted to show how particular theories arise to rescue what people want to preserve and others to reject what people think inappropriate for Christian belief. That procedure, however obvious, ends up in a muddle, only a fraction of which I have described. There is a sea of views, a sea to drown in. For all these views cannot be true at the same time, in the sense that they lay claim to historical truth about Jesus. Their very multiplicity makes one sceptical. Nor is that the only thing.

The whole network of theories which presuppose one another assumes that Schweitzer was right in his view that Jesus was an apocalyptic prophet, who announced the end of time. But nowadays a question mark is being placed even against that (read David Flusser or Marcus Borg).

6. *Albert Schweitzer's lesson*

Like Reimarus' *Fragments*, Schweitzer's book, too, has become a kind of stone in the pond: a centre, or better a starting point, of lines which determine the future. If you can measure the importance of books by their effect, then Schweitzer's *Quest of the Historical Jesus* and Reimarus' *Fragments* are of equal stature.

Let's look again at the splendid sentence in which Schweitzer describes the results of the historical investigation. It seemed as if we were about to encounter the historical Jesus, 'but he did not stay, but went past our time and returned to his own'. In the previous section I explained what Schweitzer meant by 'Jesus returned to his own time': Jesus was an apocalyptist and thus irrevocably of a past time. But before that, Schweitzer says that it did not seem like this. We thought for a while that the investigation would finally bring us to the real Jesus, the living Jesus of flesh and blood as he lived and died in Palestine. Why has this expectation not been realized? What makes it, after the event, an illusion?

It is because the investigators, with whatever good intentions they set out, adapted the picture of Jesus to their time; they removed from the Gospels whatever in their view did not fit and brought out what they could use. All these patterns of 'the life of Jesus' are reconstructions, says Schweitzer, modernizations of the image of Jesus which have to make him acceptable to the eyes of the time in which their creator lived and to which he himself was clearly also obligated. Great moral teacher, educator of the human race, you name it, they cooked it. As was fitting in the age of Romanticism, they were in search of the religious personality named Jesus, the genius without equal, describing and explaining.

We should not be misled by the word 'adapt'. In orthodox circles people understood (and understand) it to mean a sell-out of the Christian message of salvation to the spirit of the time, in an desire to get into the good books of science and culture. In this context adaptation has negative connotations; it amounts to denying, a betrayal of the faith.

Schweitzer saw things differently. Adaptation was necessary, was unavoidable; it wasn't betrayal but the need to survive. But *is* adaptation possible? It's like an elastic band: if you stretch it too far, it breaks. There is a point where adaptation stops: what has to be adapted can be so stretched and torn apart that we honestly have to say we are no longer talking about the same thing.

So a historian mustn't adapt: that's what it amounts to. Schweitzer himself didn't: he wanted to remain strictly honest towards his material. If Jesus is an apocalyptist, then that is what he is, and we mustn't make him into anything else but recognize that we are rid of him. All those lives of Jesus, tumbling over one another, so seriously and accurately constructed by the researchers, aren't the result of historical investigation but rather of the dream of the researcher projected back on to the past, Jesus as the research peels him from the tradition. The theologians of the Enlightenment do that by removing things: everything that has to do with performing miracles (the Enlightenment was allergic to it) is removed from the image of Jesus. According to the attractive summary by K. T. Heim (himself a theologian of the Enlightenment), Jesus did not do miracles; he was himself a miracle.

The Romanticism of the nineteenth century simply added to this. The information given in the Gospels about Jesus is too meagre for it to be possible to distil his personality (the 'hot item' of Romanticism) from it. So Romanticism filled in the gaps. With lofty features, if one wanted to preserve Jesus as the object of faith. Or as a psychopath (Ernest Renan, Emil Ludwig), if one though him only an eerie man. Be this as it may, what came out was Jesus according to Heim, according to Strauss, according to Baur, according to Haeckel, according to Renan – to mention only a few names who at that time produced a great deal of material.

How could investigators bring out so many sides? Because according to Schweitzer, the Gospels give us too few facts to distil a life of Jesus from. They lure the researcher to cross frontiers: the lack of facts is the root of the historical problems.

So is Schweitzer's book a fatal blow to historical investigation of Jesus of Nazareth? Not at all. Even in his view, that investigation is certainly both a legitimate and a necessary occupation. But what he encountered wasn't a historical investigation: the theologians of the Enlightenment weren't interested in history, and many theologians of the age of Romanticism no more so. Moreover those who were interested had no biographical interest (although they said that they had). The authentic Jesus whom they conjured up was the one that they desired. There is nothing against beginning there; all researchers begin with a preliminary judgment, otherwise they see nothing but loose facts with no connection between them. But 'prior knowledge' needs to be open to fundamental correction from the facts of research. If one already knows everything (if one began with more than 'prior knowledge'), one no longer needs to investigate. Moreover we can say that of most of the figures that Schweitzer discusses: they really didn't need to investigate anything; they already knew it.

Unfortunately the same applies to church orthodoxy; it knew it already and therefore had no need for research. The failures of the quest for the authentic Jesus also give it a kind of 'There you are' feeling: for it, the impossibility of getting a grip on Jesus was not a consequence of a shortage of facts (as Schweitzer thought) but a sign of his divine origin. God doesn't allow himself to be caught by investigators! No, of course not, but according to the church's own doctrine Jesus was also truly man, and so it had to be possible to trace him historically. In my view, to say that this is impossible because of his divine nature is to make a virtue out of necessity.

7. Schweitzer himself

How did things develop? That isn't just a historical question. Christianity today is being overwhelmed by an avalanche of images of Jesus, each more remarkable than the one before. To unravel the mechanism behind this phenomenon we can still follow Schweitzer.

Let's begin with the way in which Schweitzer himself went further. At first sight he too wanted to offer a sketch of the historical Jesus. That sounds paradoxical: the man who shows how all these constructions go wrong himself offers one. But he does so deliberately. As we have noted, Schweitzer thought that Jesus of Nazareth saw himself as the bringer of salvation in the end time, as an apocalyptic figure we can no longer make anything of. But in his view that cannot alter the fact that the historical roots of Christianity lie in the person of Jesus. To say Christianity is to say Jesus, and to say Jesus is to say Christianity.

But in that case we are no longer talking of Jesus as he was, but about the effects of Jesus, about what went out from him. Historically speaking, the historical Jesus is interesting, but he doesn't do anything. What they made and (still) make of him is 'Christianity', and historical investigation cannot say anything about that (e.g. in terms of good or bad). So Schweitzer answers the question how things must go on by picking up what for him (Schweitzer) remained as 'the effects of Jesus' appearance': Christianity as an ethic, impressively depicted in the ethics of Jesus, in his unconditional dedication to the Creator's command, and in the strictness of what has come to be called the Sermon on the Mount (read Matthew 5–7). It may be that we cannot follow this ethic; it was an 'interim ethic' which derived its radical rules from belief in the approaching end of this world, which Jesus expected. An interim ethic is an ethic without compromises: if the time is very short, what is the point of regulations which reckon that the centuries will continue to roll on endlessly? If your right hand makes you sin, cut it off: it is better to enter the kingdom of heaven with one hand than with two hands to be lost in eternal fire. That – if you think that such statements were meant literally – is interim ethics.

Meanwhile the world has failed to come to an end and the belief that it will do has proved an illusion; not only has the so-called return been delayed all too long (the first generations of Christians already had problems with this) but it will never come: it rests on a misunderstanding, that of taking the apocalyptic pictures of history literally. Moreover the history of Christianity can best be seen as a story of believers who have to come to terms (read II Peter 3.1–16) with an eschatological expectation which amounted to nothing. That is how, to give an example, Schweitzer also explained baptism and eucharist: originally they were a seal of belonging to the small flock of the end-time, but they were reforged into sacraments by means of which the church can distribute grace to believers. The ethic of Jesus, too, in terms of his commandments, is no longer possible in the original way. The unconditional character which marks the ethical imperative is the only thing that we can take from it.

Schweitzer did much more. As a philosopher of culture he later argued for a mystical view of life. But I shall not discuss that further, nor shall I discuss his medical work in Lambarene.

8. *The 'new quest'*

After Schweitzer the investigation fell silent. Doubt about discovering
the historical truth increased. Historical investigation seemed to be leading to a dead end? Is that a bad thing? No, even good comes out of it,
said people like Bultmann: faith and historical investigation aren't compatible, nor do they need to be. Historical investigation is unavoidable:
it goes with the business of scholarship, and so too therefore does
investigation into Jesus life. But whether or not we get far with that
investigation, the faith of a Christian is not an effect or a consequence
of the knowledge of historical or other objective facts. Coming to faith
happens through confrontation with the Word that is put into words,
just as it was formerly put into words in Jesus. That is what makes
Christianity Christianity. What may make the minister, the professor,
any believer serviceable is the Word made history, not the knowledge of
this history.

From Bultmann's standpoint the quest for the historical Jesus can
thus be quietly stopped. Jesus must have lived, died and been crucified,
but that is all that we need historically. That is what someone like
Kierkegaard thought, and Bultmann joined him.

But in that case why do we have all those Gospel narratives? Are they
any use? Do they have no significance for the Christian gospel? For
Bultmann's pupils, to say that was to go too far. I shall not investigate
their opposition, but they scored a point. How do you explain Jesus'
death? Why was he despised and rejected, and by whom? Why didn't he
die a natural death, but ended up on a cross? To think all this unimportant for faith is to go much too far; it obscures essential aspects of
Jesus' life, what he had to say and what he did, and does so because of
dogmatic prejudice. So there was a revolt against the old master by his
pupils. Thus investigation of Jesus as a historical figure started again
under the name 'New Quest'.

The Christian message has a confrontational character; it certainly
scares people out of their skins. But for what purpose? There were a
great many answers to this question. For authentic humanity, for freedom from the establishment, for unconventional behaviour and other
such characteristics that were high on the list in the 1960s and 1970s.
Jesus wasn't just a spoilsport but an inspirer; believing wasn't just being
told that you were bankrupt but also a change of life, a conversion. In
its most outspoken form, the New Quest ended up with Jesus as a model
for humankind: believing is being a fellow human being or, to put it the
other way round, being a fellow human being is believing.

In this form the new quest was short-lived. It was too much a flare-up in the Bultmann school, opposition to far-reaching historical scepticism. The real question was not an exegetical one but was on the verge of systematic theology: What is the meaning of the historical investigation of Jesus' life for faith? As a historical figure is Jesus indispensable for Christian faith, and if so, why? In an impressive work published in the Netherlands in 1974 (but not in English until 1979), *Jesus,* Edward Schillebeeckx gave this question an appropriate answer.

9. *Qumran and Hag Hammadi. A deluge of facts*

Times have changed again. The incredible number of pictures of Jesus with which we are harassed today (if I may put it that way) again bewilders the onlooker. There is work round the corner for a new Albert Schweitzer to survey all these Jesus pictures and to judge their historical truth. One step towards that has already been taken by Gerd Theissen and Annette Merz in their big book *The Historical Jesus.* I won't attempt it myself, since I am not an exegete or a historian. All I do is to read the work of such specialists and draw my own conclusions.

The new wave of historical reconstructions was started off by the amazing discoveries at Qumran. A shepherd from the region around the Dead Sea made the find of his life: a large number of jars which proved to contain complete scrolls of books and fragments of scrolls of books, coming from a religious community which had settled there around the beginning of our era. Secondly, there were discoveries at Nag Hammadi, a hill in southern Egypt, which on excavation proved to contain a complete papyrus library from the fourth century, clearly hidden by a group of enlightened Christians to keep them safe. Because there have been detailed accounts of Qumran and Nag Hammadi in all kinds of books and journals, here I shall limit myself to touching on what I need for my story.

Qumran casts new light on the prehistory of the Gospels, on the religious context in which Jesus appeared, and thus helps us to understand the Gospels better. The Nag Hammadi library increases our knowledge of what came later, what happened after the appearance of Jesus. Both provide new insights in their areas, though these are not as radical as some sensational journalists with their sweeping statements would have us believe. Thus the discoveries of Qumran are said to bring about the bankruptcy of Christianity, at all events to show that it was not at all original, and there are other tall stories like that. Sheer nonsense, said the people who had studied the texts, and now that the scrolls have been made available to the public, anyone can check them. Whether Jesus had contact with people from the Qumran community and whether John the Baptist was perhaps a member of it are interesting questions, but what is more important for us is the insight that Qumran gives us into, for example, the religious language used in the world of Jesus, and the way it shows us which religious groups he was more akin to (to the amazement of readers of the Bible, the Pharisees) and those to which he was less so.

The Gnostic writings of Nag Hammadi have been available to the public since 1970. The scenario is repeating itself: sensation-seeking journalists have pounced on them, and again we have been able to read that the Christian church deliberately kept quiet about the truth about its past (Gnosticism as its rival). Add the discovery of the religion of other cultures, and people's uncertainty about their own religion and culture in Western Europe, and the door again becomes wide open again to new constructions of the historical Jesus. Now the Nag Hammadi writings in fact make it clear that Gnosticism meant a good deal more in early Christianity than emerges from many official church confessions. But here too we must see the limits: the Gnosticism of Nag Hammadi is post-Jesus, and there is no proof or even indication that Jesus himself was entangled in Gnosticism. I shall be returning to the Gnostic Jesus shortly.

First, there are a number of authors who can be included in the most recent generation of researchers. Most of them write in a very readable way and make exciting reading (the Americans are particularly prominent here), but in the end the reader gets the feeling that Goethe attributes to Faust: 'There I am, poor fool, and am no wiser than before'. We have to chose from a very varied christological platter, but on what basis?

In his book *Gospel Truth*, Graham Stanton argues with Carsten P. Thiede over a papyrus fragment from the Qumran caves which according to Thiede contains a Q fragment of ten letters dating from around AD 40 to 50 (Q is an abbreviation of the German word *Quelle* – according to some scholars a source predating Mark. We shall come back to that). But there is one recalcitrant letter in that fragment which virtually rules out Thiede's view, quite apart from all other objections. Crossan assumes a Cross Gospel from which he distils the view that belief in Jesus already existed before Easter, and so the squabbling over an exalted Lord isn't at all necessary. In his view the resurrection stories are to be read as stories which are intended to legitimate levels of authority in the Christian community: whoever has seen him may be a leader. Marcus J. Borg, a representative of the Californian Jesus Seminar, disputes the view that Jesus was an apocalyptic figure who expected the end of the world (I have already been talking about this), and in so doing undermines almost all of German New Testament scholarship. Whether he is right is not for me to say. Somewhat triumphantly he announces as the conclusion of his investigation that Jesus is not divine. One gets the idea that he thinks that he is the first to claim this. Robert Funk draws Jesus off to the New Age; Klaus Berger defends the tradition, but not all that sweepingly by comparison with someone like Luke T. Johnson in his *The Misguided Quest for the Historical Jesus and the Truth of the Traditional Gospels* (the title speaks for itself). This is only a fraction of the total number of Jesus books which have appeared so far, and the stream continues to flow. Indeed the importance of *Jesus Matters* (den Heyer) is clear.

Some historical discoveries that the reader will make in these works, and some interpretations of them, will be right, and others will not. That can be said a priori, since once again the bottom line is the author's theological programme. This is not a programme for debunking the church's Christ, which is how the quest once begun: that phase has long since been *passé*. The issue now is more the discovery of a new Jesus, one whom we people of the twentieth century can go along with, as Marcus Borg puts it.

10. *The Gnostic Jesus. Robert Funk and 'New Age'*

The Gnostic Jesus is a perfect example of the most recent historical quest as a theological programme. All the lines of the new approach converge in this picture of Jesus: the Nag Hammadi discoveries, the need to reckon with the apocalyptic Jesus and the religious trend towards inwardness as a place to discover God.

First the 'Gnostic'. What we call Gnosticism today is the name for a spiritual current which in part accompanied the rising Christian church as a kind of rival and in part put down roots within the church itself, though there too it developed a kind of rival position over against church orthodoxy. The result was a reversal: the church began to outdo Gnosticism, regarded the trend as a heresy of the first order and firmly drove it out of the church. Hence the hypothesis about the Nag Hammadi library: enlightened Gnostic Christians are said to have found a refuge there, books and all.

Gnosticism comes from the Greek 'gnosis', which literally means 'knowledge'. However, in the Gnostic sphere it means 'higher knowledge', comparable with the way in which the apostle Paul speaks of it in I Corinthians 2.6–16. The need for this higher knowledge, gnosis, permeated the whole culture of the ancient world, Christian and non-Christian, and has all the characteristics of religion: gnosis is saving knowledge, a deeper insight into reality. We needn't seek true life in the outside world, the body, the world, matter; it isn't there: the outside world lets down the trust that people place in it. Human beings will always remain strangers there. Life lies in the inner world: the interior, the soul, the spirit, the divine spark as the origin of human beings. To go outside for God is a mistake: look for him within, in your own self. I shall leave aside the fantasy world with the help of which the Gnostic initiates clothed these thoughts, and the variants in their systems, which were both impressive and fantastic, and go on to the theological programme, the construction of a Jesus who fits the New Age, Jesus in the garb of New Age thinking. By this New Age we must understand the post-Christian age, not as a counter-movement to Christian faith (New Age is not that), but as a movement which contains the Christian faith and possibly takes from it what it can use.

Thus, as for example Robert W.Funk points out, we are seeking the post-Christian Jesus, a Jesus of whom we can make something today, not only brought out from under the material of the church's christology, as in the former attempt, but now stripped of the material of Christianity. According to Funk's account we then arrive at the Gnostic Jesus. Jesus certainly got a glimpse of what the world is really like – here I am following Funk further – i.e. from God's perspective. He gave evidence of that in what, to use technical terms, are called parables and aphorisms, and with the help of these we can try to unravel the world of his ideas. So Jesus – I would comment in passing – is a wisdom teacher (that fits the Gnosticism) and no longer an apocalyptist. To discover Jesus' ideas we need to get not only above the church's Christ but also above the Gospels, since these do not present the authentic Jesus, but rather a distortion. We must replace the model of the *external* redeemer, who comes into the world from outside (the evangelists and the early church stamped that model on us), with the model that follows the myth of the *inward* redeemer: the helper helps us from within, teaches us to defend ourselves inwardly against the time and culture which seek to destroy our humanity. Then follow Funk's attacks on McDonald religion, on religion as fast food, with an impressive final remark: the iconoclast is the authentic Jesus, not the icon which the church has made of him.

For this last we should thank Funk. However, as a researcher he presents us with rather more. And we are left with a somewhat uncomfortable feeling. Funk wants another Jesus, a new picture of Jesus, Jesus as the inward redeemer, and he presents that as the result of historical research. But in fact he is engaged in a reconstruction of Jesus, this time as the inward redeemer, very much in line with the great respect that Gnosticism is enjoying today in New Age thinking. Gnosticism, more knowledge of Gnosticism than we had hitherto, is certainly the result of historical research. But that does not say anything about Jesus as a Gnostic. That is a theory which hangs on a very thin thread, the thread of the dating, for example, of the (Gnostic) Gospel of Thomas. There is no proof for the view that this Gospel is just as old as the Gospels that we know, if not older. In other words, it seems to me that to say that the Gnostic Jesus is the real Jesus is an unsubstantiated assertion. It can be supported by the argument that the New Testament writers eliminated from their narrative everything that smacked of Gnosticism, a clever piece of deception. But there is not a single piece of evidence for such a conspiracy theory. Others refer to the fact that Jesus never condemned Gnosticism, never had anything against reincarnation, and so on. But anything can be done with such arguments. So it is a construction, nor is that the worst thing; it is a construction which has no text and no dating, only the strong need to construct a post-Christian Jesus.

3

The mythical Christ. From Strauss to Bultmann

1. David Friedrich Strauss and the mythical Christ

Reimarus (see the first chapter) read the Gospels as a historical account of the life of Jesus, but an account which twisted the facts: the Gospels as pious deception, as a falsification of history. The result was an explosion of historical research into the authentic Jesus, but this did not produce any satisfying result: historical investigation did not bring the authentic Jesus to light.

However, at a very early stage David Friedrich Strauss (he died in 1874) had proclaimed that the Gospels do not present history. Stopping that historical research will show all the more clearly how the Gospels are being read wrongly. They are not accounts of Jesus' life, as both church orthodoxy and the friends of Reimarus thought, but an account of what people saw in him. Moreover, according to Strauss, it does not matter whether what is described in them really happened or not. The Jesus of the Gospels is the mythical Christ, a product of the pious imagination of ordinary people, of simple Jews of the first century, who attached their messianic expectations to Jesus of Nazareth. What makes Jesus important is not his historical truths but the messianic idea (I am paraphrasing him freely).

So Strauss began on the other side: he wanted to solve Reimarus' problem from the side of the text. To explain these remarkable writings that we call Gospels, we need religious imagination, not the dry old historians who wanted to reconstruct a historical Jesus from these texts. Lessing had said that 'what really happened' can never form the basis for faith, and look, according to Strauss we can quietly leave 'what really happened' aside. The Christ of the church is a mythical entity.

1. According to Strauss, in any case we can forget the quest for a historical Jesus, in any form. Moreover, in opposition to many of his contemporaries, he does not outline a real 'Life of Jesus', although he did give a later edition of his notorious investigation this title. The

stories of the New Testament are to be kept and not to be demythologized (I know that the term was only coined later) by a historical
approach, since that robs them of their force.

2. What are myths? Unhistorical stories, however they came into
being, in which a religious community knows itself to be grounded, they
belong to the world of giving meaning. What must be sought in the
myths is that which according to their adherents is constitutive of
human existence. Rationalists forget the mythical character of the
Gospel stories and make them into history, which in turn has to be
checked against 'what really happened'. But that rests on a misunderstanding. The Gospel stories tell us how the first followers of Jesus
thought about God, and thus they speak the language of myth.

3. What does myth have to tell *us*? Not something about Jesus of
Nazareth, but something about God, human beings and the world. The
myth of the figure of Christ represents a truth which we also talk about
today, a truth of all times which must therefore go on being told. The
Christ figure as God-man is the unveiling of the oneness of the All
(Strauss's term), in which as human beings we have a part. God is present not only in this one human being ('it does not please the deity to
pour himself out in one example') but in the whole of humankind.

4. The notion of mythical stories which a community saw as constitutive for its existence helped Strauss to get rid of the prejudice that
the evangelists were motivated by malice. The rationalists saw clearly
that the Gospels do not contain any supernatural truths. But, according
to Strauss, they do not contain any history either.

5. By Jewish popular fantasy Strauss means what today we would call
a messianic future expectation: 'the consciousness of believers'. The
confessors, the believers, are speaking in the stories. Jesus is Christ
because and in so far as he was dressed in the garb of expectation:
historically he is of no interest to us. He indeed lived, but there is no
need to bother about how he lived. In the last resort the question is not
about Jesus but about the expectation that someone who believes in him
must have.

2. *The mythical Christ does not need a historical Jesus*

Strauss's standpoint found little approval in his own generation (later he
too more or less abandoned it). For his contemporaries, the quest of the
historical Jesus remained the trump card. An end to it came only when
Schweitzer (see the previous chapter) irrefutably established that in any
case Jesus was not the good nineteenth-century figure whom research

held him to be – at least that within that framework, so much had to be stripped from him that there was nothing left – but rather the seer who saw the good world falling to pieces, the prophet of the end time.

Only around the beginning of the twentieth century did serious successors to Strauss appear. A first consequence of his work was that if the issue is not the so-called historical Jesus but the mythical Christ, this figure need not even have existed. The myth is the idea on which everything turns. Take, for example, the idea that God dwells among human beings. Now that fact could also be expressed without being illustrated in Jesus as Christ. So radical theologians, even some historians, appeared, who claimed not only that Jesus did not need to have lived to make Christianity explicable (Strauss did not go further than that) but that he never lived at all. In Germany, Bruno Bauer was not averse to this position and in Britain G.A.Wells has argued it.

Another development was rather less crude, but followed the same line. Of course Jesus lived; Christianity is inconceivable without his person. But we are then talking about an actual state of affairs. That is the make-up of Christianity: it begins with Jesus. But need it also continue with Jesus? Yes. However, not in so far as he is the Christ, but because according to the laws of social psychology the Christian church cannot exist without the figure of Christ: otherwise it would fall apart. As Christ, Jesus is the necessary condition for both the present and future existence of Christianity, and so he must remain.

This was the view of Ernst Troeltsch (who died in 1923). In his view (though this was not always the same), Jesus was the bearer not so much of a myth as of a social and religious necessity. If we want the Christian church to continue to exist, we must also want Jesus as the Christ.

Here Troeltsch remains near Strauss: the anonymous piety of Christianity is the basis for the Christ figure and thus for Christianity. The significance of Jesus subsequently became a theme of Christian doctrine, but that is only after the event and not fundamental.

I know that this is not all there is to say about Troeltsch. He pondered, and was engaged in a search for a point outside the stream of history from which a judgment could be made on history without falling back on revealed truths, as pre-Enlightenment theology did. Moreover he put the question 'Who is Jesus?' in another, wider context, that of the scientific explanation for the origin of Christianity. Of course the figure of Jesus is needed for this, but along what course did that process develop?

3. 'God on earth'. Jesus as God-in-our-midst

A historical explanation of Christianity will always have to fall back on the figure of Jesus. Nineteenth-century historical criticism understood that well, as is evident from its diligent work. But how did Jesus develop into the church's Christ? That was the question which was raised by Strauss's work. A fantasy of the community, all right, but how did such a thing develop? Can that be traced?

A whole generation of theological practitioners set out to answer this question when (for the moment) the historians had talked themselves out. William Wrede (whom we have already met) made the first move in methodology: treat Christianity as a piece of the history of religion, in other words, just as you would treat any other religions. That produces an honest result. Troeltsch (we have also already met him) adopted this approach, but wrestled with the price that has to be paid for it: in that case the special position of Christianity among the other religions (the so-called absoluteness of Christianity) has to be given up. The historian of religion Wilhelm Bousset (died 1920) went furthest in this direction.

The time of the New Testament, Bousset argued, is not a separate time which calls for a separate treatment; we must deal with it as we deal with the early church. So there must be no division between the two spheres. Away too with the division between the history of Christianity and the history of religion. We see the processes that we perceive in other religions also at work in the rise of Christianity. Bousset wanted to work from A to Z with what I would call the principle of 'great religious minds think alike'. But what he comes out with is of only partial interest for us. Of course he wasn't the only one who wanted to explain the origin of Christianity, as the Jesus movement, in this way; there were others who arrived at other results. According to Bousset, Jesus, once 'exported' to the non-Jewish world, underwent the fate of divinization in accordance with the dominant religious longings of the time. Here he was thinking of the enormous influence of the ancient mystery religions, so called because they celebrated the mystery of God's presence in their meetings. Once the mystery religions gained a firm footing on Hellenistic soil, Christian assemblies took over this model: in their weekly celebrations Jesus was worshipped as God-in-their-midst. He was the real but secret Kyrios (Lord), the only one who was really worth worshipping.

So not only did Jesus fit into this time; according to Bousset he also met people's radical religious needs. They need to be able to lose themselves, to go outside themselves, to surrender themselves totally: religion gives them the space for that, too. That was also the case with rising Christianity; it followed the laws of religious needs. According to Bousset, these needs therefore come before the person of Jesus of Nazareth; Jesus became their chosen vehicle. Moreover, according to Bousset and his supporters, the one, fixed immovable view of Jesus Christ, unchanged in Christian memory, as Son of God, our Lord, is an effect of the religious treatment to which Jesus was already subjected in the earliest time. The Christ is a product of human religion generally. Jesus is made an idol, and idols are raised to superhuman proportions. They have to be capable of being worshipped; but we can only worship God. That is where an itinerant Son of God inevitably ends up. So the doctrine of two natures is the effect of a religious need: that is not what Bousset and his school said literally, but that is what it amounts to.

Bousset reminds me of the 1992 Kirchentag in Munich to which the Dalai Lama had also been invited. He attracted almost all the participants to whatever room he was in and whatever platform he appeared on, although his address always consisted of the same incontrovertible truths like justice, no war, living in peace, and so on. It amazed me. A German housewife sitting next to me explained: 'You can see what young people want: a God on earth.' According to Bousset, that's how it was with Jesus. We must go to his worshippers, to their world, to understand how Jesus could develop into the Christ, the Son of God.

Bousset thought that this world was the Hellenistic world. There should be an end to explanations of the Jesus movement in terms of Judaism (which his predecessor Albrecht Ritschl still thought necessary). Jesus could never have become God in this context. The background to the classical christology, the doctrine of two natures, is not Jewish but Hellenistic religion, especially the mystery religions. We shall see that, given all that Bousset argued, this conclusion was not so strange.

4. *The gospel of Jesus the preacher*

'The gospel of Jesus' is an ambiguous expression. We can take it in two ways: the gospel in the sense of 'preached by Jesus' or the gospel with Jesus as the subject of the preaching (here, oddly enough, the subject is at the same time the object). Jesus as preacher or Jesus as the object of preaching, which do we choose?

Adolf von Harnack (died 1930) remarked that Jesus does not occur in the gospel. What he meant by that was that Jesus did not preach himself, and so we mustn't do that either. Orthodoxy thinks differently, as Harnack (the 'von' is usually omitted) was aware; moreover, his argument is directed against orthodox, conservative Christianity with its christology of the two natures (the divine and the human) in the one person of Jesus. Like Bousset, whom I discussed in the previous section, Harnack thought the doctrine of two natures a product of Hellenistic culture. Strauss had already said that the criticism of Christian dogma is its own history, and Harnack agreed with him. The history of dogma consists in a slow but sure distancing from the original Jesus of Nazareth.

It is clear that Harnack thus wants to return to the so-called historical Jesus. And he had a reason for doing so: like his predecessors, he sought to get rid of the dogmatic Christ of the church. But something strange happens. Harnack wants a historical basis for Christianity: we can be happy with that. He wants to reconstruct this basis as non-Hellenistic. We can also be happy with that. So it would be most natural for him to return to the Jewish origin of Jesus. Already in 1905 a biblical scholar like Wellhausen (died 1918) had neatly remarked that Jesus was not the first Christian but a Jew (Bultmann was later to follow him). But Harnack could not or would not approve of this, for that would put Jesus in the framework of the religion of the Old Testament and Judaism, and like most of his contemporaries (and many Christians to the present day), Harnack thought that this would amount to a relapse into an outdated religion. In his view we cannot learn what is Christian from the Old Testament. This is crude language, and it can get even cruder. In his study of Marcion (who saw the God of the Old Testament as a secondary God, not the real one), Harnack even pronounces a kind of Christian anathema on the Old Testament: still to retain it in his time as a canon for doctrine and preaching is in his view a phenomenon of religious and ecclesiastical paralysis.

In his days that was part of the tradition: the New Testament is the real Bible, God is the God of love, and the Old Testament knows nothing of that. Christianity has not only grown out of Judaism but is superior to Judaism. However, here – in a way quite remarkable for a historian – Harnack misses the boat: the need for de-Hellenizing brought him back to the need for the historical Jesus, but when he has to give him a place in history he peels him from his Jewish context. Is Judaism superseded? In that case the religion of Christ is also superseded. How can this conclusion be true if at the same time one wants to go back to Jesus as the proclaimer (rather than as the one proclaimed)? Here Harnack gets stuck, as we see. When it comes to the historical

Jesus, Harnack, like the others, depicts him in accordance with his own wishes, and thus loses sight of even the most obvious fact (Jesus as a Jew).

5. *The preached Christ. The Gospels as community theology*

To the present day, the standpoint of orthodoxy has been diametrically opposed to the gospel as preached by Jesus: Jesus *is* preached, he is the content of the proclamation. Here I am referring to someone like Karl Barth, in whose theology Jesus is even made the exclusive subject of Christian preaching. There is only one word of God, Jesus Christ, and thus there is only one proclamation. Of course Jesus himself also preached, no one denies that, but the real proclamation of the Christian church is the proclamation of Christ. In this way, orthodoxy has traditionally defended its disregard for historical criticism. Karl Barth, too, seems to have had no interest in it; he pushed it to one side as irrelevant, and in this way continued the standpoint of conservative theology: the church is not about the historical Jesus but about the preached Christ.

Already at the beginning of the twentieth century this standpoint – it is not the historical Jesus but the preached Christ, the Christ of faith, who is important – was being defended with vigour. That seems to be nothing new; didn't the Christian church do the same thing in terms of the classical doctrine of two natures? But there is a snake in the grass: the Christ of faith is played off against the historical Jesus, and a price has to be paid for that. Quite apart from all kinds of other insoluble questions which it provokes, it seems identical to the line taken by David Friedrich Strauss. History is of no importance: the Gospels are about the mythical Christ. If by the word 'mythical' we do not think of folk tales but of what Strauss understood by it – the believing (Jewish) community sees Jesus as its Christ, the Gospel story is a testimony to how believers feel – then the Christ of faith, the Christ of the community, is none other than Strauss's mythical Christ: christology is community theology.

This parallel between the mythical Christ and the proclaimed Christ seems to me to be indisputable: history is not important for either of them. I deliberately say 'parallel', because neither the orthodoxy of earlier days nor that of today (for example Karl Barth) meant or means that: moreover one cannot impute anything like that to it. Simply in terms of the content of proclamation, there is a world of difference between Strauss and conservative orthodoxy. However, there is an unmistakable parallel: those who do not respect history end up with unhistorical myth in one of its many manifestations. A lack of interest in the question who the real Jesus was ends up in a Christ who is left hanging in the air.

The question is of course whether that is so bad, in the sense of being unacceptable to Christian belief. I think that it is, and will explain why later. Anything goes in christology if there is no direct line from Jesus of Nazareth to the proclaimed Christ. But before I get to that, I shall first follow out the line with which I am presently engaged, by sketching out the current of a different way of thinking (and its consequences).

6. *Continuity or discontinuity between the historical Jesus and the preached Christ*

As I have demonstrated, theologians orientated on the church could live with community *theology* in place of community *fantasy*. Really there was nothing against calling the Jesus of the Gospels (and thus the Christ) the view of faith held by the first Christian communities. That makes the Gospels easier to understand: we can see them as the preaching of the Christian church or, if you like, as its theology about Jesus, and thus as its christology.

So everything fell splendidly into line. How could the Gospels present Jesus so clearly as the Son of God from the beginning? Because their story is a story of faith that they were only able to write down after the end of Jesus' life. They write as it were with retrospective force about Jesus: the story begins at the beginning, but the narrator already knows the end, the resurrection of the crucified Jesus. In this sense the confessing community is speaking in the Gospels.

So there is no objection to how things are presented. However, a close analysis of the Gospel stories allows another conclusion: they are stories of faith. But in that case one condition must be fulfilled: the preached Christ and the Jesus who preached and went around Palestine, the Jesus of flesh and blood, Jesus of Nazareth, must be the same, if the church's teaching is not to go up in smoke (viz. myth). Thus a remarkable problem developed which dominated the discussions for years after the Second World War: the problem of the continuity between Jesus of Nazareth and the preached Christ. For conservative theologians this continuity was essential: the one who was exalted had to be the same as the one who was humiliated and vice versa; otherwise there was no longer a gospel. Or, to put it another way, the Christ of preaching, the Christ of faith = the risen Christ, and the risen Christ must be the same as Jesus who walked around in Palestine.

That's attractive. But if this sum is to work out, then we must accept the resurrection of Jesus as a historical fact. The continuity between Jesus of Nazareth and the Christ of preaching rests on it as a bridge rests on its piers. There is no continuity without resurrection as a historical fact. At that point the complications begin.

Is the preached Christ the risen Jesus of flesh and blood? Quite apart from the possibility of establishing that beyond dispute (see below), not everyone was ready to speak so crudely about the resurrection of Jesus (as one event among others). So there was a split: on the one hand were the more conservative theologians who had no objection to faith as a community theology, provided (and only provided) that the continuity between the preached Christ and Jesus of Nazareth was maintained. And on the other were theologians (above all researchers) who thought that there is more discontinuity than continuity: the preached Christ may then have Jesus of Nazareth as its content, but in that case this Jesus is quite different from Jesus as he had seen himself.

A horrible dilemma! Discontinuity between Jesus of Nazareth and the preached Christ – but in that case the preached Christ is left hanging in the air. Those who keep with the community get away with it, but then they have to show this continuity historically. And in that case the whole story begins all over again from the beginning: the basis of faith, certainty about the truth, again becomes dependent on scholarship, in this case historical research into the resurrection of Jesus. We are back with Lessing, who rightly thought it impossible for faith to be dependent on scholarship for its certainty.

7. *Bultmann. Community theology and kerygma*

Bultmann, whom we encountered earlier, has left his mark on christology, even among people who did not want to accept his solution of the problem of continuity and discontinuity. His view of things deserves a separate section.

According to Bultmann, we do not know much about Jesus of Nazareth as a historical person. He went round as a preacher, proclaimed the kingdom of God and died on a cross. It is improbable that he thought of himself as the eschatological bringer of salvation. Thus Bultmann opted for William Wrede and not for Schweitzer: Jesus of Nazareth did not come forward as messiah. But even if we knew more about him, it would be unimportant for us. Jesus of Nazareth and his preaching belong to the presuppositions of the New Testament preaching, not to that preaching itself. For that we must keep to the significance which the first community attached to him. It is the community which saw him as the eschatological bringer of salvation, as messiah. So in the Gospels we do not encounter Jesus of Nazareth, but Jesus in the meaning attached to him by the believing community, Jesus as the one who is preached. And to the present day, faith has to do only with the Christ who is preached.

For Bultmann, (*a*) the historical person of Jesus of Nazareth has no importance for preaching except that he must have lived, and (*b*) the awareness of faith in the first community is the source of the preaching of Christ. That sounds like David Friedrich Strauss. How is that?

1. Why is Bultmann so uninterested in the results of historical research? Because historical events are not the content of Christian proclamation. That would make 'believing' the acceptance either of truths of a universal kind (as liberal theology thought), or historical truths (the standpoint of orthodoxy). 'Believing' is something different. It arises through hearing the Word of God that is proclaimed by the church. Proclamation is the key term in Bultmann's theological scheme.

2. Bultmann distils this view from what he sees as the community theology of the Gospels. The believers knew that in Jesus they were confronted with the Word of God, and so they portrayed him as the eschatological bringer of salvation sent by God, the bringer of salvation in the end time. This 'end time' must not be taken literally but reduced to what people wanted to express by it (called 'demythologizing' by Bultmann and his school): in Jesus they encountered the word of God. I would remark in passing that where Bultmann wanted to demythologize, someone like Heinrich Ott wanted to leave the mythical world of the Gospels intact. He thought that religion can express itself only in the language of myth. But Ott didn't get to grips with this; he was too early in the discussion to do so.

3. So we must regain what the community meant when it exalted the historical Jesus to become an eschatological figure. Proclaiming Jesus can only be confronting people with God's word, or really I should say confronting people with the speaking God himself. Moreover that is also what we in the church mean by 'proclaiming Christ'. This is not just *about* the ultimate concern; it *is* the ultimate concern in human life, the same ultimate concern that the first community experienced in its confrontation with Jesus. It is not a report *about* the eschatological event; it *is* the eschatological event that confronts people with the 'end', *their own* end. Or to put it more precisely: where the Word touches a person, there 'the end', the eschaton, *happens*. Bultmann calls this almost impracticable revaluation of Christian preaching, introducing a

God who speaks, *kerygma*. That is Greek for proclamation and serves as a marker for the special position he assigns to preaching.

4. Can one then, as a human being, introduce God who speaks? No, but it is precisely there that the mystery of proclamation lies, as did the mystery of the Messiah in the Gospels. Can a human being, an ordinary human being, who moreover ends his life on the cross, confront us with God's last, decisive word? Jesus' hearers took offence at this, says the first community. In other words, they had to choose between going along and going away. That is also the case now with Christian proclamation: because the Word of God appears under the form of its opposite (human beings are speaking), the hearer is faced with an unavoidable choice: take offence at this paradoxical form of God's action towards us, stumble over it (of course the most natural course), or rise in it to a new life.

5. Thus Bultmann maintains a kind of continuity between then and now. Not between Jesus of Nazareth and the proclaimed Christ, but between the God who spoke then (in Jesus) and the God who speaks now (in the proclamation). God is not the sum of a number of truths about God. God happens always: all that we can say of God is what God does in us. God can be expressed only as an experience of/in our humanity.

6. Being touched by the Word leads to 'believing', but we must then learn 'faith' as a new way of being. Bultmann calls this being detached from the world, in the way in which Paul describes that in I Corinthians 7: he also calls it possessing as if we did not possess, a kind of eschatological existence. 'In the world but not of the world' is the terminology used in the Gospel of John. That is also an aspect of faith, but the question is whether it is all that the proclamation of Christ has to offer.

7. Yet another question. If Jesus as they saw him then is not in any way even a bit of a source (I am deliberately piling all these epithets up together), but only a product of community theology, then in Bultmann the kerygmatic Christ is literally left hanging in the air. And that is the intention, Bultmann would say: the Word speaks here; either you hear it or you don't. Only the cross is indispensable as a historical event for Bultmann: as a demonstration of his starting point that revelation takes place only in the form of its opposite. Otherwise there would be no scandal and offence and people would not sense that they faced the decision of their lives. So the cross is a model of revelation.

8. Karl Barth realized that Bultmann was going to get stuck here: you really get rid of all christology if the cross is no more than a model of revelation. Indeed. But Barth also got stuck.

8. *Barth and Bultmann. Friends and opposite extremes*

Karl Barth was Bultmann's friend at the start. Both wanted to distance themselves from anything that made believers possessors of the truth. Truth that is possessed isn't truth, at least not the truth of faith. It is theory, and no faith emerges from theory. For that God's word is needed. If you call the Bible God's word, then again you face the same problem: we would then possess God's word. That cannot be. God's word is God himself speaking, God who spoke in Jesus Christ. Certainly the Bible reports that (we have no other information), but the Bible cannot take the place of the God who speaks, of the Word that takes up the word. Barth will later call the Bible a form of the Word of God and thus again make the Bible both a given and unassailable authority of revelation.

All right, they began as friends: no truths about God, but God who speaks the Word. But what is 'the Word'? That requires further definition. We have in some way to be able to measure that we have come into contact with the Word, otherwise anything can be called the Word! At that point the ways of Barth and Bultmann part. In Bultmann the Word is recognized as Word by what it does in a person: it becomes the occasion for a new way of living. Karl Barth thought that one had to be able to recognize the Word of God by its content, by Jesus Christ, and he wrote a *Church Dogmatics* in at least thirteen volumes to demonstrate this criterion (Jesus Christ). The two ended up as 'warring brothers'. Bultmann remained true to the starting point, Barth deviated: he thought that truths about God and Jesus have to be proclaimed; Christians have to believe in order to be able to be Christians.

The mountain of truths in the *Church Dogmatics* is difficult to reconcile with 'the Word speaks the word'. Added to that, Barth not only seems to know too much but is also unwilling to take any account of the Gospels as community theology. He again treats them as historical narratives which reveal Jesus as God's Son. But I shall leave things there.

The controversy between Barth and Bultmann can be reduced to their position *vis-à-vis* Kierkegaard: how does a person become contemporaneous with Jesus of Nazareth? Barth was initially even fascinated by Kierkegaard, certainly in his criticism of official Christianity, but he dropped Kierkegaard when he saw from Bultmann where he would end up if he took this course. Barth bridges the gulf between past and present by the preaching of Jesus as the crucified and risen Lord, the Christ of faith: that is the traditional way. Bultmann remains faithful to Kierkegaard; he too has the gulf between then and now bridged by proclamation, but the proclamation has become the kerygma, the word that confronts human beings with God in the form of their opposite. The cross is not believed in, but as a model form of revelation is an 'invitation to believe' (as Kierkegaard puts it), an invitation to an eschatological mode of existence. Karl Barth – it seems to me rightly – found that too little.

4

The Gospels: Jesus as packaged by faith

1. *Texts not of, but about, Jesus*

In this chapter I must retrace my steps. The historical Jesus and the mythical Christ may be diametrically opposed to each other, even to the degree that they may not be reduced to each other, but the dispute over the two approaches has at least had one advantage: we have a better insight into the unique character of the Gospels. Under pressure it has become quite clear that the evangelists were not historians, nor did they practise falsehood in their writings, the charge made against them by Reimarus. But in that case what were they? What was their concern? What is the unique character of the Gospels?

This question is of cardinal importance for our expectations of the Gospels. We are almost exclusively dependent on the texts of the Gospels for our knowledge of Jesus, who he was, what he did and what he said. We do not have anything else. I shall be going into this unique character of the Gospels, but first here are two comments.

1. In this chapter, unless otherwise indicated, by 'the Gospels' I mean the three so-called Synoptic Gospels, Matthew, Mark and Luke. They bear this name because in all three Jesus' life runs along similar lines; that in turn happens because all three begin from a common basis (sources), quite apart from the use that Matthew and Luke make of Mark as a source. And what about the Gospel of John? That not only models Jesus' life on another pattern, but according to experts is also more theological than the other Gospels; at any rate, it is historically less reliable. Of course that doesn't mean that John doesn't contain any additions known to him from his own tradition.

2. There is a good reason for saying 'almost exclusively dependent'. Like the Old Testament, the New Testament is a collection of divergent, independent writings which came into being independently of one another. There is more in it than the text of the Gospels, so here and there – especially with the apostle Paul – a tradition may crop up which goes back to witnesses of Jesus' life. In addition, almost inevitably, there

are also extra-biblical accounts of Jesus' activity. There are not many of them: some are obscure, some are disputed; but there are also some which are beyond question reliable reports. Those who do not want to rely on the Gospels because they contain partisan accounts can, for example, turn to writers of this period, like Tacitus, who in his *Annals* (XV, 44) gives a description of the atrocious cruelties to which the emperor Nero subjected the Christians of Rome, and in that connection comes to Christ, to whom Christians owe their name. The idea that Jesus did not exist seems to me, historically speaking, to be just a partisan standpoint. Whether what the church has said about him is true is of course quite a different question.

Thus by and large we have only the text of the Gospels, texts which are *about* Jesus. The peculiar nature of this situation becomes evident when we reflect that we do not have a single text *from* Jesus. We have no writings from him, as we have writings of Plato or Aristotle, no authorized tradition of what he said; all we have is others who tell of him and say what he said. This is community fantasy, said David Friedrich Strauss, and we mustn't look for history in it. It is community theology, said both Bultmann and the more conservative researchers. But whatever it is, at all events here Jesus' followers are speaking. So this is confessional language, the belief of the first Christian community, Jesus as faith saw him and worshipped him. It is presented in story form, in all the evangelists, but 'story' need not mean 'historical'; it is (provisionally) a narrative form. It is for historical investigation to discover what happened, including what Jesus really said.

It is the view of faith, but that is not all there is to be said. How did the evangelists come to write their works, and what was their purpose? That too is a question which we cannot pass over, for the evangelists come from a later period than, for example, the letters of Paul. There already was a kind of Jesus community both in Palestine and outside it, and there was already preaching about Jesus, by apostles and lay people; in short, Jesus had already become a kind of centre of a religious movement. So we can best imagine that the evangelists were people who said: 'We shall tell you in rather more detail who this Jesus who is preached to you really was'. Thus the Gospels are not pure preaching, nor pure history, but fill in what we then call a hiatus in knowledge: what the evangelists really want to do is to open a book about him (who is preached everywhere).

Now that may seem a simple statement, but the more closely the textual side of the Gospels was investigated with this purpose (function) in view, the greater the complications proved to be: not one preached

Jesus but a multiplicity of pictures of Jesus emerged. There were not just four of them, one picture of Jesus for each Gospel, since it proved possible to split these pictures, too, into their composite parts. The so-called Christ of the scriptures does not exist except as a mosaic, made up of multicoloured stones, which can constantly be combined in new ways.

2. *Four theological treatises*

As used to be customary in a Reformed family, my father read from the Bible at every meal (i.e. three times a day). When the Gospels came round, I remember that he didn't use the traditional Bible but a so-called harmony of the Gospels. A certain Tatian already produced such a work as early as the second half of the second century. Fragments of it have been handed down in different languages (Syriac, Coptic, Arabic), and today are very useful for reconstructing the earliest versions of the text of the Gospels. Tatian, who had a critical mind, undertook this work because he was offended by the far-reaching contradictions between the four Gospels. There are indeed quite a lot of them, and the church father Origen was even afraid that they could cause people to lose their faith. Tatian made a discovery: he put the four Gospels side by side and constructed a harmony of them which smoothed out historical unevennesses, a kind of second-century 'life of Jesus'.

In the kind of Gospel harmony from which my father read aloud, the parallel passages of the Gospels were put side by side, as far as possible in the same historical order, so that one could see at a glance 1. where the Gospels ran parallel and where they didn't; 2. whether they reproduced the same story or the same argument with the same words or not; and 3. where one had something which others omitted. With the help of such a harmony you can see very clearly, for example, how much John diverges from the Synoptic Gospels.

My father took the reliability of Scripture seriously; the differences between the Gospels could not be substantial, and so he arrived at his harmony. It had to help him preserve the unity of the Gospels. Nevertheless he was perpetuating a misunderstanding here which had continued from Tatian to the beginning of the twentieth century, the misunderstanding that the Gospels have to be read as historical accounts. But that isn't the case. Behind the differences which Tatian (and my father) came across, there is something else: differences in views of Jesus. They need not immediately be blown up to enormous proportions, but there are and remain clear differences which can only be regarded as different views that the evangelists hold.

That's easy to see. The evangelists follow the same pattern of the story, but despite the suggestion that it is historical, they deal freely with the sequence of Jesus' words and actions. For example, Matthew collects together all kinds of sayings of Jesus into the so-called Sermon on the Mount (Matt. 5–7), which he has followed by the collection of a number of miracle stories (Matthew 8–9). But in Mark, as all readers can discover for themselves, these miracle stories are spread over a large number of chapters (1, 4, 5, 2, 5, 10, 3, 6). Matthew is composing and sees nothing against changing Mark. We can also see this with the others: the pericopes (passages which in themselves form a unity) aren't always in the same place; they can clearly be shifted to meet the demands of the story as *this* evangelist wants to tell it. Luke has put in his chapter 11 Jesus' great 'Woe to you . . .' against the Pharisees and scribes which appears in Matthew 23 (in Luke the scribes are teachers of the law); in Matthew this discourse is preceded by the dispute over the question how the Christ can at the same time be called David's Son and David's Lord (22.41–46), whereas Luke does not relate that until his chapter 20 (41–44). The historical course of events thus cannot have been the main issue in the story for the evangelist; it was more the framework that he used. Within that framework he unfolded his view of Jesus.

3. Evangelists as redactors

Once one has discovered that the evangelists are moving blocks and pieces of tradition around, it becomes interesting to identify these blocks, as it were to give them fixed labels. Mission discourses, disputes, healing stories – off the cuff it is easy to point out a number which keep recurring. They form clear stereotypes, which have become established in making Jesus known everywhere. Each has its own purpose, which can be investigated further. What is this purpose? Did for example the disputes between Jesus and the Pharisees really take place like this, or is this polemic, a first sign of the controversy between Jews and Christians? Is this a bit of community theology? And what happened to these pericopes in the process of tradition? How did the Gospels come into being in that process? And why, in that case, are there four Gospels instead of just one? Although no uniform answers can be given to all these questions, it is clear that a whole history, a history of development, preceded the Gospels as we know them. To reduce it to the simplest scheme: the story of Jesus began as oral tradition which continued in clusters, clusters of stereotyped preaching. In a subsequent phase these were written down as pericopes, which in turn redactors made into our Gospels: the texts in which the many trickles and streams of tradition finally ended up.

So the evangelists are redactors, and one of the main questions of the professional exegetes is: which Gospel took over what in framing the preaching in its own story and how did it do so? Luke is a good example of this. 'I have investigated everything', he says at the beginning of his Gospel (Luke 1.1), and then he produces a version which diverges considerably from the other Gospels he had seen. The collectors clearly each had a purpose of his own. Otherwise, to put it somewhat schematically, they would have left everything as they found it.

We could compare the investigation of the Gospels with the investigation of the paintwork of a house: we begin on the outside where the top layer is, perhaps with some ornamentation. If we scrape that off, we get down to a previous coat, then to another coat, and finally to the primer. Something like that. The history of the formation of the Gospels must then be described in reverse order.

First came Jesus, as the primer: that sounds somewhat irreverent, but it does clarify how our Gospels came into being. Experts have established that the Gospel of Mark consists to a great degree of the surface that we can call the primer. Another basic layer has even been given its own name; it is described with the letter Q (from the German word *Quelle*, source). The narrators began by developing this first layer further, adding, revising and editing; finally came the redactors under whose names the Gospels were published, Matthew, Mark, Luke and John.

And each had his own purpose! So to make a harmony is to go in precisely the opposite direction. These differences mustn't just be swept away; they are the essence of the evangelist, his speciality, the reason why he wanted to write one more book although there were already standard stories in circulation. John is the evangelist who goes furthest with such a theology of his own. For example, in the Gospel of John Jesus uses the term 'kingdom of God' only once, whereas it is a key term in the Synoptic Gospels. But it isn't far from the truth also to speak of a theology of Matthew, Mark and Luke. Luke, who writes for the rich and therefore devotes so much attention to standing up for the poor; Matthew, with his school of Jewish Christians, who for example finds it inappropriate to say that Jesus 'could not do any mighty work' in Nazareth (Mark 6.5) and changes the 'could not' into he 'did not' do many mighty works there (Matthew 13.58). Whatever other features they may display, in that respect the Gospels are all distinctive theological treatises.

4. First read what it says

Everything begins with reading exactly what is said. By that I mean not only everything good, but also everything problematical: everything that faithful believers experience as an attack on their faith. The exegetes are blamed, they are said to make everything unnecessarily complicated, to apply little or nothing of what is said there to themselves, and so on. Now of course that can happen, but on the whole it is precisely the other way round. The exegetes read exactly the texts that are under their noses and note that things are quite different from what the average churchgoer usually thinks. 'Just read, what is there isn't there', a line from the poet Martinus Nijhoff, has become a proverbial saying in all kinds of new theological approaches. The saying points out that the question is one of the meaning that a text has to offer, and we don't discover that until we've carefully analysed the grammar and the words. That adds up. But before we're in a position to say 'what is there isn't there', we must first have read exactly what is there and what isn't, letter by letter and word by word. Otherwise every attempt at the meaning is a mere guess.

First let me give an example of inexact reading that made an impression on me. Years ago, following the traditional Dutch translation, I spoke of 'the murderer on the cross', until one day an exegete made me read the text properly, and then the word proved no longer to be 'murderer' but 'robber'. That also appears it in the new translation of the Dutch Bible society, but many people continue to say 'murderer'. Why? It seems to me to indicate how the language of the Bible in general and the Gospels in particular comes across to the average churchgoer, namely as liturgical language. They hear well-known sounds, expressions which are familiar and sound familiar. That is also what so many people want in a Sunday sermon: no deviation from what they have always heard, as that breaks out of the familiar circle, the reassurance for which they go to church. Of course there is nothing against going to church for reassurance, and I don't mean this passage as a criticism. But to experience the Gospels as liturgical language means getting used to a particular interpretation which can no longer justify itself from the text of the Gospel. From this perspective, to read the text exactly is an obstacle. Not only does it require effort and patience, which is not given to everyone, but it is also unsettling. So such a liturgical way of dealing with the Gospels is very understandable. However, those who adopt it can no longer be allowed to be cross with exegetes who read the text exactly and then come up against problems which churchgoers have overlooked

Here is an example of this kind of problem, to which I shall return in the next section. In Mark 10.17–18 we read about a man who asks Jesus, '"Good master, what must I do to inherit eternal life?" And Jesus said to him, "Why do you call me good? No one is good but God alone."' Luke 18.18 has the same text. But if we open Matthew, we read in 19.16–17: 'And look, someone came to him and said, "Good master, what must I do to inherit eternal life?" He said to him, "Why do you ask me concerning the good? One is good."' Exact reading – as any serious reader of the Bible will have discovered – shows that the texts do not agree. What is behind this? Why doesn't Matthew, like Luke, simply take over the text of Mark?

Certainly not, as some Christian exegetes conjecture, because although Jesus knew better, he was here adapting himself to the Jewish way of thinking, in which attaining blessedness is made dependent on doing good works. That is an interpretation which wants to safeguard the Christian doctrine of grace, but has nothing to do with the texts. The first difficulty is the use of the word 'good'. Matthew makes it look as if Jesus does not want us to talk about *the good* as a characteristic of our actions. But in Mark and Luke Jesus thinks it wrong for *him* to be called good. Clearly Matthew thought that was going too far: he keeps Jesus' criticism of 'good', but twists it so that it no longer applies to Jesus himself. A bit of a view of Jesus, if you like: Matthew's theology? Certainly, read the commentaries, and they all agree with Matthew that the text of Mark and Luke really doesn't justice to Jesus' divinity (or sinlessness, as others want to render 'good').

But which did Jesus say: 'Why do you call me good?' or 'Why do you ask me about the good?'? Whom must we believe? Do Mark and Luke have the original text in which – unfortunately – the words about Jesus are not theologically correct, whereas Matthew is unfaithful to the original text by improving Mark and Luke? We needn't exaggerate the difference to discover the real point. That is not whether or not we may call Jesus 'good', but whether Jesus really said what the evangelists attribute to him.

5. Jesus-authentic sayings

'Now compare that with what Jesus himself said,' I read a while ago in a church paper. It was about Jesus as the Son of God, or more precisely about whether Jesus saw himself as Son of God, and the intention was clearly to pick passages out of the Gospels. The church paper thought what most people think: the Gospels are closest to the source, to Jesus as a historical figure. If the evangelist relates that Jesus says 'I am the son of God', then that is what he said. This presupposition is a misunderstanding, as I have shown in the previous sections. Nevertheless, let's examine the Gospels to see what Jesus, according to the evangelists, said about himself. I shall take as my starting point the story set at Caesarea Philippi. There Jesus asks his disciples, 'Who do people say that I am?' (in Matthew, who the Son of man is)? The disciples' answers are meant to prompt an answer from them: 'Who do you say that I am?' 'You are the Christ,' says Peter in Mark 8.29. According to Luke 9.20, Peter says 'the Christ of God' and in Matthew (16.16) we have 'You are the Christ, the son of the living God'. Matthew has the longest text, the words which the Christian church preferred. Now precisely what did Jesus say? That seems a strange question; aren't we looking for what Jesus himself said? Now the remarkable thing is that nowhere in the Synoptic Gospels did Jesus call himself Son of God. We have indirect testimonies and the wording of these doesn't agree.

Take the interrogation before the Sanhedrin. In Mark 14.61–62 the conversation with the high priest runs as follows: '"Are you the Christ the Son of the Blessed?" And Jesus said to him, "I am, and you shall see the Son of man seated at the right hand of Power and coming with the clouds of heaven."' In Luke we read that the Sanhedrin asks Jesus, 'Are you then the Son of God?', Jesus replies, 'You yourself say that I am' (Luke 22.70). Matthew's version diverges: 'And the high priest said to him: "I abjure you by the living God, that you tell us whether you are the Christ, the son of the living God." And Jesus said to him, "You have said it."' Again, 'Son of God' does not come from Jesus' own lips, but from the lips of others. The only statement that can be regarded as a confirmation from Jesus' side ('I am', in Mark 14) is thwarted by Jesus himself by his move from 'Son' to 'Son of man'. Did he think that better? Is the Son of man someone else? Is the evangelist making things difficult for us here by joining different traditions together? Even if we have to regard the evidence I have presented here as echoes of Jesus' own testimony, the question remains: did he call himself Son of God, or the Christ, the Son of the Blessed, or the Christ, the Son of the living

God? That is not of course a point for someone who makes no distinction between these terms, or only makes liturgical use of them, but *is* there no difference?

What did Jesus really say? Here is an example which makes the problem acute. We read in Matthew 28.10 that after his resurrection Jesus says to the women to whom he appears, 'Go and tell my brothers to go to Galilee, there they shall see me.' Did he really say that? For in Luke 24.36, according to the evangelist, Jesus' first appearance to his disciples took place in Jerusalem, on the evening of the day of his resurrection. Had they gone to Galilee, then they would have so to speak missed him.

The list of differences in the tradition could be made much longer. It is not as if there were just the redactors whose hand we can clearly recognize, so clearly that we can even reconstruct their theological interest. As we have seen, the redactors stand at the end of a history of tradition which I described in the previous section as layer upon layer painted over what the first narrators had to say.

As time has gone on, scholars have identified such layers increasingly clearly and then have gone on to ask from which layer which sayings of Jesus come. It's tricky, the circular argument is obvious: the characteristics of a layer of tradition are at the same time being used as evidence for its existence. Of course that isn't on. They are and remain hypotheses: one cannot go further.

But that creates a new problem: not every researcher presents the same hypothesis. Some presuppositions are shared by almost all, for example the existence of a source Q (or even a pre-Mark), which we have already encountered. But even then not everyone attributes the same parts of the text to Q, or, more generally, not everyone puts the same saying of Jesus in the same layer. Exegetes work out what comes from Jesus himself and what doesn't on the basis of what they regard as the first layer. Edward Schillebeeckx has coined the term 'Jesus-authentic': it's bad Dutch (and bad English), but it gives a strong and succinct indication of the issue: what to the best of our knowledge comes from Jesus himself and what doesn't. For a long time the discussion about this ran along the lines: whatever isn't Jewish comes from Jesus. It was later supplemented with: whatever isn't Jewish *and* early Christian comes from Jesus. That gambles that a characteristic of authentic sayings of Jesus is that they cannot be derived from anywhere else. But Jesus was a Jew, so it is very forced to presuppose that only sayings which cannot be fitted into Jewish faith are Jesus-authentic sayings.

There is no real solution. We can be sure that a certain number of sayings were spoken by Jesus himself. Schillebeeckx includes Matthew

11.25–27 among them and bases his christology on it. In addition there are a number of sayings which certainly do not come from Jesus, but have been attributed to him by one of the groups or persons involved with the tradition. Take for example the words with which Peter is made the head of the church, Matthew 16.18. Or what Jesus says of himself in the Gospel according to John, 'I am the bread of life' (John 6.48), 'I am the life of the world' (John 8.12), expressions which must be read as: according to John, Jesus is the bread of life and the light of the world. It is extremely improbable that Jesus said this himself. Between these two extremes comes a large group of sayings which he may have spoken himself or which may have been attributed to him by a narrator or redactor – we cannot be certain. Take the saying of Jesus in Mark 10.45: 'the Son of man did not come to be served but to serve and to give his life as a ransom for many'. This plays a key role in the discussion of what 'the atonement' means, but did Jesus really say it? There is great disagreement over this among scholars.

That doesn't mean that such sayings as Mark 10.45 have lost their value. At all events they go back to a very old interpretation of Jesus' life and death – provided, of course that we may read that the Son of man = Jesus. But that doesn't prevent us from concluding that there is no unanimity as to what is Jesus-authentic in the Gospels and what is not. Exact reading ends in an impasse.

6. *An end to the cutting up?*

Discovering the layers, detaching them from the Gospel text as a whole with a scalpel (this gets sharper, the more time goes on) and opening them up, and then with their help establishing what is Jesus-authentic and what isn't is an art which specialists practise with skill, and there is no objection to their method. But this comes close to a kind of vivisection of the theological treatise called 'Gospel': the patient itself (the text) dies from it. Am I exaggerating? No. It is hard to see the multiplicity of views about what can be regarded as Jesus-authentic and what cannot other than as a real disaster: a dissected text produces a dissected Jesus, and we avoid this only by rigorously maintaining the authenticity of those sayings of Jesus which the investigator or lay person thinks important or appropriate to his person. These are legitimated by demonstrating that they come from the basic layer of the account. I realize that it can be hardly otherwise, but, to put it mildly, the image of Jesus doesn't become any clearer. So how do we get any further, if there is any further?

Certainly there is one way of stopping the scissors: to get back to the text as it is. Leave the Gospels as they are, don't cut them into bits again, accept that we have no basis to stand on other than the texts as they are. Put an end to the distinction between what is Jesus-authentic and what isn't, between what is and what is not historically verified (or at least verifiable), and there will again be a breathing space for faith.

It has already been argued that we should go back to the text as we have it, and people have done this. To do so we have to go back to the Old Testament, and in it particularly to the five books of Moses, the so-called Pentateuch (*penta* is Greek for 'five'). For more than two centuries, with varying success and in a more or less convincing way, scholars have tried to distinguish the different strands in the tradition from one another, to attribute them to a number of separate narrators, each with their own characteristics. These have constantly been further refined, so that in the end it has been hard to see the wood for the trees. That provoked the call for a return to the text which had been handed down. Redactors? All right, but – according to the well-known maxim of F. H. Breukelman – R = R, the redactor is our rabbi. To read the Old Testament is to read the text and not fragments of text.

Now we cannot make a direct comparison between the Pentateuch and the Gospels. The problems of method with which the investigation of the Pentateuch wrestled are in part the same as those in the investigation of the formation of the Gospels, for example the question whether what are identified as characteristics of a narrative tradition can at the same time be accepted as proof of the evidence of this tradition. But simply because of the different lengths of time over which the tradition was formed, the difference between the two kinds of investigation is too great for us to lump them together. Nor is that what I mean. The point of agreement is a call to return to the text as it is and not to make use of the scissors. Let it be the redactor, who produced the Gospels in their present form, and who down the centuries has been the teacher and the informant of the Christian church. He had reasons for doing what he did. So don't let's cut into pieces the unity that he produced and thus frustrate the testimony on which the Christian faith has established itself.

The words I am using to describe this standpoint already show that we can find this return to the text of the evangelists themselves above all in conservative Christian circles. Their argument that the evangelist did not do this for no good reason, that he had a plan, is a telling one. There is nothing against this way of dealing with the Gospels. Indeed, we have to adopt it, since we have only these texts. In a later chapter I shall show that treating the text as text, i.e. in the form in which it has been handed down, has also gained popularity outside conservative circles: the Gospels can also be treated as literature. The question, however, is whether this gets us any further.

At all events, everything doesn't remain as it was, as people had hoped. As far as the Gospels are concerned, 'what it was' is the result of an inexact reading, introducing harmony where the evangelists introduced differences. So we can say that the redactor is our teacher and informer: but which of the four? If we make the Gospels literature, we come up against precisely the same problems. It is hard to ask literary critics to read less exactly for the sake of believing Christians.

The most important question is something else. Asking which parts of the book of Genesis come from the source J and which from E and P (I am following the jargon of the scholars) doesn't establish anything prior to the text, far less the question whether Abraham really said what is attributed to him. But the question whether Jesus said what the evangelists report is a different matter. Even conservative circles will think that an extremely important question. But they solve it by explaining all the words attributed to Jesus as Jesus-authentic. So they solve the problem with a dogmatic theory about the infallibility of the biblical authors. That takes us round in a circle. For that is how the problem began: historical research challenged dogmatic theory by putting question-marks after 'really happened' and 'really said'.

If we keep to the texts as they are, we have indeed stopped cutting up. But that – it should be noted – is at the cost of historical investigation, which is now excluded. Conversely, those who want to continue with historical investigation, into the Jesus who lived, who spoke and what he said then, must keep on cutting up, using the scalpel and everything else that goes with it; at all events, they must take all this into account in the way in which they deal with the Gospels. That seems to me to be the solution, but I shall postpone going on to it and first continue along the track that I am following here.

II

From Meaning to 'Meaningful'

We belong to language and history before they
belong to us

(*David Tracy*)

5

'Do you understand what you are reading?'

1. 'Understanding' as a return to the past

'The Ethiopian eunuch' is the name of the story told in Acts 8. A man, a black man, was travelling from Jerusalem back to his own country, and on the way, sitting in his coach, he was reading a book, as we might do in the train today. He met up with an evangelist, who asked him, 'Do you understand what you are reading?' Now the eunuch happened to be reading an old book, the prophet Isaiah, and had got to the passage which mentions a mysterious figure called 'the servant of the Lord'. The clarity of the eunuch's reply leaves nothing to be desired. 'How can I?,' he says, 'for there is no one to show me.' The sequel is well known: beginning with these lines from Isaiah, the evangelist brings him the good news of Jesus Christ. The man is so attracted by this preaching that he stops the carriage – when he sees water somewhere – and has himself baptized by the evangelist.

I have used this story because it illustrates what people have for centuries understood as exposition (exegesis) of the Bible. The eunuch knew what a servant was, and he will also have known what or who is meant by this Lord, but he couldn't make out the expression 'servant of the Lord', let alone what or who the prophet Isaiah meant by it. That had to be explained to him first. 'Exegesis' is showing someone round a writing, and 'understanding' is the result of this exegesis: 1. being able to grasp the meaning of words, expressions, passages from a book (any book) and 2. knowing what the words and expressions used point to, to what person or event.

Now the exegesis of the Bible is a particularly complicated matter. The Bible is a writing, or rather a collection of writings, from the past. So are the Gospels. The exegesis of such writings requires the exegete to understand the meaning of the words and discover who or what they refer to; it requires the exegete to undertake something like a journey into the past, to learn the language, to get acclimatized to an earlier period, to the spirit of this time and this particular author. So 'exegesis'

in the sense in which I am now using the word has become a very important discipline in Christian theology. How shall we understand the
documents of the Christian faith which come from times that lie far
behind us, if no one shows us? Established translations have already
understood this and therefore often provide notes at the bottom of the
page of the translated text of the Bible. In this way generations of
Christians have come to understand the text of the Bible better.

But of course information about the past isn't everything. It is
necessary to return to the present with what we have understood. And
a great problem begins here, familiar to everyone who has done Bible
study (as it was called when I was a student preacher). Exegesis as a
journey backwards is all very well, but the journey must be a return
journey, otherwise it makes no sense and everything remains in the past.
What has been found must have meaning for the present; it must do
something for us. But how do we achieve that? Clergy above all faced
this question, because they were the men (or women) who had been
burdened with the application of what had been discovered. As exegetes
they have to uncover the past, and as clergy they have to say what it
means for the present.

Consequently, the sermons of the clergy used to have a clear structure: first there were two points with a historical or dogmatic exposition
of the text, and then in the third point came the application, the moment
at which those who had gone to sleep had to be woken up. The one was
impossible without the other. What one had to think when reading 'Son
of man' was one thing, a necessary preparation, but what the Son of
man meant today was a different matter. Exegesis was one thing and
application in the form of the sermon was another.

2. 'Today if you will hear his voice.' Bultmann and 'understanding'

Understanding was seen as an expedition into the past and then a return
with booty which had to be brought up to date in the so-called application. 'But I don't call that understanding,' said Bultmann. We have
already come across his name earlier, and we could see how drastically
he questioned what was taken for granted about text and interpretation.

According to Bultmann, understanding happens only where the
Gospel says or does something to us. Of course a grasp of the text is
necessary for that, exegesis in the sense in which I used the word in the
previous section: becoming wise to the past, knowing what the words
mean and what they refer to. But even if I know what 'Son of man'
means, or 'Servant of the Lord', and over and above that know that this

refers to Jesus, the gospel has not yet become meaningful. For one can speak of 'understanding' only when one is addressed by the gospel.

That is a statement with which Bultmann as it were starts a new page: understanding the Bible means making it meaningful. The old model, first back to the past and take what emerges for you there into the present and try to apply it there, is laid aside. Bultmann combines exegesis and application, so that there is no separate application. 'Understanding' is a matter of being addressed by the gospel *today*.

Bultmann can talk like this because for him the gospel itself is already a sermon: he doesn't read it *a priori* as information about the past; or, to put it more strongly, in so far as it tells about the past it is uninteresting, only a condition for 'understanding', good for historians and no more. The Christian church must use the gospel in such a way that the community hears it as proclamation (I shall leave on one side the complicated business which Bultmann thinks necessary to achieve this), or, to use his own terminology once again, as kerygma, summons ('Today if you will hear his voice'). Only if you hear it as a call which does something to you, have you understood it.

What does it do then? At this point Bultmann seems to want to have the best of both worlds. For he already tells the readers (or the hearers) *what* the text does to them: to put it in as Lutheran a way as possible (Bultmann was a Lutheran), it brings them to their knees. That means that a bit of dogmatism begins to guide the understanding of the Gospels; the text has already had its say. So Bultmann begins from the present, the meaning of the gospel for my life, today, but at the same time he has already established this meaning. However, he can't really do that. If it really is the case that 'understanding' emerges when a writing, a text, including the text of the Gospel, tells us something or does something to us, then we must be consistent and leave open *whether* it does anything to us and if so *what*, and not state *a priori* that we have really understood it only if we go down on our knees.

Another prejudice of Bultmann's is that he mixes up his view of 'understanding' (it must indicate more than 'back to the past') with his view of the kerygma as bridging the gulf between past and present. Therefore he keeps repeating that believing = 'understanding': an equation which can only be understood properly when we see what he means by 'understanding', namely being touched by the Word. Nevertheless, Bultmann stood at a crossroads, and with his demand that 'meaning' must be something for today, for the present, he took a path which later became a broad way followed by many others.

3. Ebeling. The Word and the words

Someone like Gerhard Ebeling has gone a good deal further. For him, too, the understanding of scripture in general and of the Gospels in particular means a good deal more than digging in the past and then going to the present and applying them there. There is 'understanding' only when someone has been addressed by the Word of God. But Ebeling will not have anything to do with Bultmann's actualism – the Word of God is the speaking God himself, and just as the first community knows that it is confronted here in Jesus, so we learn that in the kerygma. Along with all kinds of objections that need not concern us here, Ebeling thinks that this is far too limited a view of the Word of God. Here all we can really say about God is what God does to us on the spot: the Word cannot be expressed more than that. And in fact, as we may recall, that is almost precisely what Bultmann said. But that means that God remains outside ordinary life; the Word remains outside our words. And didn't it appear precisely there, in the figure of Jesus?

In fact, for Ebeling 'understanding' is a far broader event than in Bultmann: not so much a thunderbolt (or better, a flash of lighting) from a clear sky as a process of understanding that challenges, a process in which the gospel becomes meaningful for the hearer. Words are needed for that, ordinary human words, like the sermon. Ebeling puts the sermon between God who speaks and human beings who listen, and the sermon must have this effect, can have this effect, since words can become meaningful for a person. What does 'becoming meaningful' amount to? It is the way in which the gospel shows us our place before God. So – to put it briefly – 'understanding' is not the interpretation of a text. The texts interpret us, make clear to us who we are before God.

That is a striking formulation, the opposite of what we are used to, but it indicates, all the more clearly, that Ebeling has said good-bye to 'understanding' as such a journey into the past. 'Understanding' takes place today as Word-event, to use Ebeling's term, and by 'Word' he means that God shows us our place through the usual human words of preaching. The Word works through the words.

Here Ebeling has gone one step further than Bultmann. Still modestly, and packaged in a great deal of theology (Ebeling is a systematic theologian and not, like Bultmann, a biblical scholar), he gives a foretaste of what the prevailing theory will become: making the texts themselves do their work, but as texts, as human words. This means not reading the Gospels like historians, as documents which seek to provide enlightenment about the past; not reading them in the manner of the scholars of religion, who turned them into religious fantasy or mythology (which then in turn has to be demythologized); nor even reading them as proclamation in action, as the word of God that thunders at us and bowls us over, but reading them as texts which tell us in human words about Jesus, his words and actions and what happened to him. We then hope and expect that the words, these ordinary words, become meaningful for us = that the Word is expressed in the words.

We can see that, like Bultmann, Ebeling cannot let go of this preference for the Word, for preaching. The whole of his theology is built on this; theology is really a 'preaching aid'. And because (again, just as with Bultmann) the word is always identified with Jesus, in Ebeling, too, all the attention is focussed on Jesus. But this is Jesus as a historical figure, as the Gospels tell his story. These stories, the tradition about Jesus, form the material for preaching.

Hence the greater space that Ebeling gives to the historical Jesus, the Jesus of that time. This is not meant as a return to the time before Albert Schweitzer, but is rather intended to make room for the texts themselves, to give them the chance of being meaningful for us who live now. Having arrived at this point, we encounter the same problem that we encountered in Bultmann. 'Understanding' is a free process, so it would be consistent for human beings themselves to establish the meaning of the gospel. But we do not find this conclusion in Ebeling. Like Bultmann, he puts his view of 'understanding' in theological dress: the issue is not just 'understanding', but hearing the Word of God in the words (viz. preaching). And for him, too – in classical Lutheran fashion – the issue is the Word-event through which people learn to see themselves as sinners and righteous. What we have to understand is really already fixed. All too fixed, we could well say. For we may have an idea of what the Gospels are about – we must have an idea, otherwise we wouldn't read them – but if this is more than an idea, if what they are about is already completely fixed, we needn't read any more: we already know it all. I shall be returning to this point at the end of this chapter.

I have already indicated in passing where this theological dress comes from. It is an attempt to answer – still – a tormenting question which is as old as Lessing: how do we fill in the ditch between the past (Jesus then) and the present (us today)? By 'understanding', and 'understanding' means being addressed by the gospel itself. When using the word 'gospel', Bultmann is thinking of the God who speaks today, the Word that the first disciples encountered in Jesus and which we – today – encounter in the kerygma. When using the word 'gospel' (in a much more concrete way), Ebeling is thinking of the stories, the parables, in short the words which the Word (viz. Jesus) needs in order to come to us (viz. to become significant for us).

4. *Meaning*

Before I go any further, some clarification is needed about the meaning of the word 'meaning', otherwise it will cause confusion. The context in which the term occurs determines the content that we give to it. Talking about barometric pressure, the weather forecaster says 'That means rain'. Someone talking to his beloved asks her, 'Do I mean anything to you today?' And so on. I shall not go at length here into the possible contexts (and thus the different meanings of 'meaning'), but limit myself to the two that I have mentioned so far.

1. I begin with 'meaning' in the sense of the meaning of a word, where 'word' stands for words (plural), expressions, clauses or sentences that we hear or read. By 'meaning', we then mean two things: those words, clauses or sentences point to something or someone and at the same time say something about that. I have taken the examples that I mentioned (the Servant of the Lord, the Son of man, sitting at the right hand of God) from the Gospels: they show us how the two sides of the meaning of a word belong together. If no one can tell us to whom these terms refer (for example, to Jesus), we do not know who they're about, and if no one can clarify for us what is said about Jesus by them, we are just as far away, and the reference doesn't help us. Both aspects of the meaning of the word make it necessary for us to have an interpreter (usually called an exegete in theology) to understand the Gospels. These are writings which came into being in a distant past, written in a foreign language, and about situations and events in which we didn't take part. Knowing one's way around such a text is usually called comprehending it.

2. But 'meaning' can also relate to the question whether the words, expressions, in short, the gospel or a passage from it speak to us, say something to us. Of course comprehending the words is an indispensable precondition for this: in fact there is a *Theological Dictionary of the New Testament* which goes into the question of comprehension from A to Z. Only then do we know what we have to have in mind in connection with 'scribe' or 'servant of Jesus Christ'; we can understand what the dispute between Jesus and the Pharisees is about, to mention just one thing. But that is not the same thing as 'being addressed' by what is written there.

Jesus is a good example of the difference between two meanings of 'meaning'. What does Jesus mean? According to Matthew, saviour ('He shall save his people from their sins', 1.21). In that case we are talking about the meaning of Jesus as a name, i.e. 'meaning' in the first connection: the meaning of a word. But I can also ask: What is the meaning of Jesus for me? In that case, the question is one of 'meaning' in the sense of Jesus saying or doing something to me. I am addressed by what the evangelists say about him. Jesus has become meaningful for me.

In this (second) context, 'expound' usually means interpret, the art of arriving at an understanding of a text, and 'understanding' is then that what first was 'put into words', a writing, a piece of text, a passage from the Gospel, becomes 'meaningful' through interpretation. I choose this formulation to show that 'understanding' is about a change of make-up: words become 'meaningful'. The question how that comes about, where this meaning comes from, forms the beginning of a new approach, which is called hermeneutics.

5. Hermeneutics as the art of interpretation

People like Bultmann and Ebeling are representatives of a much wider movement, which has become well known under the name of the 'hermeneutical shift': hermeneutics as a change in philosophy, another approach, even a counter-movement to, let's say, positivism. In theology it performs the same function. What is hermeneutics?

1. Of course the term 'hermeneutics' was also used before the shift. The professor under whom I studied the exegesis of the New Testament understood it as the conditions for defining the presuppositions which play a role in exegesis (view of language, epistemology), and the rules of the art of interpretation. 'Biblical hermeneutics' was a direct consequence of this: the Bible was a special writing, God's Word, and thus other presuppositions applied in its exposition (the infallibility of Holy Scripture, no contradictions, etc.), different from those connected with 'ordinary' writings from the past.

2. What is new is a much broader view of hermeneutics, or rather of those presuppositions of which hermeneutics must take account as the art of interpreting. For one thing, previously insufficient attention was paid to them: everything that people say about the world, absolutely everything, relates to the world as they see it. This isn't an objective world, but the world 'according to': according to the Indians, the Western European peoples, the Blacks and so on. Sometimes there is a colossal difference between these worlds and sometimes they more or less coincide, but the speaker always so to speak appears in them, in

what is presented or shown to us as reality. In short, the world is the world in its meaning for the speaker. 'Meaning' isn't something subsequently attached to an object that initially is still without it. Or, to pick up the previous section: our world is the world which is 'meaningful'; there is no other world. So we can confidently read what something or someone is as what someone or something means to the people who talk about it.

From this perspective there is no philosophy which is not at least hermeneutics. People themselves are involved in all expressions of their lives. Their world is 'meaningful' (as something that has been made) and is thus dependent on interpretation if it is to say something to us. But I shall not go further into that. I shall limit myself to texts from former times, and again focus on our Gospels.

3. Such a text from the past is not an objective account but a story in which the author himself appears, with all that he thinks, discovers, feels and knows as a child of his time. In the next chapter I shall give an extensive account of what that means for our view of the text of the Gospels. Here first of all I shall describe what it means for the exegete. This position is different from that of our Reformed forefathers. Just as the author appears in his account, so too the exegete appears in his exegesis, again with all that he or she thinks, knows, feels and discovers as a child of his or her time. So Bultmann was right: 'understanding' *cannot* come about through a return to the past, for in that case we would be acting 1. as if the Gospels were an account with no contribution from their authors, a so-called objective account, and 2. as if in our journey into the past we had detached ourselves from the present. As if that were possible!

4. That's how the theologians did often treat the Gospels (and the whole of the Bible). The meaning was there; it was pulled out of the past and lay there, like a fish on dry land. So people were fond of talking about translating. They thought that this word indicated well that there were difficulties of access to the meaning of the Gospels for so-called modern men and women; however, these had to do not so much with the actual meaning as with expressing this meaning. So this view of things isn't right: that's why I prefer to talk about interpreting rather than translating. In doing so I am indicating that authors are involved in their accounts and exegetes in their exegesis.

5. Thus the 'understanding' of writings (from former times or now) comes about through interpreting, and if my description is right, it is clear that interpretation involves a good deal of relativity and uncertainty. Interpretation, 1. goes through a very complicated process. One

can lay down rules for it, as classical hermeneutics did, and indeed that is necessary – rules for exegesis in terms of what I have called the meaning of words – but even if one knows everything about 'Son of man', everything about 'coming with the clouds of heaven', everything about Nazareth and Bethlehem, Jesus still hasn't yet become 'meaningful' for today. And that is what we mean by interpretation: expounding Jesus in such a way that people of today are going to find him 'meaningful'. Do rules also need to be made here, or must we wait to see whether Jesus says or does anything for the people of today? Interpretation is 2. also a tricky undertaking! Suppose I try to work out what in my view makes Jesus someone who is meaningful for human beings in the world. I interpret the Gospel, but who interprets me, the interpreter? I am always bringing myself in as interpreter. Is that taken into account in my interpretation? Do I myself take it into account? And how far am I involved in it? 'Becoming meaningful' seems to be almost an incomprehensible process. I shall go into it further in a moment.

6. By way of a (necessary) detour, here is a short note on critical hermeneutics. Hitherto my basic assumption has been that we want Jesus to become 'meaningful'. This is interpretation in the service of the continuation of a tradition of faith: Jesus important then, Jesus important now. But one could also imagine that people or states of affairs which were formerly thought important are in our view not at all so today. Take enlightened despotism as a political system: the king knows best. We think quite differently about that from people of former times; we definitely don't want to continue this tradition, since we see enlightened despotism as tyranny rather than as a blessing. So interpretation is criticism, and indeed we can't do without it. We can harness interpretation both to what we want to continue and what we don't want to continue.

6. How does Jesus become 'meaningful'? 'Content' and text

'Becoming meaningful' begins with a slight conscious or unconscious sense of knowing where to begin, or at least of thinking that one knows. I must already understand something about a computer if I plan to go on a PC course. That applies to all kinds of knowledge, including knowledge of God, said Plato. You wouldn't care about God unless you already knew something about him. The same thing is necessary to understand the gospel of Jesus. No 'understanding' develops, Jesus does not become 'meaningful', unless we have a bit of an idea what the Gospel turns on, a sense of what Karl Barth called 'the content' of the

Gospel. There would be no interpretation unless the 'content' were somewhere pre-programmed into the reader. The role played by the 'content' in understanding the Gospel is thus a key role, in more than one respect.

Of course there has long been a fleeting idea of what the 'content' of the Gospels could be. It consists in what we have been told about the meaning of Jesus, i.e. in the knowledge of the Christian tradition into which we are born: the gospel is ultimately about none other than Jesus. So we have not just a fleeting idea, but a bucketful of ideas: Jesus does not need to become meaningful; we already know his meaning. And oddly enough, it also works the other way round. If we already know everything, there is nothing left to be curious about. But that will come later.

First the 'content' we begin with in the Gospels. As I have said, this is offered to us by the Christian church. Down the centuries the church formed the religious context in which the reading of the Gospels took place. So it also formulated the content of the reading, what makes Jesus 'significant' and therefore what makes us prick up our ears. The Christian church thus provided readers as it were with the guide which indicated what would be encountered in the gospel. The 'content' was clear. Except that it didn't always take the same form.

There was a time – the time of the church fathers – when human transitoriness was the great stumbling-block in life and people were offered participation in God's immortal nature as the 'content' of the gospel. For the Middle Ages, life was suffering, just as for the Reformation sinners and their guilt were central: what the gospel had to offer to people who were troubled by that was its 'content'. Today, for many people life is the suffering of injustice: for women, being a woman is often tantamount to being marginalized. There are yet other questions which cry out for an answer. Are *they* what leads us today to the 'content', from which the gospel of Jesus derives its significance for the people of our time? Or are they perhaps (temporary) lures which will soon disappear again?

This much is clear: without some 'content' as a guide (in its most general formulation, we discover in it how people become human), the gospel does not begin to speak and Jesus does not become meaningful. We read with prior knowledge, with a pre-supposition, a kind of preju- dice about what is to be expected, otherwise we wouldn't read.

But there is also another side to this: the more firmly this prior know- ledge was established, the more crudely the Christian church formulated what the meaning of Jesus is, and the less people needed to read

Matthew, Mark, Luke and John: they already knew it all. That's also
how it often is in practice, to the present day: many faithful churchgoers
do not read the Gospels (to keep just to them), because they think that
they know what is in them. But there is again another side to that. The
more the power of the church crumbles, the freer readers feel to deviate
from the prescribed direction: they themselves read the text again and
make it their own. That can happen on all sides, as we shall see, for in
principle the modern reader too can only begin by having a guess at
what the issue is, a guess at the 'content' which makes Jesus meaningful. How does one know whether this guess is right? One doesn't know
in advance; all kinds of things can happen even as one reads, and one
can end up with another content. The meaning of Jesus is as it were a
provisional scheme: it has an aura of provisionality, of relativity, about
it which we cannot remove and which we mustn't want to remove. If we
did, we would miss the boat, for any provisional scheme that we may
make of Jesus' meaning must legitimate itself by the text of the Gospel.
I shall come back to that in the next chapter. The text either confirms
or does not confirm our provisional scheme.

The 'content', the pointer, or whatever name we want to give it,
sometimes consists in a greater whole from which Jesus derives his
meaning. How we arrive at that, where this comes from, is thus a constantly recurring, extremely important, question. If the tradition of faith
in the Christian church no longer works well as a pointer, we can try to
improve it by broadening the framework. Someone like Schillebeeckx
describes Jesus' meaning in the framework of the human history of
suffering. Grollenberg saw Jesus as a way to peaceful co-existence.
Which framework do we chose? Do we have to choose? But that already
takes me too far ahead of myself. These questions come later.

7. 'Do you understand what you are reading?' = Does Jesus become 'meaningful'?

Despite all the complications, this chapter has been about a simple question: how does Jesus become 'meaningful' for us instead of being 'mere
words'?

1. The complications have to do with getting rid of the misunderstanding that to discover Jesus' meaning is to discover from the past
what he said and what he did, his life and his fate. Here one doesn't get
beyond 'that's interesting' unless the meaning is already laid down in
the dogma of Christian teaching. And indeed, if that is the case, time
and again exegesis again simply amounts to bringing up the past. Isn't

the rest known? That approach takes its revenge: the meaning of Jesus gets lost. He becomes 'meaningful' only if 'understanding' follows the course of interpretation.

2. As I have already suggested earlier, 'understanding' is a free process. It cannot be guided; it happens as it happens; in other words, nothing happens or great deal happens, one is talking about something or talking about nothing, as with 'a good book'. As practice shows, people think differently about this. Why? Because only the readers (or the hearers) can say whether a work or a bit of a work means something in the sense of being 'meaningful' to them. The meaning comes from the reader. It cannot be forced on the reader, not even the meaning of the Jesus of the Gospels. What Jesus does to us = what we do to him. Or to quote Gadamer, an important philosopher of our century: understanding is not reproduction (of the past) but production of meaning. Or yet again (and more briefly)': 'What did Jesus say?' is not the point but what Jesus *says*. Only we can answer this question.

3. Is that strange? Not as strange as it seems. Didn't we want to go back from the chopped-up Gospels to the Gospels as writings, as text? In that case they must be treated as text, as we treat literature, and when it comes to literature, 'Beauty is in the eye of the beholder.' That too is strange. If the meaning of Jesus can be derived only from us as readers, what more does the exposition of a passage of a text from the Gospels offer? Is there something else to expound, or is anything possible, and is it all just as good? In the next chapter I shall show that precisely this anxious question, precisely this idea that we have got into an impasse, forms the niche in which new forms of exegesis can nestle.

4. Another bit of theology: we see why Bultmann and Ebeling (to keep to those two) could not surrender themselves totally to hermeneutics. The gulf which separates the past and the present is bridged if Jesus comes to mean something for us. But if 'meaning' comes from the reader, from ourselves, who live in the present, then we ourselves have crossed this gulf. That was going too far for both theologians, and so they stop half way: or rather, they maintain that the Gospels have a normative content.

6

Text and exegesis. The literary Christ

1. Language as 'putting into speech'

The Gospels are writings, texts, as I shall say from now on, and texts consist of language. There is more to be said about them, but at least they consist of language, and thus are subject to the same characteristics, peculiarities, unexpected jumps as any other expressions of language. So what is language?

Language is an ambiguous word in English. By it you can mean what foreigners have to learn if they want to live in Britain: the language as it is described in the textbooks. How humanity arrived at language (in this sense) and why there are so many different languages is just as complicated a problem as the question where and when our mind began to play a role. I shall leave that on one side and content myself with saying that language is a collection of words with the help of which people, through an endless series of possible combinations, can put 'into words' what they want to communicate. This is true of all languages, and so I shall speak of language (in the singular). Language is the most perfected means by which human beings can communicate with one another. It's fine to use hands and feet to make something clear to one another; to make love is even finer; but without language intercourse is a thin event.

So language is a means. With the help of language we put ourselves and our world into speech. I shall be concerned here with language in this sense, in other words language as 'speech'. Two aspects of this will concern us. First of all we know our world and ourselves only as a world 'put into speech'. In this sense, the reality in which we find ourselves is always translated reality. Some thinkers draw from this the conclusion that there is only a 'linguistic' reality, in the sense that outside our language there is nothing. Thus there is no point in testing statements. This necessarily ends up in testing them by other statements, testing language by language, and so on, and one can't call that testing. However, this conclusion won't do; it gives in too soon. The inability to go outside language does not in itself mean that there is nothing outside language. Were that the case, nothing new could enter our world, and I cannot accept that.

Reality put into speech is reality as human beings see it. That is the second important aspect here. If I say that our world is one 'of language', I mean that with their speaking, their speech, people are not doing philosophy but putting into words the world as they experience it. Speech is the world and the world is speech, so in speech we encounter the interpreted world. The whole of life consists of interpretation; this statement from the previous chapter finds its foundation here. And to interpret texts is to interpret interpretations – that is also the case.

Thus from the language by which people understand one another we can always reconstruct how people think about themselves and their world. From language *as speech*, not from language in the first sense of the world, language as it occurs in the textbooks. That has also in fact been claimed: for example, that it would be possible from Hebrew vocabulary, Hebrew grammar, Hebrew declensions and conjugations, to infer how the Israelites thought about human beings and the world. And because the Israelites are the people of the revelation – thus the argument – it is of great importance for us to note this language, Hebrew: the language itself is said to have revelatory content.

Quite apart from the appeal to revelation, that's an exaggerated view. Of course vocabulary and terminology differ from culture to culture, depending on all kinds of factors which define a culture, from climate to the level of development. But one cannot go any further. What people think is not expressed in the language as a system (the grammar, the idiom, the declensions and so on), so one cannot say that language (as a system) channels the thought of those who are born within this language. We don't know which came first, thought or language. We can discover what people thought of life in a particular linguistic community, their interpretation of existence, from the way in which they put their life *into speech*.

Of course language as speech introduces a collective element of interpretation. People communicate with one another with the help of language; that means (literally) that they share something, and what could that mean if not that by and large they maintain the same values: a free person is better off than a slave, life is better than death, and so on. That collective element is strongly present in traditional communities, but the more a society develops, the more speech can also be used to oppose the code. But again language (speech) is needed for that.

Language (speech) remains the binding element between people, *the* means of communication. Whether communication comes about is of course another question.

Language as interpreted reality entails two things: 1. the speaker is not the onlooker but the actor, the inhabitant of the world, and: 2. in his or her speaking this world always comes back put into speech: speech is always *about* something. No matter what a person says! People want everything when they have a say (with good reason that 'speaking' is called the performance of a speech-action). They speak in order to inform, to moan, to rejoice, to complain or to praise God. But none of that alters the fact that the speaker is always talking about *something*, bringing a bit of the world on stage. Speaking is performing, and performing includes interpreting.

2. *Text as textile*

The Gospels are composed not only of language, but also of text; if I may put it that way, they arise out of the material 'text'. Language as speech is, as the word already says, first and foremost spoken language. Texts are also language, but this is language set down in writing, written language. It is language set down in writing, in which later individuals can read what earlier individuals have expressed, written language, and as such a record of interpretations. That is also true of the Gospels. Taken as text they convey interpretation, in the sense of interpretation of Jesus: of his life, work and death. Hence the official name is (just look at the titles given in the translations of the Bible): Gospel *according to* Matthew, Mark, etc.

Where language has become text, written word, a number of complications arise which I am going to discuss in this chapter. In the case of the Gospels (as text) these complications mount up, when we think that they were preceded by oral tradition, which was continued in written versions, which in their turn were again collected into a unity by a redactor, say Matthew, with his own theological views. I described that process in the previous chapter; now I am taking the opportunity of bringing to light the questions with which texts from the past, for example those from the Gospel according to Matthew, confront us.

Matthew is a writing from a distant past, in a language which has become alien to us. As for language = putting into speech, Matthew puts Jesus into speech as people experienced him, using terms which we no longer know or use. This will be familiar to those who have the Gospels at their fingertips: the Son of man who will come with the clouds of

heaven to divide the sheep and the goats, the resurrection of Jesus, however differently it is told to us in the four Gospels – this doesn't surprise
us; these are sacred texts. But what are the texts really saying? Granted,
we have translated them from the Greek (translation is already a form
of interpretation), but that is not enough: we must give text *and* interpretation of the language (the speech) of Matthew, Mark and so on, and
that is not as simple a business as the average reader imagines.

To mention the most important point first of all: the Gospel text
consists of words, sentences, ideas, stories and so on by means of which
the evangelists express the significance which they attach to Jesus. But
where do they get these words from? Answer: they find them in the
language (speech) which was already there. Even the stories. Think of
the resurrection of the young man of Nain (Luke 7.11–17): whether it
really happened or not, such stories were well known in the vocabulary
of the Jewish people (see I Kings 17.17–24). The evangelist can make
use of material which has already played a role earlier; he recycles existing terms, notions and stories. A well-known example is Mary's song of
praise in Luke 1, which is constructed (composed, one might almost
say) from Miriam's song of praise (Exodus 15) and that of Hannah (I
Samuel 2).

The reuse of words, expressions and notions is the distinctive character of any use of language. *What* one says, one says with language which
already has a whole history behind it. That we communicate with one
another through such a language is a miracle, natural though it may
seem to us. In written language that is of course the case, but there we
have the advantage that by a close investigation of the preceding texts
we can retrace the way by which particular expressions and notions
have come down to us.

To focus our thought, take the titles which were given to Jesus:
Messiah, Son of man, the Son, and so on. These are all current notions
which the evangelists use to indicate how important Jesus was to them.
But what were they thinking of when, for example, they called Jesus
'messiah'? The world of Jesus' day was teeming with ideas of a messiah.
Or take the expression 'Son of man'. It comes from Daniel 7, but is that
the passage which we must think of, or should we think rather of all
kinds of discussions of this figure in the so-called apocryphal books?
What undertones keep echoing? If we as readers want to understand
what the text is about, and moreover want this text to be meaningful,
then we have to know that.

Language (speech) is a storehouse of meanings, and so too is the language of the Gospels. So a text, say the text of Matthew, is something

like (to go over to another metaphor) a mixture of old pieces of wool; it is textile, a weave of words that are used, recycled language, the meaning of which we have to try to establish through exegesis.

3. A text is an orphan

But why don't we ask Matthew himself (or Luke or Mark) what he means when Jesus is called the Christ? The question is obvious, but let's see how far we can get with an answer.

To begin with, who is Matthew? We have seen that this Gospel consists of fragments of theology about Jesus: Matthew is a redactor. So it is already not so simple to arrive at Matthew's meaning. That is easier with the Gospel of John. John tells his own story; he makes use of the same stories and words as the other evangelists, but he is more markedly present as a redactor with his own theology than they are. He tells and does that with an explicit purpose, 'that you may believe that Jesus is the Son of God, and believing have life in his name' (John 20.31).

But there are meanings and meanings. We know what John intends with his Gospel. But do we also know what he means when he says that the true worshippers of God will worship in spirit and in truth (John 4.23)? In any case we cannot ask him, since he is no longer there. That's the great difference between reading a text and hearing a narrator. We can see and hear the narrator: we see his facial expressions, hear the way in which he raises his voice now and then, notice that he makes gestures to emphasize his meaning, and if even then his story isn't clear to us we can ask him: What do you mean? Tell us again, because we don't understand it properly.

In the case of a writer who has written a story, that isn't always possible (where do we find him or her?). It is certainly impossible in the case of a writer from the past like John. The writer writes, and after that lets go of what has been written. That's the definition of a text: a story or an exposition, let go by the writer. Plato said that a book is an orphan: it no longer has a father. It goes its own way and from then on plays a role of its own. The author and his or her intentions no longer play a part. The book has become the readers' and they do what they want with it. That happens to all books and collections, including the New Testament Gospels. The writers no longer have any say about their writings. The readers do: for them these mean something or – just as possible – nothing.

To investigate what the author of a writing from the distant past meant isn't forbidden, it's quite natural. And the investigation isn't always hopeless or doomed to failure. But it's plain as a pikestaff that we can no longer ask the author himself. So how are we to discover his meaning? Can we put ourselves in Paul's thought-processes? Become of one mind with the apostle? But how will we know when we get there? The only one who could tell us, Paul himself, is no longer there. We have only the text as it lies before us, and that is what we have to deal with.

To the present day, traditional theology and preaching think differently here; they do not find the meaning of the biblical authors any problem, and if they do, then it is a problem of a lesser order. The experts are there to bring us back to Paul's meaning if it escapes us. But is that really true? If the meaning is no problem, then we can be content with reading the words and stories of the Gospel 'as it stands'; indeed we may just as well put it all on a tape and play it in times of need or longing. In reality we don't do that; even Christians faithful to the Bible don't do that, but interpret just like everyone else. Every Sunday sermon is interpretation, but because today's sermon sounds just like yesterday's sermon and the sermon of the day before that, it seems as if no interpretation is involved. That's a mistake: the interpretation doesn't strike us because it is held captive in a straitjacket of traditional, orthodox exposition.

4. The readers take their revenge

Traditional orthodoxy is tedious. That is particularly the case with its sermons: they're always the same. The hearers are told in advance what the Bible will say (according to the minister). Basically that's because as far as possible the readers are kept inactive; they have to remain outside the text. Even deliberately, since there cannot and may not be any other interpretation than the one that they are being given. For orthodoxy, creativity is no virtue.

But the readers are still there! I shall take this up again later. For times have changed, and a flood of new exegesis of the Gospels, even of the whole Bible, has appeared – often to the bewilderment of church and theology. I think that readers are taking their revenge: for too long they have been excluded and now they are getting involved. They can do so because two movements are converging and have given them the room that they need as readers. One is the reformulation of 'understanding', to which I devoted the previous chapter. 'Understanding' is more than just looking into the past: not only what Jesus *said* but what he *says*.

I have clarified the second line above: a text, even that of the Gospels (or rather, especially that of the Gospels), is textile, a weave of words which are involved in a recycling process. There is no term, word or notion used to describe Jesus which has not been used already. Today's readers are continuing that never-ending process and putting themselves into it; they have their own ideas, what strikes them, and with words and notions from their own world they again present to those who come after them what they have made of the speech of their predecessors.

There are two openings which the current approach to a text from the past ('What does Matthew mean?') have reversed: the meaning of a text comes about through the reader; it consists in what the reader makes of the text. In its most extreme form, this means that the text is an occasion to shape one's own thoughts on the subject presented in the text. No more than that.

And indeed it has to be said that without readers a text is nothing. Jesus becomes 'meaningful' not in what Matthew meant (if we could discover that) by his story of Jesus but in what the readers of today read into it. Does that open the floodgates? Is anything possible? In any case a great deal is possible. Bit by bit readers form a picture of the Jesus of the Gospels. Or bit by bit they drop the traditional picture which they had. That too can happen. A large number of variations are still possible, guided by a whole series of prejudgments, as we shall see. Thus in principle anything is indeed possible.

5. *The weight of a text*

At this stage it seems as if everyone is making what they will of the text. Indeed that happens, as is clear from practice. From the Gnostic Jesus to Jesus as the feminine man, to mention all the interpretations which are friendly to Jesus, it's all in the game. Reading is free and reading is the same thing as discovering a meaning in Matthew's text. We find that to be the case in 'ordinary reading', and enjoy it; we make something of it. Why should that be inappropriate in reading Matthew? To forbid this is to forbid reading. From this perspective it is understandable that for centuries the Roman Catholic Church forbade ordinary church people (laity) to read the Bible: they made of it what they thought good, and that was rather different from what the church (the clergy) themselves thought good. However, that time – fortunately – is past: no church any longer forbids the untrained to read the Bible.

What does still happen is what orthodoxy has been doing from time immemorial: it lays down the meaning in terms of a standard exposition, of an unchangeable formulation of the 'content' of the Gospel, and in so doing again robs the Bible of its freedom. There is no such thing as a standard exegesis. Even a legal text (and here we have something which is tremendously precise) does not have a standard exposition, as jurisprudence indicates. Jurisprudence consists of the way in which lawyers look case by case at how they must expound the law.

So the real frontier lies elsewhere, as this example shows: there is also still a text. Exegesis has to do with an independent entity, a written word. Everything is possible, people can make what they will of Jesus, as for example Matthew has described him, but not everything that they make of him is equally good, in the sense that not everything can appeal with equal justification to the text of Matthew. Just as the text of the law precedes the lawyer's exposition, so the Gospel of Matthew precedes the reader, and continues to do so. That's what a text is for.

So the text has a weight of its own, a power of its own, over against the reader, who is (also) a power. That is even the only reason why the text is read: because it puts its own weight on the scales. If that wasn't the case, why would one pick it up?

I am deliberately introducing the word 'power'. It suggests that something emanates from the text, and that is also the case. One can read Matthew (to keep to him) in a slovenly way, quickly; one can take him over because one thinks that one already knows what is there ('I've read it so often'): in short, in reading a good deal can go wrong. Then the text opposes itself as text. Over time it even proves to have an element of granite in it, because it offers so much resistance to those who do not take it seriously. This element of granite is the advantage that the text has over the prejudices which hearing a living speaker raises. The text keeps coming back, if not in one reader then in another, and keeps putting a question-mark against the understanding. In other words, it always compels a re-reading.

Finally, the text has both priority over readers and also a greater weight than they do. I once read that the relationship between text and reader could be clarified by seeing the text as the score of a piece of music. Is the score the piece of music itself or not? Yes and no. It is nothing unless the music is performed, but the reverse is also true: there is nothing for the orchestra or pianist to perform if there is no score. Every performance is a rendering, an interpretation. The one isn't the other, but they are all interpretations of one and the same score, and they all have to be able to defend themselves in the face of the score. In other words, the meaning that we give to Jesus is free, completely free. But unless we treat the text responsibly, we are no longer talking about the

Jesus of the evangelists, or, to put it more strongly, the text of the Gospels need not even be there.

6. *Matthew is more than a literary text*

The Gospels are texts and must therefore be treated as texts. No 'biblical hermeneutic' or anything of that kind can evade profane rules in interpreting them. The Gospels don't need that at all. But what kind of text are they? That's a relevant question. In genre, is Matthew something like Homer or Shakespeare? Is Matthew literature? Yes, of course it is also that. The whole Bible, including the evangelists, can be read as a literary product; there is nothing against that. On the contrary, Matthew lends himself admirably to it, and many people have spent golden hours reading him. But it cannot be maintained that – to put it in an exaggerated way – the Gospels are exhausted by their literary aspect.

To begin with, people don't just read Matthew for their pleasure, as if it was a novel. Or rather – again – it is possible to read Matthew for literary needs, just as in the end it can be made into a libretto for passion music. But that isn't the reason why people have picked it up from the time it was written to the present day, and still pick it up. Literature is disinterested; people read it for pleasure, for beauty or to be shocked – it makes no difference. People read Matthew because they expect something from it, insight into God and themselves, comfort in suffering, encouragement, guidance for their lives, and so on. The expectations with which people read the Gospels ('read' here is a schematic term for 'occupy themselves with') are religious and not aesthetic. If people don't have this expectation, they aren't hungry, and why then should they eat? This is a first indication of why the Gospels aren't to be treated as a literary product.

Moreover that doesn't work without doing violence to them. In literature all that counts is the text, and in principle references to facts outside the text are unnecessary. The text isn't a transparency through which we may look at an outside world, which is what it is really all about; it is self-sufficient. In form, a hero slaying a monster is a historical story, but no one investigates who the hero might have been, since we know that this is a literary expression. There is no colleague of Sherlock Holmes who is called Dr Watson; he exists only in a series of stories. The text itself and nothing but the text; in the case of a literary creation we look no further. We don't step outside the story, even if such a literary text goes back to historical events. Think, for example, of Shakespeare's Hamlet. Stories about a tragedy at the Danish court may certainly have inspired Shakespeare in writing his play, but what he writes doesn't become greater or different if we try to investigate the historical background. It is the literary text that makes Hamlet. With Matthew things are different. I can illustrate that from an example that I once read (in a book by David Norton), a comparison between Hamlet's mother and Mary the mother of Jesus. It makes no difference to our understanding of Shakespeare's play whether or not Hamlet was an only child. We needn't investigate the question, since at least in Shakespeare's play Hamlet is a product of the imagination, clothed in the words which Shakespeare speaks about him. The text makes Hamlet and not vice versa; Hamlet (as a historical figure) doesn't make the text. The question whether Hamlet ever existed has even become unimportant. That's what literature is for.

In a text like Matthew's, things are quite different. Questions like 'Did Mary have another son?' 'Was Joseph the natural father of Jesus?' 'Was Jesus married?' and so on are important. Readers are very interested in them, for however much fiction they also encounter, they read the Gospels as information about a certain person called Jesus of Nazareth. Other answers than the conventional ones would give a twist to the story told by the evangelists which would immediately amount to changing their meaning. Mary could no longer be called 'ever virgin' (for most Roman Catholic Christians an insurmountable obstacle) and for Joseph to be the natural father of Jesus would remove Jesus from his divine pedestal for many Christians, of whatever confession. Matthew not only refers to other (previous) texts, but also invites us to look through his text to what lies outside the text, in this case historical events. Certainly they are packaged in the text, but they are facts which were already there before Matthew's text and had to be told to others precisely through the story. The text of Matthew is certainly a transparency through which we can (even must) look to something behind the text. Why otherwise are there four Gospels, which in many respects follow the same narrative pattern? That can only mean that there is a historical event that stands behind the text and could continue to be told in at least four different versions. That seems to me sufficient argument in favour of the view that we do justice to the Gospels only if we do not see them as a merely literary creation which must be treated by purely literary means.

7. *The literary Christ. Has the Word become text?*

Although they wouldn't dream of regarding the Gospels as a purely literary creation, many Christians today *treat* them as if they were. I see this as a retreat, a last attempt to get out of the morass of 'Did it happen or didn't it?' The advantage of a purely literary approach is that one is finished with that bother for good. But does it get us any further? What is the price that has to be paid? Here are a couple of things to think about.

1. The purely literary approach (in the way in which one deals with *Hamlet*) ends up in an endless retreat into the use and reuse of the material, what I called the recycling process. The exegesis gets drowned in this, because then there is nothing else. Unfortunately. For the literary approach is taken in order to avoid cutting up the Gospels – what is Jesus-authentic and what isn't. But it takes us from the frying pan into the fire: at all events no further than we were before. Jesus' significance has not become clearer, except that all can make what they like of him. There is no longer any 'content' to guide the reader, or rather, anything will serve as 'content'. In its moderate form, this view of the Gospels leads to declaring the question 'what really happened?' secondary; in its thoroughgoing form Jesus becomes a literary figure: after the historical Jesus and the mythical Christ there is now the literary Christ.

2. For the historical person of Jesus, the one with which the religious text had begun, has forfeited his place as a person dating from the beginning of our era. Under pressure he disappears into the text and gets submerged in it. To offer a variation on a line from the Gospel of John: the Word did not become flesh but text; Jesus gets caught up in what he means. Is that on, or is it the same as going up in smoke? Does the text speak only when the historical question has been silenced?

3. If 'reality' in shorthand = what is meaningful for us, then Jesus indeed goes up in smoke, since in that case anything can be made of him. Where that goes too far is obvious: you cannot make a historical person, someone who lived at one time, into just anything. Jesus was the occasion for the Gospels, for their composition, and not the product of them. The Jesus of flesh and blood must be 'meaningful', but when it is a substitute for 'flesh and blood' I see 'meaning' as a misunderstanding. Without texts about Jesus, there is no Jesus for us to perceive who could be 'meaningful' for us, but without a historical Jesus of flesh and blood we would be just in the same position: there would be no texts in which he is described to us. In short, he must have been, in order to be able to be 'meaningful' for us.

8. *Abstract or figurative christology?*

We have reached the critical point: if Jesus is not to be dissolved into the meaning which people attach to him, then a reference to what lies outside the text, to a person who lived at that time and was called Jesus, is essential. This historical person sparked off the process of giving meaning and governs it. Without reference to this person, reference as a foundation, we are back at D. F. Strauss: the literary Christ is the same as the mythical Christ.

Let me clarify what I mean by describing the difference between figurative and abstract, non-figurative art (with apologies for this generalized terminology). There are no rules for an abstract painting. The painter is free to put a yellow stripe here, a patch of dark green there, and elsewhere red triangles (for example), as he likes, so far as it all corresponds to what his intentions, say what he finds attractive. Figurative art has a different procedure: the artist has a notion which he wants to put on canvas, in his own way; other figurative artists would paint the same subject differently, but the subject is what the painting begins with. Otherwise this isn't figurative art. A painter who paints 'from life', 'from nature' or 'figuratively', as I have summed it up, isn't free. There is a subject that he wants to paint, and that subject exerts some compulsion; it must appear on the canvas in some version. Otherwise this is no longer 'painting from life'. A Christian christology acts in the same way. Jesus of Nazareth, as a figure from the past, is compellingly present in it, with name and surname, or it is not Christian christology.

7

Come tonight with stories

1. *The power of the story*

Many theologians, preachers and pastors over recent years have been charmed by the narrative character of the Bible, at least of large parts of it. One might say that this is a kind of rediscovery. Why not allow ourselves to be governed by this form and set the story above preaching or dogmatics? It can bring liberation from a great deal of bother, if only from disputes over doctrinal arguments. Stories convey more and say things more quickly than the best argument. Moreover they are good for adults and not just (as people thought earlier) for children. Stories carry listeners along with them and almost automatically draw them into the community of the story-tellers, the community of faith.

There, at random, are a few advantages of the story. What is the power of the story? It offers us the chance of living it, of identifying ourselves with people in the story. Where that happens, stories can be very important for our lives, and the deeper they go into life, the more important they are. Stories do not appeal to our minds, at least only to our minds, but to another level of our existence, the emotions. They are often models, invitations to discipleship, and in this way give shape to our lives. The Good Samaritan, a parable of Jesus, is one such exemplary story: Jesus did not even need to say 'Go and do likewise', because we had understood that already (Luke 10.25–37). Like so many parables of Jesus, this parable speaks to us one hundred times more strongly than, for example, an argument by the apostle Paul, in I Corinthians 13, on love (unless we heard Tony Blair reading it at the funeral of Princess Diana).

That is also true of the stories *about* Jesus which the evangelists tell us: they do something to us; they do far more to us than the teaching of the Catechism, and certainly far more than the most perfectly developed doctrine of the two natures of Jesus united in one person.

So we mustn't underestimate the power of the story, and it is certainly not my intention to do that in this chapter. I agree with those scholars who, in the footsteps of Paul Ricoeur, see something mysterious in the story, a power which other expressions of language (language as speech) do not have. Letting stories loose is like letting doves fly, and in the religious language of Christianity doves are the symbol of the Spirit of God. Nevertheless, I am using this chapter also to put a question mark against the enthusiasm which goes with the rediscovery of the story. By that I do not mean what all too easily is made a didactic trick to present the Christian message of salvation appropriately once again. I mean the story itself as a genre. The power of the story, which cannot be underestimated, is a discovery which has developed from the story as literature; it is, shall we say, a literary discovery. That makes it clear why I am devoting a whole chapter to it. We can treat a story as a story, with all that is associated with the term, but is the purpose of this that we then do away with history?

2. *Kinds of stories*

To prevent a word, the one word 'story', from running away with us and taking us where we do not want to go because it is so attractive, first it must be said that there are stories and stories, or better, that there are different kinds of stories. The last thing we must do is to talk about just one kind, for if we do, something will certainly go wrong.

Stories are always about something, and not always about the same thing. If they have formative power, that mysterious potency which I mentioned in the previous section – and there is no reason to doubt this – then it matters what story we tell. Stories are also told which have a negative power over people, which put them on the wrong footing. Think of the shameful stories that were told in Europe about the Jews and which cost the lives of millions of Jewish men, women and children. They too are stories with power! Or – something quite different – think of the stories about great discoveries of gold in the Far West of the United States, which made thousands of good citizens lose their heads, finally to die of their own lack of gold. To quote an appropriate proverb, when we go deeper into the genre of story, all that glistens is not gold.

In principle, we even need to put a question mark here. Stories always come from the survivors, the successful, the people who were lucky enough to be able to tell them. You only tell your story when you've 'made it'. Stories *about* people, about others, are always images created by the strong, the winners. Unfortunate people have nothing; there's nothing to tell. However, there are people who may not have a story but do exist, though they stand outside the formation of images, do not appear in them and do not join in. Had Jesus been arrested and put to death, not as a well-known teacher but as a Jew from the second cross-street in Bethany, we should never have heard of him, and he would have left no image behind. As it is, we read powerful stories about him in the Gospels, written after his death, by people who saw what they first thought to be a failure turn into a blessing. Jesus was no longer a 'loser' but someone with a story. This immediately shows us that all stories about a strong person also have an intrinsic strength. Again, the story isn't everything – a critical person can't avoid thinking that.

A first reason for not immediately ruling out argument, critical or constructive, is that it remains a necessary ingredient of interpersonal dealings, if only because we have to assess the story by an argument: which stories are good, which aren't, and why. Just as we can only make it clear by rational argument that rational argument isn't everything. It is inevitable that we have to establish what we say and don't say about a story by means of an argument.

3. True but didn't truly happen. Examples

A story has to have a storyteller, and what he tells, the story, is modelled on history: it presents things as events. Whether what the storyteller reports really happened or whether we have to regard it as quasi-historical is another question. That will be my first point.

If it isn't part of the definition of a story that it must really have happened, the power of the story cannot lie here, at least not in the first instance. Take the story that the Batavians came down the Rhine a hundred years before Christ and settled in the Low Countries, and that the Dutch are their descendants. Unfortunately, Batavians never came down the Rhine, far less are the Dutch descended from them. The story is unhistorical, but for more than a century it inflated Dutch patriotism like a balloon. The story had power; it called on the Dutch to live as 'descendants of those brave warriors'. In the 1930s, at school I still joined in the song which passionately told the story of the Batavians.

I shall call this genre of story – the story as an example, as a model, as a demonstration of how things go or must not go – the didactic story. Countless stories from the Old and New Testaments are stories which can be best read as examples; their formative power lies in the possibility that we can rediscover ourselves in them: sometimes as consolation or encouragement, sometimes also as a warning. Of course that isn't always true. Take a story like that of Jephthah, who robbed his daughter of her future because of a promise that he had made at an unguarded moment (Judges 11.30–40), or the story that Jesus cursed a barren fig tree (Matthew 21.18–22). Those are stories the force of which we don't understand, so they cannot teach us anything. We pass over them, as we have enough favourite stories apart from them. If we talk about them we say, 'Yes, that's how it is, life gets confused, that's how people are.' Those stories are true. But did they really happen? Did Abraham really pretend that Sarah was his sister (Genesis 12.10–20) because he feared for his life? Perhaps he did, perhaps he didn't, but no one is interested in that. We read the story because we find it so human: the great Abraham, the hero of the faith, also proves to be a frightened little man, as Nico ter Linden tells it. The Old Testament teems with such stories, which we can say are true but didn't really happen. We keep them as examples, not because they inform us about someone. The story about Abraham could just as well be about someone else: it wouldn't lose anything as a result. Moreover that in fact happens: it is told about Isaac in virtually the same terms (Genesis 26.1–35).

Of course such stories don't just provide examples of recognizable human weakness; on the contrary, most continue to do work so well because they give us pictures of the faith. In the New Testament Abraham is regarded as *the* great model of faith (Galatians 3.1–14); or take the cloud of witnesses, the heroes of faith from the letter to the Hebrews. Many preachers have thought it quite reasonable to take models from the Old Testament of faithfulness, of rock-firm faith in God or of honest repentance (David). This used to be called preaching by example. Such preaching doesn't ask whether anyone was really sawn in pieces for the faith (v.37), and who that might have been.

4. *True but didn't truly happen. The creation stories*

To a much greater degree, 'true but didn't truly happen' applies to the creation stories of the great religions, including those related at the beginning of the book of Genesis. They have parallels in the stories of the Babylonians, the Egyptians and many other peoples. They didn't truly happen, at least as far as we living today are concerned, but does that make them untrue? And the stories which follow: Cain kills his brother Abel; Noah and his whole family go into the ark with two (or seven) of all the animals. Did it truly happen? No, no one believes that (except for a number of those fundamentalist Christians who every now and then go on an expedition to find Mount Ararat), but we mustn't read them in that way. They don't give us any information about the past. So in that sense they didn't truly happen. But are they true? Certainly, but to see how we must examine such stories, the creation stories of the Old Testament and those of other religions, to discover what meaning they had for the narrators: simply by telling them, people explained to one another how the world was, what was their place in it, for example their identity as a people, and to what powers they were subject. They take up the great themes of human history: fratricide, the corruption of humankind, all the devastating catastrophes, human arrogance – read Ellen van Wolde on the subject.

Since the time of the Enlightenment such primal stories have been called 'religious myths'. Regardless of how they were understood by those who originally told them, for us, myths are stories which did not truly happen and yet are true. By now it is becoming clear that the word 'true' can function in two different connections: it can indicate 'what happened', in which case we have 'story' as the history of events. But it can also be related to the enlightening of human existence, which occurs in the mythical story. 'True' now means that we subscribe to this enlightenment.

Of course we don't always do that: let that be clear! Myths look at the world from the perspective of the storyteller of the time. Sometimes we have an eye for what he saw, and at others he opens our eyes! But sometimes we also think differently. God made the woman from one of Adam's ribs – that's how you know the place of the woman in the world, says the narrator of Genesis 2. But there we switch off: at least, I don't know anyone who continues to tell this story in order to show women their place today.

Or take the aftermath of the flood: old Noah curses his (grand)son Ham and prophesies to him that for ever he will serve the descendants of Shem (the patriarch of the Semites). The story shows the peoples their place. The hierarchy which the narrator experiences in his time is derived from former times, from primal times, and everything that is 'primal' is for ever. So Ham must serve Shem for ever. But is there anyone who still takes over this element from the mythical stories – now that apartheid has been abolished even in South Africa – as guidance?

So we see that whatever we take over from the creation stories, we are the ones who are making the choices, and clearly we have our criteria for doing so. The stories must fit in with what we already know as a value or truth; otherwise we leave them for what they are. That is a second reason for not getting rid of the argument in favour of the story.

5. *True and truly happened? The Gospels*

Stories as examples, as myths, needn't have truly happened to be true. The question is whether we can also read the Gospel stories about Jesus in terms of 'didn't truly happen but true'. Let's begin with an example that poses no problem: the story in which the evangelist tells how Jesus raised a young man from the dead in the village of Nain (Luke 7.11–17). This story has nothing to do with what 'truly happened'; the world would have been too small had it truly happened. Jesus' fame would have hastened before him; he would have been venerated beyond bounds and worshipped as a miracle-worker, and would never have been crucified. So this didn't really happen, any more than did the resurrection of Lazarus (John 11.1–44). We must read such stories like the other stories about resurrections from the dead (read I Kings 17 or II Kings 3): he *could* have done it, given his divine calling. So even if it never happened, the story hasn't lost its meaning. What it means is that Jesus masters death, and to the degree that Jesus is active in God's name, God is lord over death. Death doesn't have the last word and there is hope which extends beyond death and the grave. To spread this truth further, people told the story (which didn't really happen) about the young man of Nain. So there are stories which continue to be told purely for what I now call their meaning. The fact that they didn't happen does not rob them of any of their power.

But there are stories and stories, and there are also stories that must have happened if they are to retain their force the 'truly happened' is the key to the story. Surely we can't be indifferent to whether the genocide in Rwanda and the war crimes in Kosovo really took place or not? No one will say that these are stories and it is unimportant whether or not they really happened. Or think of the famous lines from the poem by Leo Vroman:

> Come tonight with stories
> how war has disappeared
> and repeat them a hundred times
> each time I shall weep.

What is there to weep (with joy about) if war has not truly disappeared, if nothing has happened? The verse has lost its meaning. If we apply that to the Gospel stories, surely these must have happened, must truly have happened, or at least some of them must have happened if they are to preserve their power? Or can we say that this doesn't matter, that we can go on telling the stories even if it is clear that they didn't happen: we carry the stories along with us and fill them with values and the truths that they convey? Is that enough?

6. 'Truly happened' as important. The miracles

'Jesus who walked on the water'; that's a short summary of what we are told in Matthew 14.22–33. Jesus had been left behind alone to pray, and he had meanwhile sent his disciples to cross to the other side. But they had the wind against them, and when Jesus saw how worn out they were, he came over the waters to them. Anyone can read the rest of the story in Matthew 14; it's too good to pass over. Did it really happen? That's a tricky question. At the beginning of the Enlightenment it became a test case for true religion. The Enlightenment thought that true religion had nothing to do with miracles; on the contrary, miracles spoiled faith, made it superstition, so Jesus didn't really walk on the water. In that case what did happen? Clearly the biblical scholars didn't dare to dismiss the story altogether, so they dreamed up all kinds of things. There was a sandbank which the disciples hadn't noticed; Jesus walked on a log which was half-submerged (so it couldn't be seen), and so on. It's clear that the miracle couldn't be a miracle but had to be explained in natural terms.

That sort of controversy is a thing of the past. It isn't that miracles shouldn't or couldn't happen, but if one allows this possibility to one's own religion, why then refuse it to others! In that case more people than Jesus walked on water, and the world is teeming with miracles. And then they are also no longer special, and miracle stories lose their importance.

That immediately gives us a good way in. 'Jesus who walked on the water', do we attach importance to it or is it already intrinsically important? No, however we want to interpret the story (for example, Jesus is lord of nature), all that we want to get out of it can also be said without the story. Whether it happened, 'really happened', is of no importance.

As a contrast I shall take the story of Jesus' crucifixion. That can only be told as something that 'really happened'. It has an intrinsic importance, a religious importance, the sacrifice of Jesus' life as 'the lamb of God who takes away the sins of the world'. Christianity would totally change its character, indeed wouldn't need to exist, if we had to conclude that there never was a cross on which Jesus had been hung.

To come to a (provisional) conclusion. Sometimes it is important whether a Gospel story 'really happened', even of vital importance; sometimes that doesn't add anything and we do best to live with 'quasi-historical'. But everything depends on what religious importance (importance of faith) is attached to it. Of course that importance is no guarantee that something 'really happened', let alone that something is a historical event because faith claims that it is. Christian faith cannot do without some things: that is the issue. It cannot do without Jesus of Nazareth, born, lived, died, buried and risen again (whatever that may be). Not everything needs to have happened as described, and there can be a good deal of subjectivity in the stories; they can be filled in with a good deal of legend (and that applies even to the stories which I have said are of essential importance), but we cannot say that they never 'really happened'. Or rather, we can, but in that case we are left with Christianity as a myth.

7. *Story as a myth that gives meaning*

We have seen that myths are unhistorical. In the century that lies behind us that has even shaped terminology. To make out that stories are a myth meant – and often still means – a kind of debunking. When journalists call underground opposition in the Netherlands during the war a myth, they mean that people have the wrong idea of it; it wasn't really that, there was little of it. A story that has been proved unhistorical is a myth.

'Inauthentic'- that's the critical side of the concept. Therefore according to Bultmann we must demythologize, as he called it, the world of New Testament ideas. The world-view that apostles and evangelists had then doesn't fit with our concepts. Moreover we have to soak off their message from their view of the world, as children do with pictures on transfers. And like them, we throw away what we have left.

But things can change. In Bultmann's day there were already theologians who thought that myths were the primal form of all religion, and that so-called demythologizing could end up in disaster, in a clear-out of religion. Today they are being proved right. For precisely the same reasons why the term was banished around fifty years ago, today it is being reintroduced. Precisely because myths are unhistorical, today they are popular; they fit into the religious revival which characterizes the end of our century; they are brought from everywhere, as far away as the Andes. And all this in order to fill a gap, a void, a lack of meaning from which Western culture is said to suffer.

Whether this last comment is true I shall leave to one side. For what

concerns me here is that we have at last come on the track of the
upgrading of the story. By story is meant Christianity as a myth which
gives meaning. What Lyotard has called 'the end of the great narratives'
is the end of the myths in which Europe has hitherto found meaning and
from which has drawn its self-confidence: socialism, rationality as an
organizing principle, and not least Christianity. Again, whether that is
true is a question which lies outside my argument. My question is
whether Christianity can be understood as a myth which gives meaning.
My answer would be that this happens, that in the last years of this
century it has even become popular to see Christianity in this way, and
as a result Christianity has gained in popularity (which is not something
to be scorned). It rides on the waves of myth as opposition, as a refuge
from the digital world in which we have got mixed up. But must we be
happy with this friendship? I doubt it. 'Myth' is in any case a perverse
terminology, one which puts us on the wrong track. By that I mean that
we can certainly include Christianity among the great narratives of our
world, the myths that give meaning, but in that case we place ourselves
outside it – though that is not meant methodologically. 'A myth which
provides meaning' is a sociological or, if you like, a socio-philosophical
term; it puts us on a different level from that of religion.

If religious people are so eager to put their religion in a non-religious
framework, something is up. This seems to me to be a kind of last resort
for Christians: they want to preserve what they have but don't want to
have too much bother with it, and certainly don't want to enter into a
confrontation with the scientific world in which they live. If the category
of 'story' gets one out of the dispute over what 'really happened', then
Christianity is only a myth which gives meaning.

Is that possible – in the specific sense of: can Christianity continue as
a myth? Empirically speaking, yes and no. Yes, if we think of
Christianity as a cultural entity. To the present day the European world
derives from it a large number of elements which serve to give meaning.
But this 'yes' isn't as firm as we would like. 'Meaning' describes a com-
munal world of values and certainties which people share with one
another, preferably without having to think about them too much.
Religions are capable above all of giving meaning. Christianity achieved
that in Europe. To use Peter Berger's attractive phrase, it spread a
heavenly canopy over everyday life. That canopy is no longer there, not
because religion has gone away and we live in post-Christian times, but
because there are more religions. Religious plurality is undermining the
unity of European culture and is the real threat to all certainties which
Christian faith hitherto thought that it possessed. Moreover, that again

explains why so many people are taking refuge in Christianity as a story, a myth which provides meaning: it gets them out of the problem of what is truth and what isn't.

Can Christianity go on as a myth? Why not? But Christianity itself needn't want that. I was talking about truth, a term which indicates that faith also contains an element of knowledge, what is called a cognitive element. To make Christianity a myth means leaving out that element. Even then Jesus can go on for years, address many people ('Jesus Christ Superstar') and spread blessing everywhere. But I would venture to doubt whether the Christian faith will survive that, or to put it more strongly, whether a Christianity which has no message about Jesus as a historical phenomenon is still Christianity.

8. *Literary fiction cannot replace history*

Beyond doubt the Gospel stories can continue to be told and do their work as story, in other words exercise power, even without raising the question of whether they 'truly happened'. It would be in conflict with reality to deny that, and moreover it would be quite pedantic: as if everyone had to become involved in the historical problems which are posed by 'story'. Of course it's nonsense; people can go on telling the Gospel stories, and it is clear what impact they can have on a person.

So there is certainly power in stories, but the specific power of a story, any story, is given in and bound up with its content: with 1. *what* is told in it and 2. *why* it goes on being told. It is indissolubly bound up with both these. That also applies to the Jesus stories (to sum them up like this for the sake of convenience). They have a different content from Snow White and the Seven Dwarfs or Rumpelstiltskin. The origin of the Jesus story is different (there really was someone who . . .) and there were (and still are) different reasons for continuing to tell it (for us he really meant 'the end'). The Jesus stories would never have been told, and would never have gone on being told, had there not been someone under the name of Jesus who led a quite remarkable life. So it cannot be true that they are just a literary fiction.

To be brief, the Gospel stories do not fall under the category of 'true but didn't truly happen' (although they also include stories which didn't really happen); they aren't examples (although they can also be plundered for those), nor are they primal stories or myths (although they illuminate our existence), but information about the importance of a historical person, about someone with a name (which historical persons have) and a fate. The life and death of this one person mentioned by name is the only reason why the evangelists began their story.

So we keep arriving at the same watershed: literary fiction or (also) historical information; myth which gives meaning or (also) the report of the life of one J of N. That isn't surprising, for in its existence and ongoing existence Christianity goes back to someone who lived at the beginning of our era. Christianity would never have been had Jesus never been, and moreover his existence is an essential element of the content of the faith of Christians, indeed even the legitimation of their existence, the only legitimation. Christians would be crazy if they were to throw away an accord with historical reality: they would be throwing themselves away. The historical Jesus is the branch on which they sit, and that is something one never saws off.

I will do best to trust in the power of the Gospel stories. But if they are compelling, it is not because of a mythological idiom, or a psychoanalytical depth structure (as brought out by Eugen Drewermann), or a literary power that they have. All these things may be present and do their work, but what Paul Ricoeur calls the 'semantic potency' can only be connected with the person about whom they report and all that is given with this person, and that is quite a lot! We need only remember that along with Jesus comes the whole of the Jewish religion, the God of the Old Testament, and this is a different power from that of literature.

8

Christology as reception history

1. History of the New Testament revelation of God?

'Christology' is the usual name for the church's teaching about Jesus
Christ. Jesus is the name that he got from his mother; Christ (or the
Christ) is the name which his followers gave him: in so doing they indicated what Jesus of Nazareth meant for them. Slowly a multiplicity of
christologies came into being. There are a great many types, and the
church christology is only one of the many possible (and real) christologies in circulation. 'Christology' is thus any more or less orderly
exposition of the meaning which a community has given to Jesus. How
have so many come into being?

I shall describe the history which underlies this as a reception history,
a term which I take from literary criticism and which – roughly speaking – covers the investigation of the way in which books were received
by their readers. That is not completely by the book, for unlike Plato,
Calvin or Spinoza, Jesus is not an author who left behind any written
work. So in the case of the reception of the Gospels I must first discuss
the reception of Jesus himself by his first hearers, and as we shall see,
even that is not the real beginning. But once this hurdle has been got
over, in other words, as soon as books or writings appear about Jesus,
the panorama of a real reception history unfolds. What did the first
users of the Gospels do with these first writings, how did they assimilate
them, what did they make of them? What views about Jesus – new and
different views – in turn arose out of the Gospels? We can investigate
this reception history down to the present day. Of course I shall not be
doing that exhaustively; that would go beyond my ability and my com-
petence, nor is it necessary. It is enough to extract a few telling moments
from it.

By seeing the assimilation of the tradition as reception history we put
ourselves on the side of the receivers. That's unusual. Almost automatically the attention of the church and theology is paid to the one

engaged in handing down: does he hand down what needs to be handed down? This interest is normative by nature. 'Reception' doesn't look at that but follows the course of events. I shall also be doing that in this chapter, so it is descriptive by nature: what did people make of Jesus in the course of history? Judging is something quite different, and in this chapter I shall hardly venture on it, because the discovery of a criterion for testing christologies is a difficult task, if it is possible at all! In the first instance everything is on one line: the evangelists, the church's doctrine of the two natures of Jesus Christ, the historical Jesus, are all stages in the reception history of Jesus of Nazareth. No one of these has any advantage over another; that is a firm feature of christology as reception history.

Was there no perception earlier of the variety of interpretations of Jesus of Nazareth? Yes, but it bore another name, for example 'history of the revelation of God'. Here the investigators examined what historical circumstances led to a yet broader interpretation of the life and death of Jesus, but at the same time made it clear that all these divergent meanings were 1. already contained in a 'nutshell' in what Jesus himself had said about himself, and 2. could fall back on the 'guarantee' of God's revelation in the New Testament.

The history of the revelation of God is the opposite of a reception history. The underlying thought is not what readers do with writings (the reception), but what they have to do with them (and above all what they have not to do with them). I shall come back to this. To begin with preaching is to begin with a *must*, with what people have to believe. What they really believe and above all why they believe as they do it is what a reception history is needed for.

2. *How did Jesus see himself?*

The Gospels portray Jesus as seen through the life of his followers. So really we first have to take a step back and ask, 'How did Jesus see himself?' What his followers relate about Jesus, their view, must be connected in one way or another with the view that Jesus had of himself. Can we get behind that?

It isn't simple. The Gospels contain information, but in terms of interpretation: this is Jesus as packaged by faith. If it is at all possible to peel Jesus' own view of himself from this packaging, it can only be in the form of a reconstruction. That means avoiding the pitfalls of which Albert Schweitzer warned us. The members of the Jesus Seminar (Borg, Funk) – I mentioned this group earlier – have not been deterred by him, and again the question of what Jesus really did and what in his preaching is Jesus-authentic and what is not is being raised quite openly. Nor is that all. What was the meaning of the words with which Jesus spoke of himself, and did his audience share his views when he was talking about the Son of man? Can we get behind this?

We are going in the right direction if we study the historical context in which Jesus appeared: what people thought then, what terms they used, in what sense they did so, and more of that kind of question. For example, what did a term like 'the kingdom of heaven' or 'son of God' mean in Jesus' day? If an answer is to be given to these questions – assuming that Jesus himself in fact used this terminology – we are getting close to what Jesus thought about himself.

E. P. Sanders is a reliable investigator in this area. He has no hidden theological agenda, like the historians whom Albert Schweitzer castigated: he doesn't need to prove anything. According to Sanders, we can say with certainty that Jesus saw himself in a special relationship to God (think of the Father-son imagery) and that he performed miracles (he healed the sick, stilled the storm), drove out evil spirits, was aware of being a preacher authenticated by God to announce the kingdom of heaven and to call the people to repentance. The focal point of this preaching was the message of God's mercy to sinners. What he stood for was bringing the people back to God – that is a short summary of his sense of vocation. We can add that not only did Jesus see his death coming, but he also accepted it: he saw it as a sacrifice that he had to offer.

That isn't a great deal, above all if we still have to leave aside the sense in which Jesus saw his death as a sacrifice. Let's think back to the argument between William Wrede and Albert Schweitzer about Jesus' self-awareness of being Messiah: did Jesus feel that he was Messiah or not? This question too isn't easy to answer; at any rate, Jesus himself cannot be captured by the use of this name. But did he call himself God's son? That certainly seems to have been the case, but 'son' was normal religious language in Jesus' days and it was often used. And wasn't Israel itself often called ' the son' (Hosea 11.1; cf. Matthew 2.15)? More strongly, we hear the apostle Paul exclaim that all are sons of God (Galatians 3.26)! One might ask where the daughters are, but it's certain that 'son of God ' is not an expression that Jesus reserved exclusively for himself.

I need say no more in this context. Where Jesus got his sense of vocation from may – historically speaking – be an interesting question; I cannot go into it here. To sum up, we can say that the Jewish world of

Jesus' day was the religious environment in which Jesus moved and that this environment gave him the language and the images, and the views about God and his work which these contained, and with the help of these he presented himself to his audience.

However variable the implication of that fact may be, one thing is clear: Jesus appeared to be quite different from what the later church suggested. He came to call his people to repentance and not to present himself as saviour of the world. For church people that is a disconcerting outcome of the investigation. In that case where does the saviour of the world come from? A second conclusion needs to be added: Jesus did not see himself as a kind of superman, in the possession of a divine nature, but as one human being among others, albeit with a special relationship to Israel's God and a special commission in his name.

That is all too little for believers, and even for many non-believers. People are so used to the idea of Jesus as God-man that they can hardly think or speak of him in other terms. But things began differently, and this discovery has its consequences.

3. The Christ of the scriptures

It is the evangelists who make Jesus the Christ. The reception history of Jesus begins with them, but not yet that of the writings about Jesus, for they wrote the first of these themselves; this is not yet reception history in the strict sense, but initially the reception of Jesus himself as a person. That comes in the oral stories about him, and afterwards the recording of them in strands of tradition (written), and finally – as its end-point – in the Gospels.

The evangelists are enthusiastic narrators: Jesus is the great light, the one sent by the Father, come to announce the kingdom, if not to bring it, to proclaim the gospel of God's mercy to the poor, to show the reflection of the new world in his miracles and healings, and meanwhile to celebrate the victory over Satan and the kingdom of evil – these are just some of the themes which indicate the impression that Jesus made on them. It is all in terms of a story which ends with his death, resurrection and ascension into heaven. His death is not the painful story of a defeat; no, he has to suffer to accomplish God's will, but God has raised him, and now he sits at God's right hand, in the place where the real power over the world is seated.

Did the evangelists make more of Jesus than Jesus thought or said about himself? They certainly did, at any rate when it came to the title messiah, which Jesus so avoided. But that isn't relevant to this element;

we must see the Gospels as an illumination of the person and the work of Jesus. Who was this man, about whom the itinerant preachers keep talking? We shall now tell you in detail, say the evangelists. To the preaching (which was already there much earlier) they add a kind of 'life of Jesus'. This is written for readers outside the limits of Judaism, including non-Jews. The end of Matthew even says that beyond any dispute: 'make all peoples my disciples' (Matthew 28.16–20). Nevertheless, the evangelists write in terms of the Jewish religious world.

In using the term 'the son', the evangelists are thinking of a special relationship between Jesus and God, and not, as is customary in the Hellenistic world, of a child fathered by God, a hybrid. Even the Gospel according to John, so much later than the Synoptic Gospels, and so much more interested in Jesus' origin in God, cannot be read in a Hellenistic spirit. John is more concerned with praising Jesus to the skies (if one may use that expression) than intent on giving Jesus a divine nature (as well as a human one). I shall be returning to John in due course.

It might perhaps be understandable that in his birth stories Luke crosses the frontiers: after all, he wrote his Gospel for Graeco-Roman readers. Luke is also the one who is in love with the title 'Lord' for Jesus, and although the Jewish Christians also already knew this terminology (*maranatha*, see I Corinthians 16.22), for Luke's Greek-speaking fellow inhabitants of the Roman empire the term 'Lord' (*kyrios* in Greek) was appropriate for indicating the divinity of the emperor. In that case isn't it natural to say that the true *kyrios* is Jesus?

I needn't go in detail here into the precise meaning of the titles of Jesus, The question is what the evangelists made of them, and whether they were thinking of the same thing. But the fact that they use them so lavishly (prophet, priest, king, messiah, son, son of man and so on), and attribute them so generously to Jesus, speaks volumes. In him they see a summary of the salvation that the world needs from God, and the world is to know that.

4. *The church's Christ*

For most Christians, the church's Christ is so familiar that it is difficult to see him as being anything other than the real Jesus. Such Christians happily leave the precise formulations to the theologians of the Christian church, but the real Jesus is the son of God, man and God at the same time, the God-man, as we read in some writings, at any rate God on earth, walking around through Palestine.

But is that the real or authentic Jesus? In its official statements the early church was more subtle; indeed it said that the Second Person of the divine Trinity had assumed human nature (Nicaea 325), but it did not mean that in the sense that God turned into a man or a man turned into God. In order to clarify that (indeed) it developed the doctrine of the two natures of Jesus, the divine and the human, which according to the Council of Chalcedon (451) were combined unconfusedly, unchangeably, indivisibly, inseparably in one person. By this formula the Council fathers wanted to kill two birds with one stone. The two natures really were two; one might not say one nature. Hence the 'unconfusedly and unchangeably'; the divine nature did not swallow up the human nature. But the two natures might not be detached from each other either: hence the 'indivisibly and inseparably'. One had to say one person.

This doctrine – the so-called doctrine of two natures – is a nice example of the thought that the early church devoted to its faith. The never-ending disputes over it show what was at stake and at the same time how a puzzle had to be solved which was really insoluble. How can two natures form one person, if each nature (the divine and the human) is thought to be integral? However many anchors the theologians put down, the construction irrevocably slips in the direction of one nature (the divine) or two persons. That is shown by the sequel (which is often forgotten). The Monophysite disputes (one or two natures? – *physis* is Greek for nature) which Chalcedon wanted to end (but did not succeed in doing) were nothing in terms of subtlety compared with the monotheletic disputes: if Jesus has two natures, does he have one will or two wills ('will' is the Greek *thelema*)? The solution to the problem is to see the human nature of Jesus as anhypostatic, without a distinctive I; or rather, the I consisted only in the divine I. The consequence of this was an unimaginable Jesus, and another heresy. I have elsewhere called this a 'jigsaw-puzzle theology', albeit a venerable one.

I must emphasize this last point; it expresses not only hard thought but also love for Christian faith. But this comes from a particular time. The church's Christ is not the real Jesus but a phase in the reception history of the Gospels: in its conception and structure, as Harnack rightly stated, it is the work of the Greek spirit on the soil of the Gospel. The early church read the New Testament with eyes which belonged to a completely different culture from that in which the Gospels had come into being. There are four centuries between the first traditions, shall we say around AD 50, and the Council of Chalcedon in 451, which definitively (as the church thought) established who Jesus was. That is the same span of time as divides us today (1999) from, say, around the end of the reign of Queen Elizabeth I. In four centuries the world, including the religious world, can change a great deal.

The son? For the evangelists this is still an elegant name for an intimate spiritual relationship with God; as we have seen, there are others who call themselves 'son'. For the church fathers the word indicates that Jesus has a substantial share in the divine nature. That was not just important for the church fathers; their faith stood and fell by it. That is the only explanation of the vigour of the fight, say, between Athanasius, Bishop of Alexandria (in the years in which he had not been driven out by the opposing party), and the learned monk Arius. I mention both names because a rhyme is associated with them. 'Two opponents always box, the Arians and the Orthodox.' That's a good expression of the relationships: that's how it was and that's how it often is today.

5. Stop at Chalcedon?

The christology of the early church, established at the Council of Chalcedon, has been elevated to become the exclusive church doctrine. It hasn't changed to the present day. So instead of writing 'established' I could have written 'set in stone'. How that came about, one can read in all the church histories: the great christological dogma came into being with a great deal of compulsion, much rivalry, even with deception and violence. That is not denied, certainly in our century: as a student I had to learn by heart all this wonderful history of heretics, emperors, empresses, princes of the church and simple monks. But, I was told, the outcome of this struggle was the best description that one can give of the mystery of the incarnation of God: with a crooked stick, in his providential rule God had struck a straight blow.

Chalcedon became unassailable. For christology that meant that the doctrine of the two natures was backed by the authority of the church leaders. If we think how powerful the Christian church has become in Europe since then, in fact being able to extend its power into the political sphere, it is not surprising that the church's christology achieved a monopoly, and became the dominant christology which saw off all possible rivals. That is, if they had not already been attacked and exterminated! I am thinking of the rediscovery of the Gnostic Jesus, stifled by the official church but now brought out from under the sand of the Egyptian desert. I certainly haven't picked the term 'stifled' out of thin air; the Gnostic movements were the heretics of the church. That we should *therefore* see the Gnostic Jesus as the authentic Jesus is not of course a conclusion with any firm basis. But that it isn't the issue.

Chalcedon became not only unassailable but also the standard of orthodoxy. For centuries, and as far as the church was concerned for eternity, this christology was established, and every concept which sought to make any innovation was set against the matrix of Chalcedon. Refinements, developments, further problems, anything was possible, except to change Chalcedon. Reformers like Luther and Calvin wanted to have changes in the church, but not in the church's teaching about Jesus Christ.

Only in the eighteenth century did the structure begin to shift and the church's Christ was replaced by the historical Jesus, by the mythical Christ, by the kerygma, and finally, as the opening of the floodgates, by a multiplicity of new pictures of Jesus, of which the end is still not in sight. Stop at Chalcedon? That was certainly the intention, and for many believing Christians still is, but there is no stopping now: the current is too strong, and the structure of christology is falling apart.

In the light of what I have called reception history, this change is understandable. And it is not a disaster for Christian faith. On the contrary, Chalcedon is rather like an artificial island of yesterday in the sea of today. Graeco-Hellenistic culture has long been a thing of the past; people have long grown out of its approach to human beings and the world; for a long time it has been an 'alien body' which could only survive as a result of church paralysis, as Harnack remarked. What he meant was that no one dared approach it, or, as the Reformed theologian H. Bavinck said: it isn't good but we have nothing better. Why nothing better? Why didn't people want something better? That's an intriguing question. But first something else.

6. Rescue operations

The classical picture of Jesus may totter, or even in many cases give way under the pressure of historical criticism, but that doesn't alter the fact that it is adhered to to the present day, and is even the official teaching of almost all denominations of the church. The great disadvantage of this is that it comes to be a kind of standpoint theology. By that I mean that 'believing' is reduced to 'believing that', believing *that* Jesus is the Son of God, that in him two natures are united in one person, and so on. The model of such a narrow view of believing, I might say *the* model, is the so-called Athanasian Creed, which is one of the three so-called ecumenical confessions of faith (= accepted by all the churches).

It doesn't come from Athanasius (it is later, from the fifth century), but has been given his name because of its doctrinal content, relating to the two natures and the divine Trinity. 'Whosoever would be saved,' the text begins, must 'keep the faith whole and undefiled', and that 'faith is this . . .' Then follows the classical doctrine of the Trinity and the doctrine of the natures, divided up into sections. To 'believe that' is a condition of one's eternal salvation.

Much more fruitful than purely insisting are the attempts to keep to the essence of Chalcedon but to introduce deviations into christology. Some seek the remedy in the view of personhood: how can we avoid making the two natures of Jesus into a completely unrecognizable human being? That is possible, for example, in the form of a spirit christology: we must understand the divine nature as an indwelling of the Spirit in the person of Jesus. The Roman Catholic theologian Piet Schoonenberg looks in this direction. Although he doesn't want to meddle with the church's dogma in any way, he was not gratefully received by the church's magisterium. 'Believing that' clearly wasn't sufficiently safeguarded.

Edward Schillebeeckx, another Roman Catholic author, does not want to get rid of the classical christology either. In fact he is looking for a new way of approaching the church's Christ, and finds this in human history as a history of suffering. Suffering is the universal doom from which Jesus derives his significance as bringer of salvation. Of course the question is whether and to what degree the doctrine of the two natures is a necessary ingredient of this christology. But I shall only touch on his view, since it is not relevant here. That also applies to the christology of Hendrikus Berkhof, which in fact leaves classical doctrine behind. He no longer needs a doctrine of two natures to say who Jesus is.

Why do so many theologians not want to let go of the doctrine of two natures? First of all, out of respect for the faith and thought of the fathers, and also – I think – out of respect for the person of Jesus himself. Both sides of the matter coincide: the psychological element, that anyone can sympathize with (we are abandoning a view of Jesus to which we have been brought up from childhood), and the element of faith. The Christian church cannot have made a mistake when it confessed Jesus as God on earth, although we can see the Hellenistic origin of the formulations. No. But 'mistake' isn't the right word; it's a form of unhistorical thinking: we are measuring former times by today. The doctrine of two natures is a link in the chain of a never-ending process of tradition, a form of community theology, but from a later community than that of the Gospels: it's the exposition of an exposition.

Bousset called God-on-earth the fulfilment of a universal religious need. That leads to a paradox which is both attractive and remarkable: from this perspective, the man who most vigorously challenged religion as a universal human need, Karl Barth, has become its greatest victim. With his theology as christology, he is following the laws of religion.

7. Religious needs

Religious needs form the motive force which keeps christology on the road. From my perspective they put into words the longings and aspirations of a time, and do so on the basis of what this time experiences as an indispensable need – I can also say as an unattainable salvation (unattainable, that is, by human beings). Put in a more scholastic way: christology is governed by soteriology, which in turn is governed by the religious needs of the time: what do people want to be saved from, and what do they want to be saved for? In other words, it is on the basis of this argument that the fundamental problems of existence stand.

I shall limit myself to a comparison – in shorthand – between the religious needs of the ancient world and those of the Enlightenment; after that I shall give some modern examples and end with a conclusion.

1. The Jesus of the Gospels enters the Hellenistic world through the preaching of the apostles. In that world, as everywhere, people stumbled over death, but the spokesmen of the culture elevated it so that it became the great doom: the transitory nature of human beings is their wretchedness, and *the* religious question is who saves human beings from annihilation. As moulded by this need, christology assumes its church form bit by bit: the great longing for the other world, the world which is not transitory, is fulfilled in Jesus. In his person the true reality makes itself known; the incorruptible God appears in corruptible flesh; the divine nature assumes the human nature. That really says it all. Here is the great saving event. Through the sacrament (moreover Gregory of Nyssa called it *pharmakon athanasias*, a medicine against death) the believer takes part in it: he takes incorruptibility into himself. We see that this argument turns on the divine nature of Jesus: through it human beings are saved. In terms of the need of the early church, the Monophysites have the oldest credentials.

2. The Enlightenment – at least in its spokesmen – had far less need of the appearance of the other world in ours; it was much more rational in its view of human existence. The great longing does not consist in the hope that one day God will come to earth, but in the ability

to control the living world. Accordingly, another model of christology is needed, a Jesus for now, a Jesus who helps people to exercise their humanity, more a pointer than the Way. To complete the picture: now that the Enlightenment has again fallen into discredit among the intellectuals, once again the need is cropping up for more, for another world, for places where the ordinary world becomes transparent and unveils something of God or divinity: if only a flicker, or if need be a recollection of a God from the past. I shall be returning to this at length in a later chapter.

3. Other religious needs or, if you like, other religious aspirations, produce another model of christology. Mission can talk of this. When the church's Christ is proclaimed in black Africa, his significance is spontaneously grasped there and put into words in terms of African needs. These are different from those from which Western missionaries begin in their christology. Jan Greven relates somewhere that for his hearers – he was involved in theological training in Congo – he could not begin with the resurrection of Jesus. People had no need of this, for 'the dead are not really dead; they surround us, although we do not see them'. An attractive example from our own time is the liberation theology of the 1970s, which is shaped by formulating the doom under which people suffer in terms of social and political injustice. This gives yet another colouring to salvation and the saviour (Jesus).

4. Needs are the support, if not the foundation, of the Christ who is preached, and thus they themselves – remarkably enough – become part of preaching. Think, for example, of Reformed orthodoxy. With the church's Christ it replaced the doom of transitoriness with that of sin, and in so doing changed the salvation of immortality into the forgiveness of sins. But needs are subject to erosion, even the need that presided over the birth of the Reformation, the need for forgiveness. For a long time it has been the regular lament of the churches of the Reformation that we aren't burdened with a sense of sin, so what do we do with the enormous emphasis on forgiveness? Thus the sum comes out at zero. Mortality? We no longer find the hereafter a matter of the utmost importance, so why do we go on preaching that after death we shall inherit eternal life? Sin? We don't fret over it, so why lecture us that we suffer from a lack of a sense of guilt? A change in religious needs undermines a christology, just as at an early period it helped it to get going. Since the Enlightenment, by common consent the process that I am describing here has accelerated. Christology has got loose from the church's chains. The price for this is the parcelling out of the church's Christ.

8. The feminist perspective. A test case

Feminism exists in many versions, and the same is also true of feminist theology. Its most important contribution is in indicating the 'masculine' character of the Bible and the tradition of the faith, which is connected with the irrefutable fact that men were the authors of both. How, for example, could a woman have written Psalm 19? The framework of this book limits me to discussing what is important for christology. Feminist theologians score a point when they observe that women play a far greater role in the life of Jesus than is usually indicated. I shall go more deeply into a couple of examples.

Women are the first to preach Jesus' resurrection (read Matthew 28; Luke 24 and John 20). I shall not discuss whether we must see that as a reprimand to the men who, when it came to the point, left Jesus in the lurch or as a legitimation of women as preachers of the Christian message (which was later reversed by men). Both options are worth considering.

Jesus is even anointed by a woman, an action which becomes far more significant than a testimonial or a farewell ceremony if we regard 'anoint' as 'appoint', confirm in office, and thus read into it what the Old Testament authors understood by it. Jesus receives his function as Christ, as Messiah, as bringer of salvation, from the hands of a woman! Whether that is a possible interpretation I do not know, but in any case it invites us to look at the place of Jesus with women's eyes. I once found in an American church paper a most attractive example of such an approach and the repercussions that it had for men. One of the editors, a woman, was discussing at length Jesus' encounter with the so-called Canaanite (we would say Palestinian) woman (Matt.15.21–28). Precisely as the story tells it, she described how Jesus initially doesn't want to listen to the woman, since he sees his mission limited to his own people (v.24). But the woman won't give way; she catches Jesus out with his own words and finally goes so far that he involuntarily changes position and also gives help to someone who doesn't come from a Jewish home. So you can see, the editor remarked at the end of her contribution, in the end it is a woman who makes Jesus understand that he must see his mission as a world mission.

The letters written in response were highly entertaining: of course they came from men, and the tone of all of them was that one cannot portray Jesus as a pupil sitting at a woman's feet. That's blasphemy, a betrayal of orthodoxy, an undermining of trust, since one would have to assume that in this phase of his messianic ministry Jesus still had things to learn, and from a woman at that. In that case, how can we trust his earlier words? Here is hurt male pride.

Compared with these examples (just a couple) of reading with the eyes of women, the idea of a Jesus who is friendly to women, or Jesus with a feminine perspective, or, even more attractively, Jesus with a balance between his anima and animus, is peanuts. It's all a guess; we don't know anything and it doesn't help anyone or anything.

We get to a crossroads when the customary question is asked whether Jesus could also have been a woman: could God also have sent his daughter? A treacherous question, one might say. Those who ask it have already got the church's christology at the back of their minds; they begin from the church's Christ, his role to bring people to God, to explain God, to be God on earth, or however people want to put it. Of course, if only a man could fulfil this role, that can only be greeted with gnashing of teeth. Moreover I can understand well why so many feminist theologians cannot accept the classical christology. If any dogma can be said to have been fashioned by men, carefully wrought and with a splendid design, then it is the teaching of the church's Christ.

But of course it doesn't help then to go on to reconstruct the image of Christ as a redeemer who is much more accessible to women. Jesus was a man, and nothing can be done about that. So we cannot put a Christa in place of Christ, as some theologians want, or a Christina, as I read in a German paper. They are all just as far removed from the Jesus who lived at the beginning of our era and over whom the church's christology began. Christology takes its own high flight if the historical Jesus is no longer of any interest, and where it flies depends on air traffic control. They can send it in all kinds of directions.

9. Wild christologies

'Our time is ripe for His ideas!' I read in a German newspaper. The headline above the article read: 'Jesus' challenging message!' Practised readers of religious literature prick up their ears somewhat suspiciously. Has the secular press caught up with the church of all ages and is it now taking off its hat to Jesus, or is this a PR stunt, not so much on behalf of Jesus as on behalf of his commentators and their publishers? Be that as it may, the christological tide is flowing, and Jesus has the current with him, or however we might like to put it. Albert Schweitzer once wrote nicely that Jesus escaped the hands of his investigators and went back to his own time. Today he is escaping his own dogma and entering our world in a multiplicity of figures, all just as arbitrary. These are certainly Christ figures; however, this no longer has anything to do with the reception of Matthew, Mark, Luke and John, but with the reception of the Christ figure, the church's Christ.

The views about him run in series: the feminine Jesus, Jesus as the liberator of the poor, the Gnostic Christ, the eco-Jesus, Jehoshua as a protester, Christ as the hidden inwardness of every human being, Jesus as a teacher of esoteric knowledge, and so on. This is only a selection. The 'and so on' indicates the never-ending story of christology. Why never-ending? Because human beings are human beings, with religious needs and aspirations, who bear the stamp of the world in which they live. If this world is no longer a unity, but has fallen apart in bits and pieces, then the religious needs also become fragmented: many series apply at the same time.

That process is reflected in the chaos of christologies today. Every religious need that arises seeks material from christology to express itself, and the more quickly the needs follow one another, the more rapidly we have a new Jesus; the more simultaneously they appear, the greater the multiplicity of pictures of Jesus. This fanning out can go on endlessly. The examples are obvious. Those I have mentioned are only a fraction, and I would have to devote more attention to them if I were to assess their value. But is it all new? It seems to me that the Christ of New Age thinking is caught up in a kind of process of fermentation that we also meet in the first centuries of Christianity. Herman van Veen, for whom the divinity of Christ is the same as the divinity within every human being, is not very different from the theologians of German idealism, and these would feel most at home in some version of the Gnostic Christ, the redeemer whom we must seek within rather than outside. And doesn't that in turn have points of contact with the pietistic children's verse about Jesus, enthroned in every lowly heart?

One can go in all directions with the figure of Christ (typifying terminology). I call the christologies that come out of this wild christologies. Jesus entered Western culture in the packaging of faith provided by the Gospels; once inside it he became the church's Christ, and once he became the Christ, he was parcelled out into wild christologies.

That immediately brings me to my definition: wild christologies aren't grafted on to the Gospels, but on to the church's Christ. To be 'touched by the figure of Christ' is no longer to be touched by Jesus but to be touched by the church's version of Jesus and to make it your own. The meaning of a meaning of a meaning – that process can go on in an endless series, both collective and personal. That is reception history.

10. *Religious authority as a concern*

The wild christologies pick up the Christian tradition, but why? They could easily begin quite independently. They already have what they aim at, their aspirations, their religious character (friendly to women, belief in reincarnation, to mention a couple); they already know the religious interests for which they stand. Why attach them to Jesus?

Let me venture an answer. The more religions there are on offer, the more uncertain we are about which of them to choose. If anything is possible, people no longer know what to do and seek a new support, an authority to confirm their choice. The Christ, or simply Christ, is brought in here because of the religious authority conveyed by his name or title.

The need can express itself spontaneously: Jesus becomes meaningful to our group (women), our ideas (New Age), our action (social improvement), at the moment when people discover points of contact for their programme in christology. As an authority, I've just said. So a little suspicion can't do any harm: nothing is more natural than to manipulate needs, above all when this is the need for a religious authority, Jesus Christ as a resource for groups which get further with the authority of his name than without it. One finds them everywhere, and even where it isn't piled on, we may ask ourselves whether this is spontaneous recognition or a case of manipulation. Or sheer nonsense. What is Jesus as animus/anima, as giver of sexual freedom ? I can't imagine anything more fashionable.

May we not then ask what we have in Jesus, for example in a nuclear age, in a world threatened with destruction as a result of ecological disasters, in a world in which, as Malcolm X said thirty years ago, people sell their own mothers if they can get anything for them? It's always possible to ask these questions, but in all honesty, if the concerns are already there, the strategies already developed, for what other reason do we still want him (Jesus) in our camp, if not for the religious authority that he can give to our ideas? I can't forget that the great model of the manipulation was (and is) hell and damnation in classical preaching: *the* way of keeping people in order. Jesus is used in the service of a concern, namely the ongoing existence of the church.

Back to my story. What the Christian church leaves behind of its christology, even if the church itself should disappear, is always still the legacy of an empty authority, an authority which is needed for certainty, and which because of its emptiness is capable of adorning a number of choices and a number of concerns. Jesus as the draught horse, as a guarantee or a recommendation. To put it rather more crudely: Christians cannot be critical enough when the question arises what this authority is being chartered for.

11. *Reception history = the history of assimilation*

He came for something quite different, to call his people back to God, but he became the Saviour of the world. That is reception history in a nutshell. Jesus is what they make of him; that's what we learn from it. So I could use the reception history of the Gospels as the axis on which we could expound the subsequent christologies, in fact the series of ways in which Jesus was given meaning for human beings and the world. For 'reception history' we can read 'history of assimilation': what people make of him, makes Jesus worth the trouble. I wouldn't have written this book, it wouldn't have had a topic, were this not the case.

Reception history clarifies a great deal. The Christ of the scriptures – or, to use a term of Lucas Grollenberg's, the 'biblified' Jesus – is no longer Jesus of Nazareth; the church's Christ is no longer the Christ of the scriptures; the historical Jesus of the nineteenth century is no longer the church's Christ; and so on. The pattern is so complicated, sometimes almost impossible to unravel, because, as I have shown, it is not a 'pure' Jesus who is named and evaluated through constantly new times, but an already legitimated, already named, already clothed Jesus (clothed in concepts), who is then declined and conjugated time and again by new generations in order to keep in the picture: he has yet more new clothes put on top of his old ones. People cannot do otherwise. They live in a particular time, in a particular culture, and it is this culture which gives them the perspective, the evaluation, the veneration of the Jesus who has been handed down to them.

Christology sums up this veneration (and the reasons for it) in what we call 'doctrine', the dogmatic account of what the Christian religion has to offer in this culture: no more than that. We mustn't exaggerate its importance. Doctrine is a wafer-thin layer, a meagre residue, that certainly tells us what people *needed* to think, but hardly what they really thought, what they really desired, and where their passions really went, as believers. For that we must go to the history books which tell us about daily life as it was lived by the Greeks, Romans, Longobards, Alemans, Franks, Saxons and so on. The investigation of a christology doesn't go that far; it's the history of theology, and at that level it contributes a small stone, a pebble, to the knowledge of the religious aspirations circulating in our world. Granted. It's a little stone, but it's big enough to leave those who look at the whole development with an uncomfortable feeling: everything is possible, but is everything equally good? Of course there is freedom of interpretation; it's a great privilege to live in a time when that has come to be taken for granted. The Christian church has no monopoly of Jesus; the stakes at which heretics were burnt have disappeared. People can and may interpret Jesus as they will. But is everything equally good? That depends on the criterion that we introduce with the term 'God'. This criterion cannot be the doctrine of two natures, however useful that may be: in itself it is a historical product. Far less can it be the benefit provided with the annexation of Jesus by a group or an individual. But in that case, what?

12. *The question of the criterion*

From the perspective of reception history, and reception history presented as the history of assimilation, for a criterion we must return to the beginning. Not in the sense that there has to be a historical Jesus by whom everything that followed his appearance is measured. Measuring would amount to chopping off, whereas it began with that process in which Jesus becomes 'meaningful' for people from time to time, from culture to culture.

1. For this reason I want to replace the term criterion by legitimation. A Christian christology needs a legitimation, and wherever we turn, we keep ending up at the same place. The historical Jesus must have a place in it, an indispensable place: he represents a primal interest that cannot be scrapped without taking the ground from under christology and thus from under Christianity. Without a historical Jesus, anything is possible.

2. The diversity of meanings which are attached to Jesus is connected with the religious needs and aspirations of a culture, and these again go back to what people – in this time and culture – experience as the human need, the problem of existence that they cannot solve themselves. A universal significance of Jesus would have to derive from a universal religious need, a problem of existence that attaches to people as people. Can such a problem be demonstrated?

3. The question brings us to the way in which a culture interprets itself. What do people experience as a doom from which they cannot rescue themselves? At this point I see the real choice which is made in a religion: it is not so much the picture of humanity which determines what people believe (that is far too vague and wide a term) as what they

experience and express as the need, as the irremovable basic misery, of human existence.

4. Now Jesus interpreted himself within the self-interpretation of Judaism. The cultural context of the evangelists is already somewhat broader, but in principle still tied to the Jewish heritage, as I shall show, and the church's Christ begins from an even wider cultural context. Is 'Jewish' the canon, standard, measure for all cultures? No, but it is the measure for what people cannot make of Jesus if a christology at least still wants to be associated with him as a historical figure. As far as I am concerned, Christian may be an ounce more than Jewish, even far more than an ounce (although?), but it must at least contain what was essential for Jesus, the religious aspirations and needs which came with his Jewishness.

5. What does this imply? A human life is lived before the face of God the creator, and it is from there that a person derives his or her high value, joy in life, self-confidence, and also his or her basic problems: as the mystic Zeeuwen remarked, people can sin against the creator, fail as guilty human beings in their responsibility to God. Jesus himself speaks and acts from this Jewish self-interpretation, and it is by this perspective that he is coloured in the New Testament. Not exclusively: it isn't just a matter of concepts like sin and guilt; suffering, anxiety, lack of freedom – all this too is human wretchedness, and in Jewish culture is even given with human failure. We shall see this.

6. Back to the legitimation. To take Jesus' Jewish faith into account seems to me to be a minimum requirement for what is 'Christian'. In what follows I shall show that this minimum demand can be observed strictly, that christologies can be tested by it, and that it implies a great deal more than might appear at first sight. For this we must go back to history; that is a given. And that is where I shall also begin the next part of the book.

III

'The Religion of Christ'

Since I have prayed the prayer from my first
years at school, it also belongs to me as a Jew.
It is universally Jewish, although in one way or
another we can see who has composed it. For
that we are grateful to our heavenly Father.

David Flusser on the Our Father

9

The contribution of the historical Jesus

1. On such a fully laden tree

From the distance it looks like a tree, a cheerful tree full of little white birds, but when we get closer we see that the birds are little white paper scrolls. When we open them up, we see that on them are written the longings, the sighs, the emotions and the aspirations of young girls and housewives, career women and old grandmothers, cancer patients and bank directors. I'm talking about Japan, and about the trees which adorn the open spaces around the Shinto temples there. At first sight it's a strange affair. In some temples they use wooden tablets instead of letters; these are then put under the tree or hung on a rack placed there for them. But the strange custom is less strange if we set it alongside, for example, the prayers (short prayers, for example) of respectable Christians, teenagers and their parents. The difference is the tangible element of letters and tablets.

There is another difference, and that is the reason for writing this section. In Shinto religion it is the tree that is fully loaded with wishes and prayers; christology as reception history shows that in Christianity Jesus is the tree, the point to which people attach the religious needs and longings that they hope Jesus will provide for.

There is nothing against this. Anything is allowed, as I emphasized in a previous section. The question is, rather: does the tree also bear fruits of its own or is everything hung on it by others? Or, to abandon the metaphor: does Jesus make his own contribution to christology, a contribution which is indissolubly given with Jesus as a historical person? If that is the case, anyone can go on to the day of judgment using Jesus as a symbol for exalting their ideals – as it pleases them. However, in that case, of course, the question is how far such a christology (if I can continue to call it such) still has anything to do with Jesus.

This last point, what it has to do with Jesus, seems to me to be a meaningful criterion for the viability of a christology, very much according to the argument that it would be odd if the tree only bore things attached to it and no fruits of buds or its own.

So by the shorthand expression 'have to do with Jesus' I understand a contribution to christology which derives from the historical person of Jesus, a contribution in the active sense of the word, deriving from his own religious needs and aspirations, and in the passive sense of his fate and life.

But surely we know hardly anything of this historical person; surely he is known to us only in the garb of those who worship him? Certainly, and moreover that makes it difficult to establish what is possible and what is not in connection with any legitimation from the life and work of Jesus of Nazareth. But the advantage is again that as a result, the threshold to a Christian christology remains extra low: by this test much is legitimate. However, that does not alter the fact that it is indispensable as a test.

In order to avoid any misunderstanding, I am not using the term 'legitimated' in the sense of what is permissible and what isn't. How could anyone prohibit anything here? It serves above all to establish whether or not we can speak of a contribution from Jesus in a particular christology, which in my perspective is a condition for a Christian christology.

2. Historical research indispensable

A christology with Jesus in it (now the expression cannot cause any misunderstandings) means going back to the scholarly discipline of historical research. But the aim is not the same as in the days of Lessing, when the issue was to safeguard what 'really happened'. Nothing needs to be safeguarded. I shall be saying more about this shortly. First, historical investigation and the way in which it is taken for granted.

1. To begin with, history is already intrinsically important – quite apart from what precisely happened and what didn't – simply because there would be no Christian faith had there been no Jesus of Nazareth. Christian faith is given with the existence of Jesus as a historical person, and thus also dependent on that existence. That given, a historical person as a starting point, also means – as is self-evident – that historical investigation represents an interest of the first order. Suppose that Jesus had never lived, or had not been crucified, or had not been a teacher, then Christianity might perhaps have continued to exist as a religion, but it would have had no other basis than the fact that it exists here and now. That must be said openly and without fear. The world

isn't lost if there is no more Christianity, nor does that do away with belief in God. All that can be said is that for a number of centuries (no more than twenty out of the hundreds of thousands known to us) our forefathers made the mistake of supposing that – if we felt called to it – we had to draw a different picture of God. For the moment, without any hesitation, I am starting from the assumption that Jesus existed. No serious investigator doubts that.

2. If nothing needs to be safeguarded, that means that in this book I am not going to solve the unresolved historical questions (which perhaps cannot even be resolved at all). Historical investigation is not my speciality, far less exegesis; and there are others who can do that better, experts whose work I am not going to do all over again, far less make an independent contribution to. Why should I want to discuss this, if certainty doesn't depend on it? All that I am doing – and advise others to do – is to wait, to see what has been discovered and of course to use my mind to distinguish between what is reasonable and what seems to be fantasy. We don't need to accept everything from historians just like that. What we hear from them is always exciting, sometimes confusing, sometimes contradictory to what we are used to hearing. Was Jesus a Gnostic teacher or wasn't he? Did he offer himself as a sacrifice or did later believers attribute that to him? Not to mention the vivid reconstructions of Jesus' life (by Funk, Borg and their Californian 'Jesus seminar'), which could easily make conservative Christians panic. That needn't be. Historical investigation doesn't present any infallible historical truths: above all, faith doesn't stand or fall by its results.

3. Its results do not provide a foundation

It is very important for Christians to know who Jesus was and what happened to him; to put it as strongly as I can, it is important for faith to know that, but the certainty of faith doesn't depend on it. Historical investigation cannot destroy anything.

1. Science, of whatever kind, doesn't secure the foundations of faith. These foundations aren't dependent on it, for faith has no foundations. Faith is faith, and does without them. All it knows is a quest, a picture, series of pictures which help us on the way towards finding God. We have freedom, complete freedom, to take that course or not. As things stand (I have written at greater length about this elsewhere), what then is the value of historical investigation into Jesus? What do we get from it? Here is an answer in the form of three comments.

2. The scope of scholarly investigation is limited. Historical research

can try to discover what happened with Jesus and what didn't, but it cannot establish that Jesus indeed, for example, was the Son of God, the Second Person of the Holy Trinity, the Suffering Servant, the Messiah, the exponent of God, the Risen Lord, and so on. That was the mistake made by both nineteenth-century orthodoxy, which is still influential today, and those who challenged it. Meanings are confessions, expressions of faith, and historical investigation has no instruments for testing them.

3. Take the statement that in Jesus God has become a human being. This can be tested by church doctrine: is it an orthodox statement? But what else? More testing is impossible. We can only understand that God has really become a human being in Jesus as a historical truth if we have first established (in the sense of 'agreed') that Jesus wasn't just Jesus but the Son of God (in the trinitarian sense of the word). If that has been established, his birth is indeed the birth of God's Son. That is not only the logical order, but also the picture that practice shows. First the church's doctrine of Jesus Christ, christology, is developed, and only when that is established does his birth become the birth of the Son of God. This – later – becomes the occasion for celebrating Christmas as the celebration of his birth. But that is to go round in a circle: historically, nothing more can be said than that at one time a human being was born, Jesus of Nazareth, who by his followers is called the Son of Man, by others the Son of God, and by yet others the Messiah – all important titles, deriving from his followers. We can see him only through their eyes: Jesus in the packaging of faith. But is that the truth about Jesus, assuming that we know what they meant by their statements?

4. To put the problem in the right perspective, take instead the Gnostic Jesus in the Gospel according to Thomas. In it Jesus figures in a completely different packaging of faith from that in our Gospels. Who is to judge who is right here? Certainly not historical investigation – and that is my point. No single christology, even that of the so-called historical Jesus, is the fruit of historical research. For the record, on the other hand it is not the case (as people thought in the nineteenth century) that there are bare facts about which subjective views were later proclaimed, as it were in a second phase; that scholarship recovers the facts, like currants from a cake, and happily leaves the subjective views to believers. That is also a misunderstanding. All facts are narrated facts, if you like proclaimed facts, and thus are always interpreted; otherwise there would be nothing to tell. I have given an extended account of that in the first chapters of this book and will not return to it here.

4. *Research cannot ruin anything. A prospect*

The minimum requirement that I make of a Christian christology brings us back to the investigation of Jesus' words and actions, his life and his fate. We must see what emerges from that. Much is uncertain, historically speaking; much consists of guesswork and inference, but there is also much that is certain. In any case one thing is as firm as a rock: Jesus was a Jew, his religion was the Jewish religion; he believed in God in a Jewish way. Whether we need it or not, in any case a christology, of whatever kind, has to be capable of being in tune with the Jewish religion. Jesus' picture of God must fit in with this, otherwise Jesus does not fit in. And what kind of a christology is that?

In putting limits to our pictures of faith, building a kind of dam against excessively wild christologies, Jesus is quite indispensable: as a historical figure, as the person who lived at that time and was called Jesus, with all the historical investigation which that involves.

But that is rather different from saying that the Christian faith stands or falls with the results of historical investigation into Jesus' life and work. That would be the case only if we had to see Jesus as God on earth, and then in the sense of 'what really happened', which could then be discovered through historical research. But God-on-earth is first of all an interpretation, a view which people attributed to the Jesus of the Gospels in a particular time and culture, a phase in reception history, albeit one which lasted a long time and left deep traces. Nevertheless it is a phase. To attach the status of 'what really happened' to this view ('God put his footsteps here') overlooks this.

Furthermore, this view is also one which causes such insuperable problems for Christian faith that I would dare to call God-on-earth a false track. I have already alluded to this earlier, and shall be shedding further light on it in this book, but here I shall offer a pointer.

The strongest argument against God-on-earth, which can be verified by historical investigation, is that Jesus himself could not have believed it. Jesus was a Jew, his religion was the Jewish religion and a Jew cannot call himself Son of God (in the trinitarian sense). That is in fundamental conflict with his faith.

But there is more. Jesus as God-on-earth implies that alongside God as a quest (Jesus' Jewish quest), suddenly a second view of God, that of God on-earth, is added to what Jesus himself believes. That means not only that the Christian quest for God, the 'Christian religion', is detached from 'the religion of Christ', Jesus' own belief, but also that Christians must engage in two quests, and need two certainties of faith:

certainty about God in heaven, a certainty which people receive when they find the One who is delineated in the quest, and in addition a historical certainty about God on earth, which is dependent on historical investigation: at least if that investigation is not by-passed, out of a fear of attacking the foundations of the faith, by making the facts 'saving facts' to which historical scholarship has no access. But can faith determine what has or has not happened?

I shall devote the rest of the book to a kind of repair of christology on the basis of this outcome.

10

Christology and 'religion of Christ'

1. The Jewish context as a starting point

Jesus was a Jew: his roots lay in Judaism and the land of the Jews was the area in which he worked. That starting point is a winner three times over. First of all, there is historical certainty about at least something in Jesus' life: whatever else is uncertain, we know that he thought about God like the Jews of his day. I use that fact, secondly, as a minimal standard to which a christology must conform if it is to be counted Christian; it cannot get round Jesus' Jewishness. And lastly, I can demonstrate from it why the existence of Jesus *as a historical person* is essential for Christianity: Christianity owes its *own* existence to this. Furthermore, only through Jesus as a historical person can Christianity legitimate itself over against Judaism.

Jesus' faith, or the 'religion of Christ', as Lessing called it, is not the Christian religion as that has developed over the course of the centuries through dogma and theology, but the Jewish religion. Jesus believed, thought and acted as Jew. Whatever of him is introduced into christ-ology, his words and actions and his life and fate, will then have to be interpreted in a way which fits in with the symbolism of his own reli-gion, Judaism. If not, the 'Christian religion' has detached itself from the 'religion of Christ', thinking that it is better informed about God than Jesus. That seems to me to introduce an irresolvable contradiction.

The Christian church got caught up in this contradiction, especially when it began to worship Jesus as God-on-earth: Christianity was new in a way of which the Jews, in its view, had no idea. Indeed they didn't, nor could they, for the last thing a Jew will do is to imagine himself as God on earth. Quite apart from the fact that the Gospels nowhere suggest it (I shall come back to John later), it is inconceivable that Jesus himself will have felt in this way.

Now we mustn't paint too uniform a picture of the Judaism of Jesus' day (or of the Judaism of today, for that matter). It had and has many currents: messianic expectations, Hasidic traditions, apocalyptic movements, Pharisaic revivalist preaching, traditional Sadducees, the Kabbalah, to mention only a few which should be familiar to Christians today. Jesus himself was part of this; it is certain that, contrary to what we used to be taught in Sunday School, he could get on well with the Pharisees and largely share their ideas; indeed he even defended them against the Sadducees. We have been able to learn that from the Qumran scrolls.

This multiplicity does not alter the fact that Jews shared with one another what I would call the quest for God: there is only one God and God is one, the *shema Israel* of Deuteronomy 6.4. The variants could be seen as modifications of this: they divided Judaism – to the present day – into factions, but do not alter the fact that these are factions of Judaism.

In this way I can be more precise in saying what I mean by the religion of Christ: not Jesus' piety, his need for prayer and silence, nor even the depth of his trusting faith: in a word, not his personal attitude, about which the theologians from the time of the Enlightenment were so keen. Quite different from Judaism, they said, and in this way hoped to banish both the doctrine of two natures and Judaism and still maintain a historical Jesus. So that doesn't work. Not even that he belonged to the specific ethnic group which is called 'Jewish'. After the extermination of the Jews in the Second World War that fact has been recognized with so much verve that it has begun to seem almost like a Christian attempt (not all that serious) at reparation. But here, just as before, the *content* of Jesus' faith disappears into the background. I want to bring it back. From A to Z this fits the Judaism of his day.

I make this fact the guideline for christology. Not in the sense that the Christian church should only repeat what Jesus has said or could have said, or that it may interpret Jesus' life and fate only as he himself interpreted it (assuming that we could discover that). Not only is that to go too far, but it robs Jesus of any possible significance in any other historical context. However, in its christology the Christian church can hardly conflict with what Jesus himself believed. In my view a christology which goes back to Jesus must meet this minimum demand.

2. *The New Testament remains within Jewish symbolism*

What becomes of Jesus' preaching and his fate when it is picked up and interpreted by the first narrators in the framework of a particular interpretation? What made him, Jesus of Nazareth, according to these narrators, into someone who has to be proclaimed, viz., Christ? Already in the New Testament Jesus is discussed within a multiplicity of inter-pretative frameworks. I shall not present all of them; that is the work of exegetes and historians, and they are far from being clear about them (if they ever will be). So I can do no more than what anyone can do, and as a non-professional select three typical traditions of interpretation from the New Testament: James, John and Paul. All three remain with-in the Jewish framework which – with a touch of exaggeration – I am defining with the help of the statement that no believing Jew can or will ever be able to say that he is of God's make-up, God on earth.

With James that is already very clear. He hardly speaks of Jesus at all, knows nothing of Pauline terms like 'justification', or when he mentions them only seems to misunderstand them. He does not speak of 'atone-ment', and this was almost unacceptable to Luther: James is 'a strawy epistle' because it lacks 'what presents Christ'. Luther was right: more than the other New Testament authors, James remains within the framework of Judaism: what he offers is not *halakhah*, but stands in this tradition. Jesus is a teacher and that's that. James represents a Christianity which still stands very close to Judaism.

The Gospel according to John can be read as the opposite pole to this; it is the least Jewish, and according to some scholars even on the verge of anti-Judaism or already beyond it. 'The Jews' – a stereotyped expres-sion in John – take the blame for the murder of Jesus. Once upon a time, as a student, I was taught that by 'the Jews' John meant the leaders of the Jewish people and not the Jewish people itself, but the damage has been done. If one says that homosexuals corrupt morality, and adds that by 'homosexuals' one means some spokesmen and women and not the group as a whole, there's nothing to be done; it encourages homo-phobia. To call John anti-Jewish is too strong; nor can one say that of the Gospel of Matthew either, where, at least in the final redaction that we know, the Jewish people is also blamed for the death of Jesus. Isn't that anti-Jewish? No, the conflicts which are presented to us are evi-dence of what are still controversies within Judaism: polemic between Jews who followed Jesus and those who did not. In John's day the formation of groups had already gone far enough for the former to feel superior to the latter: the law comes through Moses, but grace and truth through Jesus (John 1.17). That can only be read to mean that as a reli-gion, Christianity is superior to Judaism.

That isn't the only thing in which John sets the tone. His redaction of the story of Jesus has been called the most precious Gospel. That's understandable, since – whether he meant it or not – the terminology which John uses is read as a foundation, a constant foundation, under

the idea that in Jesus God came to earth. Is that the case? I shall devote
a separate section to it.

3. *Identification with God? John*

The Gospel of John seems to be balancing on the edge of identification:
whoever sees Jesus sees God; whoever knows the Son, knows the
Father. The Son has come down to earth, and after his work is done he
returns to heaven, to the Father. The most powerful identification seems
to be Jesus' statement 'I and the Father are one' (John 10.30).

But it is not the doctrine of two natures, even in embryonic form.
John uses terms which are derived from what in technical terms is called
Gnosticism or Gnosis, a view of human beings and the world which, as
I showed earlier, is enjoying especial popularity today. It uses markedly
dualistic imagery: world history consists of an endless struggle between
good and evil, light and darkness, spirit and flesh, earth and heaven, a
struggle of cosmic proportions: the light shines in darkness, and the
question is who or what will win, the darkness or the light.

John is best read against the background of this world of ideas, and
here (though not only here, of course) he differs from the three Synoptic
Gospels. Jesus is the light of the world because he comes from the world
of light; he is the bread of heaven because he comes from heaven and
returns there. He is the Son because he comes from God, belongs with
God; the Word that was with God and was God, the connecting link
between the spiritual God and the earthly, bodily creature: all things
were made through him. The Word was already the true light of the
world, but the world did not know it. That Word became flesh and
dwelt among us, and we have seen his glory, the glory of the only-
begotten Son of the Father. That is how John introduces Jesus to his
readers (John 1.1–14).

Gnostic? In the word of Gnostic ideas Jesus is the prince in disguise,
the Son of God hidden in the flesh, whose bodily nature serves only to
put the powers of darkness on the wrong track, but which is of no
further significance. John doesn't go that far, although he makes use of
the language and the thought world of Gnosticism. Perhaps we should
even see the first signs of opposition to Gnosticism in his language, as
some scholars suppose, just as the doctrine of two natures is already
meant as opposition to it (the human nature of Jesus also contributes to
this).

Be this as it may, John does not identify Jesus with God. Jesus is not
God and God is not Jesus. Nor does he say of himself that he is God,

but makes the claim that he is the true revealer of God, can interpret God because he comes from God's world. In other words, John offers no support for the 'light from light' in the Nicene Creed (325) that became the basis of the doctrine of two natures (Chalcedon 451). But he isn't a genuine Gnostic either. Gnosticism sees true life not in the union of the divine and human natures, but in the abolition of dualism, any dualism, including that between God and human beings, and in parallel to that, dualism between body and spirit. The misery of human beings lies in their fleshly existence, their earthiness, their mortality, and their redemption therefore consists in spiritualization, eternal life, rebirth, liberation from the body. We meet some of these terms in John, but he knows nothing of a devaluation of Jesus' bodily nature. The pattern of the other Gospels – Jesus suffers in his body, dies and is raised from the dead on the third day – is also followed by the evangelist John.

Discussions about the relationship between John and the Essenes (and whether the Essenes are the same group as the Qumran community, which settled there about 130 BC) are of historical interest: where does this 'clothing' of John come from? But of course they make no difference to his view.

4. *Paul*

'Is Jesus really necessary?,' we ask ourselves when reading James. 'Are we still within the Jewish context?,' is the question which arises for us with John. The third in the series, Paul, completes the picture. I shall follow him further because through his position I can demonstrate why Jesus is so necessary as a historical person and at the same time how Jesus does not disrupt the Jewish quest for God.

So what I am in fact saying is that I am giving a central place to Paul. Not because through his way of speaking (his letters are older than the Gospels that we know) we arrive at an old, if not the oldest, interpretation of Jesus. That can be disputed, and moreover why should the oldest be the best? But here we find an exegesis which presents the meaning of Jesus in terms of the symbolism of the Jewish religion, and does so in such a way that we can easily understand the significance of the exercise. I realize that I must explain this statement word by word.

To begin with: in his interpretation of Jesus, Paul remains a believing Jew. Whatever he thinks that he has to say about Jesus, he does not erode the Jewish quest for God. Indeed he tells us that himself, as Luke reports in Acts 24.14: he believes all that stands in the law and the prophets. He liked to appear in all the synagogues on his journeys; he was a very welcome guest. That means that we can expect an answer from this Paul to the question why Jesus must be added to Jewish belief in God. He must have wrestled with this question, and come to a conclusion: what is achieved with Jesus, what is his role, and why is he necessary?

Of course Christianity raised this question in the course of its history. But I do not like the time-honoured answers that have been the vogue for centuries and centuries, and are still repeated today. I don't trust them, nor do I think that they are good ones. I give more credit to Paul. He is, if not the founder, then the organizer of the Christian church, and as a Jew, indeed as someone who never wanted to be anything other than a Jew, his christology forms the starting point for him here. He undertakes his mission with the help and guidance of an interpretation of Jesus' life and death. What did he see in Jesus?

Not the first Christian. Jesus wasn't that. There would have been no Christianity had Jesus not lived and worked, but Jesus' religion was Jewish. Like that of Mary, I might add for the sake of clarity. To believe in 'the Mother of God' (as the Roman Catholic faithful like to call her) would have been impossible for her.

This simple, most trustworthy historical fact, that Jesus was a believing Jew, has had little consideration in the Christian church. No wonder, it would amount to the fact that Jesus himself, on whom Christianity turned, had held an obsolete faith. Of course no Christian could say that, and to avoid this conclusion people had to make Jesus other than he was. One cannot make the apostle Paul an accomplice in such a manoeuvre. He didn't see Jesus as the founder of a new sort of faith; on the contrary, the God of Jesus was his God and vice versa. The apostle Paul, the Christian, pursues the same quest as that in which Jesus, the Jew, was engaged.

Thus there is no contradiction, no trace of a contradiction, between the religion of Jesus and that of the Christian Paul. If there is in fact such a contradiction today, so much the worse for Christian religion. So for the third time: what did Paul see in Jesus which made him so important, so essential, and what is there behind this exalted place that Christianity has given to Jesus, if this place cannot consist in a change in the quest for God?

5. The novelty of Christianity

As an addition to the knowledge of God in Judaism, Jesus is neither necessary nor profitable for a single Jew. The added value is there only for Christianity. For Christians the meaning of Jesus, as an addition to the Jewish quest, lies in the fact that Jesus has become the way to God (the God of the Jews) for non-Jews. That is the new element that is given with Jesus, at least for Christians. Jesus is necessary as a historical person for both the origin and the ongoing existence of Christianity as Christianity. I have done my best to devise a double formula for this, as brief as possible, and I have written it down here. In my view, it indicates the place of Jesus in the Christian quest.

1. Historical investigation indicates that there is nothing in the teaching of Jesus which was not also in the teaching of the Jews. In other words, Jesus remained within the framework of the Jewish religion. This has been pointed out many times, from Strack-Billerbeck to David Flusser and Pinchas Lapide. He criticizes his contemporaries, who are Jews, but not Judaism. The most convincing proof of this seems to me that Jesus left behind the Our Father. David Flusser says that there is no Jew who cannot pray this.

2. There is nothing in Christianity that is not also in Judaism. The Jewish quest is the Christian quest. The proof of this is that since its beginning the Christian church has used the Old Testament, the Jewish Holy Scriptures, as its own holy scripture. With a good deal of moaning and groaning, with many misconceptions about the Old Testament (about which more later), but undeniably as a canonical writing, and canonical = something for building faith on.

The Jewish is the Christian, except. . . . Except what? That through Jesus, according to Christianity, the God of the Jews has also become the God of and for the Gentiles. There is good reason for saying 'according to Christianity'. It has to be acknowledged that here there was a brutal take-over of the God of the Jews: a kind of take-over. But Christianity dared to do this, spurred on by someone who was himself of Jewish origin: Paul. 'He preached Jesus to them' means that he preached to them that the God of the Jews was also the God of and for non-Jews. I shall demonstrate all the consequences of that shortly, but for the moment I can keep to this brief formula. Everything that Christians have can already be found among the Jews: the ingredients of the faith are the same, except for Jesus.

6. *The controversy*

The controversy between Jews and Christians is thus in fact fixed on Jesus. That much is certain. Increasing veneration on the one hand and increasing opposition on the other. What was the dispute really about?

We have the starting point, if not the essence, as clearly as we could want in the book of Acts. Read chapters 8, 10 and 11. Chapter 22 forms the conclusion. In it the apostle Paul defends his activity and his preaching to his fellow-believers, apparently with some success. Not only because he addresses them in their own language, but also because his account does not make anyone cross. He is allowed quietly to tell his life-story, his call and conversion, in order once to express solemnly his regret about his past. They hear all that until he speaks of his mission. The Lord (here clearly Jesus) sends him into the world: 'Depart, for I will send you far away to the Gentiles.' Then we read (v.22).

> Up to this word they listened to him; then they lifted up their voices and said, 'Away with such a fellow from the earth! For he ought not to live.'

A stone in the pond! I read this passage as a description of *the* point, *the* source of the conflict between Jew and Christian. Not the doctrine of two natures, not Jesus as the incarnate Second Person of the Holy Trinity, not – in short – 'God-on-earth'; that is what the controversy has become in the course of the history of the two religions. However, it wasn't that to begin with, but rather the claim of the followers of Jesus that since his appearance, the wall between Jew and Christian had been removed.

I do not need to bring in all kinds of passages from the New Testament. As well as the apostle Paul, we need only read Luke (both in his Gospel and in the book of Acts), and also chapter 2 of the letter to the Ephesians (vv.11–22) which has been quoted now and then, and finally the so-called mission command from Matthew 28, which must not be read as a command to compel people to become Christians, but as the freedom for non-Jews to regard the God of the Jews as their God.

There is no stopping it now: of course all this has enormous consequences for the way people talk about God. Non-Jews do that differently from Jews, present-day Jews differently from the Jews of that time; quests have to keep moving if they want to fulfil their function. But that doesn't alter the fact that the novelty of Christianity by comparison with Judaism consists in the opening of the way for non-Jews to the God of the Jews. With good reason Jesus is called 'the 'way' – viz., the way to God for non-Jews (e.g. Acts 19.9).

7. *Thijs Booy and the people of God*

I can clarify the kind of controversy I mean by a parallel. In the 1950s there was squabbling in the Dutch Reformed Churches over the significance of baptism. On the conservative side, being baptized was interpreted – very much in line with tradition – as a sign of 'belonging to God', being a member of the people of God. Only baptized people have that status, according to the strict argument, and as baptism meant infant baptism, only baptized children are God's children. Thijs Booy, a rebellious author in those days, wrote a substantial book against this, under the title *And All Young People are God's Young People*. It isn't my concern here to go into the ins and outs of this discussion; I am concerned rather with the model of the controversy. Infant baptism is directly connected with the pattern of Israel as the people of God: anyone who is born into that people belongs to that people, and receives a sign as an indication of it. In Israel this was circumcision, and the Christian church used baptism instead ('which has come in place of circumcision', as the classic baptism formula can innocently observe).

So are the others not God's people? When Thijs Booy put his finger on this sore point there was an approximate repetition of the story of Acts 22: the Reformed Churches wouldn't hear of it; this would do away with the significance of baptism as a distinctive sign and thus with the significance of the church as the people of God. So by no means were 'all young people God's young people'.

If the Reformed found Thijs Booy so difficult, how much more difficult must the Jews have found the apostle Paul, who in their firm view sold out the God of Israel, through Jesus, to the pagans!

The concept of the 'people of God' is the basis of the problem. All people are God's people, and not one people, as Judaism would have it. It cannot even be said that God brings together his people from all peoples (thus the primal notion of Christianity). That's an improvement, but it isn't enough. Is there what can be rightly called a people of God, or do the religions share out that role, and is that one of the reasons why they so easily entered into competition with one another?

I shall keep to this last point. The Christian church as a whole is in the same boat as Judaism. To reserve the name 'people of God' for a particular part of humankind, namely that part which feels involved in a particular quest for God, makes a distinction between those who are

'God's people' and those who are not. Those who belong to it have a privilege which others do not. Hundreds of thousands of times it may rest on grace as unmerited election (as responsible theology would have it), and hundreds of thousands of times it may be connected with being called to service, but it remains a privilege, and in such cases we ourselves have shared out the privilege. Those who do not belong will therefore always experience this as discrimination, arrogance, self-glorification, the appropriation of God by the other party, and so will rejoice when this division is said to be invalid. I think that the fading away of baptism – as a sign and seal that one belongs to the people of God, in contrast to others – is connected with the intuition that something is happening here which is just not on (any more).

I am not forgetting that the concept of 'people of God' can also have a good sense, especially when it values the church people over against the clergy, the laity against the hierarchy (who regard themselves as the real church, since they keep the ritual mills turning). Thus the concept has performed good service for Roman Catholic Christians, who use it to oppose the sole rule of the pope and bishops in the church. In their terms it is not those who hold office but the laity, *laicus*, the people (literally), who are the church. However, the term cannot do further service. In the past, Christianity could begin from revealed truths, and from a church which knew them and could build on them. But if that excuse no longer exists, then 'people of God' is really a self-designation. All people are 'God's people', or none are (just as good a solution). The Christian church would do well to drop this concept as a way of interpreting itself to the rest of humankind.

8. How does Paul arrive at the idea of 'Israel's God also for non-Jews?'

Paul may have travelled the world with the Gospel of Jesus, but the story has a different beginning. Jesus begins as an affair within Judaism: he is a prophet for and of the Jewish people. The Christian church read 'God has visited his people' (Luke 1.68) all too easily as: visited the church or humankind. The focal point is Israel, and Jesus became a light to the nations only after a shift in history of which no one had any notion at that time. His own people first, he himself said when a foreigner appealed to him for help (Matthew 15.21–28). Only after long pleading did he allow himself to be persuaded, and hesitantly took the vital step.

That is certainly an opening, and it needs to be taken up. But all the water in the sea cannot wash away the fact that his story takes place within the Jewish community, picks up Jewish aspirations (Jesus as the 'expectation of Israel'), discusses typically Jewish controversies, and presupposes the land of the Jews and the Jewish religious context, to the degree that large parts of the Gospels have similar stories, though their meaning would escape us were there no exegesis. That cannot be ignored, even in the case of an evangelist like Luke, who thinks about Jesus in such a cosmopolitan way. In Acts 10 and 11 (the baptism of Cornelius), he shows splendidly how difficult the first Christians (Jews!) found it to accept a Gentile. There had to be a heavenly vision to get them that far. So how do they, and how especially does Paul, arrive at the idea that God is also open to non-Jews?

I think that most of the factors can be found if we look further, but I shall limit myself to just a few. The starting point is the opposition of some Jewish groups to what Jesus saw as his mission among his own people, an opposition which resulted in his execution by the Romans. We can accept that discussions pro and con among the Jews were the result, and all looked to tradition to confirm their view. The book of Acts, which largely comes from the evangelist Luke, relates this kind of discussion at length, and we may assume that such discussions were already being held before Paul began his mission. It raises among the followers of Jesus first, the question what must be done if one's own people do not listen. In that case, one goes outside them and seeks a hearing there. That is the order that we see described at length in Acts in the case of the apostle Paul: he always goes first to the synagogue, to his own people, and when he finds the door shut there, he turns to the non-Jews, whom he calls, without embarrassment, 'the pagan'. In his letter to the Romans he later explains this attitude.

A second factor, of equal importance, is connected with this: the idea that Israel had a saving function for the world. It is not that the Jewish religion allowed no missionary elements. In Jesus' day people travelled through town and country to make converts. You make them worse than you are, says Jesus somewhere (or the first Christian community, in its polemic, Matthew 23.15), but there was missionary zeal, and it could appeal to the prophets. Take such a saying as 'a light to the nations', a passage from the prophet Isaiah, in which the Servant of the Lord is told:

> It is too light a thing that you should be my servant, to raise up the tribes of Jacob and to restore the preserved of Israel; I shall give you as a light to the nations, and that my salvation may reach to the end of the earth (Isaiah 49.6).

The servant can be Israel, but he can just as well be a separate figure; the text doesn't give any explanation of that. That makes it attractive to refer the prophecy to Israel. The light of the nations must then in the first instance be Israel; in Israel's great son this prophecy becomes reality. In any case that is what the apostle Paul makes of it (read Acts 26 or Romans 2), and after him a number of Christian theologians. Thus God does not change appearance if non-Jews can join in. Or, to put it more strongly, it is a notion within Judaism that non-Jews may also share in the salvation of the Lord.

Yet a third factor played a role: the great dissemination of Jews throughout the Roman empire. Every important city had a synagogue. Thus Jewish religion, with its strict observance of God's commandments, also enjoyed great respect among outsiders. Jews were open to ideas from outside; they were real cosmopolitans, but they remained Jewish. Paul was such a person; he lived outside Israel, and even had a Roman passport, but he remained faithful to his religion.

The situation which I am describing here explains at least in part how when Paul came to a city – Antioch, Derbe, Lystra, Corinth – he knew how to recruit groups of Christians: he fished for them so to speak in the Jewish pool. It was a great advantage that the new group (of Christians), certainly to begin with, was viewed by outsiders as a branch of the faith of the Jewish fathers and thus as a legitimate religion.

I shall stop there. It isn't my concern to give exhaustive explanations but more to explain why the involvement of non-Jews with the God of the Jewish religion is an element which had long belonged to it, and at any rate was not in conflict with it. On what conditions? At that point we can clearly see that the apostle Paul was rather different from his brothers. But that is still to come.

Guilt and penitence. The atonement

1. Jesus and the atonement as Jewish ritual

For a long time, it has been out of order to approve of Paul. He is seen as the evil genius of Christianity; he is said to have complicated everything that with Jesus was still simple and made it inaccessible to ordinary people. Take the simple discipleship of Christ which the evangelists report, and put alongside it Paul's doctrine of reconciliation and justification. What a complicated kind of Christianity he makes of it! Fodder for theologians – that was the mood, and is often the mood today.

Is this picture right? Given the purpose of this book, I shall not go into the question in detail. A lack of patience, inadequate knowledge of the matter and – it cannot be denied – a certain inaccessibility on the part of the apostle himself will all have contributed to the formation of this image. But Paul didn't contaminate everything. He interpreted Jesus, or at least did his best to interpret Jesus, in terms of the Jewish religion. One can have difficulties with that, as good friends; moreover others have interpreted him in different terms, even in the New Testament. That doesn't alter the fact that Paul exists, that his work was the basis for a good deal of the Christian foundation document (the New Testament) and that his involvement of Jesus in the Jewish religion brings in atonement as one of the focal points, and that makes us think.

Anyone who follows the apostle Paul, with his idea that the God of the Jews is also the God of non-Jews, automatically comes up against a characteristic of the God of the Jews, according to the rule that whoever says A must also say B. B is what Paul calls atonement or reconciliation, and as an extension of it justification 'by faith' instead of 'by the works of the Law' (but that comes later).

Atonement isn't a Christian invention, as is often thought or claimed; many religions know of it, including Judaism, the 'religion of Christ', the world of Jesus' faith. In Judaism atonement was a ritual which occurred annually, and was marked by sending away the so-called

scapegoat. Beyond question Jesus experienced the ritual of the Day of
Atonement many times. What Paul does in particular is to give Jesus as
key role in the ritual of atonement and thus opens up that ritual to
non-Jews. The whole of the complicated terminology of justification
and reconciliation (which is indeed fodder for theologians) is meant to
make it clear to non-Jews that God is also accessible to them. In Paul's
own words, God was in Christ reconciling *the world* to itself, and not
just the Jewish people (II Corinthians 5.19). That is what Paul wants to
express. He will doubtless have used more and other ideas for clarifying
Jesus' role, but for the sake of clarity I shall sum up his view under the
heading of atonement: to put it as briefly as possible, in the person of
Jesus the world has its scapegoat and in Good Friday its Day of
Atonement.

2. *The scapegoat: what does it stand for?*

In any catastrophe we look for a scapegoat, someone on whom we can
put the blame. Finding a 'scapegoat' is a system for passing the buck; we
are fond of using it, except in religion. Then it is a mechanism which can
expect little sympathy. 'My sins go with me to my grave,' said the poet.
He meant that he would not put the blame on other people. Amen. The
whole of Christianity should endorse that rather more clearly. No one
should put the blame on someone else, ever. The scapegoat, too, is never
ever mean in this sense. Nor is that the case with Jesus. So that misunderstanding is removed. But what does it stand for?

The scapegoat ritual as it functioned in ancient Israel is described at
length in the book of Leviticus (see especially chapter 16), and in the
New Testament the Letter to the Hebrews comes back to it (chapter 9).
I cannot quote these chapters here, but must simply note that once a
year the high priest has to lay hands on a goat, has to load it as it were
with the sins of the people, and then send it out into the wilderness. The
purpose of the ritual is clearly for the sins of the people to be carried
away, outside society. The goat carries away the evil, the moral and
religious evil, and the people is again regarded as pure. So this is a sub-
stitutionary ritual. It is clearly not an invention of strict Reformed
Christians; the Jews already used it earlier and even they were not the
first. Precisely what is its meaning?

1. René Girard, a French scholar, wants to see the scapegoat as a
representative sacrifice of reciprocal violence, a victim of 'sacred lynch-
ing', sacred because it is about the purifying violence that must stem
unholy wrath. To choose a scapegoat and vent on it the aggression

which is always present calms people's minds. So Girard sees the scapegoat as a lightning conductor: blood turns away blood and in this way the scapegoat makes culture possible.

The theory is attractive, but applied to Jesus it is sheer guesswork. Does Jesus create culture as a scapegoat, in the sense that as a deterrent he calls a halt to imitation? And is the repetition of that sacrifice in the rite of the Last Supper or eucharist meant to deter those who attend from their own violence? I see nothing of this in practice. The television presents us with a peaceful Karadzic who takes part in the liturgy according to the rite of the Orthodox Church. But above all, the symbolism in Leviticus is not that people kill the scapegoat (the animal is never killed); they promote it to the status of a substitute which – symbolically – bears evil away from the community. The purification of the people is a gift of God and not a fruit of violence.

2. The term 'exchange' is certainly appropriate. The scapegoat of Leviticus 16 changes places with the people: it has the sins and the people is pure again. Not automatically – that is worth emphasizing. The priest must say words confessing guilt and repentance over the head of the scapegoat, and only then is the animal 'laden' and can be sent into the wilderness. So to the present day, the ritual stands in the framework of a confession of guilt, of fasting and a prayer for forgiveness.

3. Is the people *regarded* as clean again? Yes, of course. Like all symbolism, reconciliation is a ritual play, an extremely serious game. Human beings aren't *made* clean by a ritual. But they are *regarded* as clean again: the ritual is so to speak an agreement between God and human beings. Of course it is devised by us (us human beings) and attributed to God: we have to wait to see what the Most High thinks of it. But that is how we see ourselves, as sinners, and that is how we get clean; our sins are carried away. That 'regarded as' returns in Paul's legalistic terminology of justification, but I shall devote a separate section to it.

4. Sending away the scapegoat is symbolic language. It stands for taking away sins in the sense of removing them from the eyes of God. God cannot see them. As a result the people is restored to its dignity as people of God. Life before God's face is of course a precarious matter: without reconciliation in the sense of the covering of evil, it is impossible.

3. *The ritual comes from below*

At present, reconciliation as a religious, doctrinal concept is unpopular, and is even open to argument in that supporters and opponents irrevocably get at odds over it. That's strange, for as a social term it has a high reputation. The newspapers are full of reconciliation, or at least attempts at it, between ethnic groups in former Yugoslavia, between blacks and whites in South Africa, between the Maoris and the New Zealanders, and so on. By reconciliation we then mean a form of conflict resolution which has more substance than 'forget it'. That isn't enough; it's too easy. I haven't heard a Jew say it to a Nazi, and that's as it should be. Elie Wiesel knows better: 'Forgive them not', he prayed, standing by the gas ovens of Auschwitz, and he's right. With 'reconciliation' we want to get through to the roots of the conflicts: violence and injustice. If that isn't removed, there is no reconciliation.

Why then is 'reconciliation' losing popularity as a notion of faith, having so long been deeply rooted in Protestantism? Partly, I think, because as Wittgenstein said we are 'bewitched' by language. 'Reconciliation', too, is just a term and all can fill it with their own associations. If we don't find what we think of as 'reconciliation' in the traditional doctrine – and we don't – then the doctrine must be tailored, refashioned. In addition, the traditional notion of reconciliation seems to be dead capital: people do nothing with it and nothing changes. Why then still hold on to it, if reconciliation doesn't imply change? Anyone who reads the previous section once again will see that things are different: repentance, conversion and change of life don't need to be added to the ritual; they form an essential substructure of it. Without repentance and conversion there is no forgiveness.

But the most important resistance comes from somewhere else: from the mixture of Above and below. 'Reconciliation', as a religious term, is originally a ritual which comes 'from below', which is set up by human beings. It isn't that God devised it and then revealed it, so that we have to believe in it; it comes from human beings, who mean something by it. Let me explain.

The roots of the evil that people do to one another – that is how I began this section – lie in injustice and violence; therefore we can never resolve conflicts unless we go back to that evil. But even then we aren't finished, for the 'evil that people to do one another' extends to God the Creator and the order that he maintains in his world. All the great religions know of an angry God, a God who appears like a storm cloud, or with his long arm can bring back a people which continues to do wrong if his order is transgressed. We needn't be concerned with the great variety of notions of this. This God must be reconciled, his anger assuaged, his disposition calmed – that's commonplace. Through rituals, and it doesn't really matter what rituals. There's a splendid example in the Old Testament in the story of Noah, who offers a sacrifice to God after the flood. Then we read:

> And when the Lord smelled the pleasing odour, the Lord said in his heart, 'I will never again curse the ground because of human beings, for the imagination of the human heart is evil from youth upwards; neither will I ever again destroy every living creature as I have done' (Gen. 8.21).

Who said that the Bible doesn't speak of God having to be calmed down? Just smell! The story of Noah isn't the only one. Of course these are primitive notions of God – I shall come back to that in a moment – but we mustn't eliminate them because of the anthropomorphic way in which God is imagined; we must try to discover why people talk about God like this and what these ideas express. God must be calmed down? Yes, because he's angry. Why is he angry? Because his order, of which justice and righteousness are the foundations, has been transgressed. No people is so primitive as not to believe in that, and in a God who does not disregard transgressions: people know that it is impossible to transgress God's order. And that brings us to the rituals, from the scapegoat to the sacrificial victims. They have only one aim: turning away the wrath of God as far as possible. So the rituals come from below, from people who see the sword of Damocles hanging above their heads and are concerned about it. The view that God has revealed himself as the one who demands satisfaction (so we have to believe that), or conversely as the one who has revealed that he does not require satisfaction (so that we don't have to believe that) misses the point of the ritual and ends up in our involving God in our ecclesiastical disputes over reconciliation. 'Reconciliation' is a ritual and thus from below, from people who were aware that they had become transgressors, were guilty; they had to do something about it, and so they offered the scapegoat or a sacrificial animal.

Here I shall first investigate what is then called the primitive notion of God which lies behind the doctrine of atonement, and in a further section look at what it means that the doctrine of atonement comes from below, has been devised by human beings.

4. *Inappropriate for God?*

We have to purge the Bible of its primitive notions of God. The early church fathers already made a plea for that. I have the idea that many modern Reformed church people think in precisely the same way. God doesn't roar, doesn't become angry, has no feelings, let alone hard feelings, and so on. Here the church fathers, following Origen, used an attractive phrase: it is *non decens deo*, inappropriate for God. The biblical authors, especially those of the Old Testament, don't speak appropriately about God: they imagine him in human form and of course that's not right. It's the task of theologians to sort out the matter and make it clear to believers that we must abandon this kind of language. At least if we belong among the enlightened.

The church leaders understood the troubles with which a more philosophical concept of God saddles believers. From a tenth-century encyclopaedia I once dug up a story by Cassian (he died in 430) about a monk who was accused by the people of having all too human a notion of God. He was summoned to the bishop, who taught him more about God, and the monk obediently promised his superior that he would do better. But the next day he was found weeping in the street, crying out loudly, '*Eheu, eheu, abstulerunt a me deum meum*' (they have taken my God away from me). He couldn't believe in God without envisaging God in a human form. That's all right, let him do so, let all those who cannot do otherwise do so. Regard the biblical language, the immature language about God, as an assimilation of the Most High to misunderstanding, to the unpolished human spirit. It's an adaptation from God's side. That would put everything right: those who are required to could preserve a pure picture of God and ordinary people a God in human form.

The nice thing is, of course, that the church teachers with their orthodox disposition – to the present day – not only improved on the Bible, although the Bible was the word of God one hundred times over, but that they embarked on this improvement on the basis of a criterion by which they measured the biblical language: whether it was appropriate or not for God. In other words, their picture of God stood in the background as a criterion. I have the idea that precisely the same mechanism is playing a part in the discussion about reconciliation and atonement: God must be reconciled, for he is angry! That cannot be, since it conflicts with what we think about God, with our picture of God, our norm for God.

Now I shall drop the term 'adaptation': it is dependent from A to Z on a view of the Bible which regards the Bible as a book dictated from above, and few people would defend this view any more. God in human form, which is so essential for all the books of the Bible, is not an adaptation by the Most High to unpolished human beings, but what we now call a metaphor, a form of pictorial language by which people say what something or someone is like, not what something or someone is, as Paul Ricoeur points out.

5. *God's human form as a metaphor*

I shall pause there for a moment to clarify what I have in mind by 'metaphor'. With metaphors we make a comparison, as with other forms of figurative language. This makes metaphors somewhat risky: they can go wrong. If I say that Audrey Hepburn is a cow, no one will understand what I am saying, because she is so slim and attractive. If I call Mike Tyson a bull, then I am immediately clear: there is no mistaking it. With these two images I am demonstrating how we use metaphors to give information to others, information as we see it. 'John is like Peter' is information about John, at least if we know who Peter is. For example, he is 'just as tall as Peter', 'just as slim', or 'just as athletic', depending on what we have been talking about.

The language of faith, of religion, consists of metaphors from A to Z, metaphors like 'John is like Peter'. Judaism, Christianity and Islam have the metaphor of God being like a human being. That is less obvious than it seems; it is a quite unique metaphor for God. Of course we can only talk about God's world in terms of our world; we are condemned to metaphors. But there are also religions which say that God is like a cat, or God is like a snake. It is typical of the religions which I have mentioned (here they are more akin than they think) that they say that God is like a human being, in human form. Here Christians are not claiming that God *is* like a human being; they *talk about* him as a human being if they want to clarify who God is and what God does.

That God has a human form has, generally speaking, become such a commonplace in the Christian language of faith that many people are no longer aware of its metaphorical character. Sometimes they even oppose the statement that we have to use metaphors, arguing that metaphors cannot provide any information. But they can, as I can again show by the example 'John is like Peter'. The problem is not their referential character, but John. Mention of John presupposes that we know John and are now getting further information about him. Do we know something about God, and does the fact that he is in human form add further information?

Within that metaphorical language-field of religion, specific metaphors come into being which people do sense as such (an indication of how little God's human form is still seem as a metaphor), one might say a metaphor in a metaphor. 'Reconciliation' belongs to that second sort. It is a special metaphor within the general metaphor of God in a human form: God is reconciled as a person whose displeasure or anger has been aroused is reconciled.

After all that I have said about metaphors, it is clear that the metaphor of reconciliation can prove confusing in more than one way. A misunderstanding can arise between the speaker and the hearer: God angry? What does this man mean by that? Metaphors can run away with us; that's another pitfall: people can draw consequences from them which are quite alien to the original user or group of users. For example: the Son of man will give his life a ransom for many (Mark 10.45). 'To whom,' asked a curious reader of the Bible at an early stage, 'is the ransom then paid?' But the speaker didn't have that in mind at all: he just wanted to say that he saw the death of the Son of man as a kind of ransoming of slaves.

Most metaphors, certainly the metaphors which talk of reconciliation, claim victims if people cannot leave them as descriptions, if *'seems like'* is replaced by *'is'*. The poor monk whom I have just mentioned was the victim of a metaphor, just as many believing Christians are today when they imagine God as a human being writ large.

But the church leaders who wanted to put the monk right were no less victims. What these eminent theologians, these profound thinkers, wanted to do was to get through to that 'is', to state what or who God is, to get beyond the metaphor (though they didn't know that term). But that's impossible: all talk about Above comes from below. Therefore all talk about Above in terms of below is always metaphorical. Some kinds of talk are better than others. Even abstract philosophical language – God as light inaccessible, as eternal being, as Being itself, as the One, and so on – is metaphorical by nature and makes sense. But it certainly doesn't help the imagination (the poor monk had lost everything when he had to think in abstract terms). God in human form does.

It is clear what meaning can be got out of that (not in animal form but in human form): the personal is the essence of God in human form. And that is precisely the canvas on which reconciliation is painted, essential for its understanding. According to Christians, the Creator is most like a 'someone'. Human beings do not transgress against a

Something, a Unity of Being, an Eternal Light, but they do transgress against a personal Creator God who has made known to human beings how he wants them to behave in his house, who imposes his rules, who does right, who tramples down the oppressor and frees the oppressed, but in no way regards the guilty as innocent. People know that, and therefore they adopt rituals of reconciliation or atonement which must turn away God's anger.

Is that inappropriate language to use of God? Must that picture be used, this time not on the basis of the idea that God has no feelings at all (which is what the classical church teachers thought), but because God is love and needn't be made to think otherwise, since his thoughts about human beings are utterly good? Doesn't he breathe sheer loving-kindness? Whatever else can be said, that seems to me to be really getting to the point. In the view of Jewish, Christian and Muslim faith God is regarded as a God who takes his creatures seriously. That is the framework in which the ritual of reconciliation belongs: guilt and repentance. A sense of this keeps us on our toes, and a loss of it de-humanizes us. We take ourselves seriously when we want to know about reconciliation.

6. Must God be reconciled?

Must God be reconciled? Metaphor or no metaphor, isn't that a primitive notion? Even more primitively, must that then happen by offering him a sacrifice, a bloody sacrifice, a Jesus who must bleed? I'm putting these things one after another so as to omit nothing of the offence that people sometimes feel at this way of presenting things. What changes here if we characterize reconciliation as a ritual from below?

First the question whether God must be reconciled. A reader of the Bible cannot escape it. We can tone down what we want, reinterpret or draw minimal conclusions, but it is as plain as a pikestaff that God, like all gods in antiquity, has to be mollified. By what ritual, and how these rituals work, has then to be explained.

Some Christians react so violently here because they forget the origin of the ritual or do not want the 'atonement' to be a ritual from below. We human beings have devised these rituals ourselves. Not simply because there have to be rituals. The ritual of atonement is the sign of an awakened conscience, as I have already suggested. People know about God's order and their own transgression of it and want to make that good. The ritual is an attempt from below to make things good Above. God has to be reconciled = we are debtors, and we know that. That is the essence of the doctrine of the atonement.

Of course 'being reconciled' can immediately go wrong, degenerate into magic, into magical rituals. Nor is that just chance; it is also demonstrated by reality: influencing God by a tasty smoking sacrifice. The story of Noah is a nice example of this; it runs on a knife edge: is it magic, or does it just recall magic in its terminology? But that isn't a serious question; it's still about what people are trying to do here.

The only serious question for faith is whether God is made to think otherwise by some means, whether the means is a cause of the change in God's disposition towards the sinner. Who knows! Even there we needn't find too many difficulties: the biblical authors may have thought that on many occasions. But to begin with the ritual of the scapegoat – there is certainly no causal thinking there. The scapegoat isn't even sacrificed, so here there can be no question of a causal way of thinking – the (bloody) sacrifice as the cause of a change in God's attitude.

But isn't it present in sacrificial practices generally? My argument is the same as before. Who is to say what the pious Israelite thought, what the biblical author meant? But how does that ritual of the scapegoat get into Israel's religious laws? Because according to Moses God accepted it, like the offering of sacrifices. Regardless of where these practices may have come from, and what religions preceded Israel in them, according to the ancient writers the God of Israel made them his own, and that says at least one thing: the ritual that is to make God favourable is not the cause of God's favourable disposition. God accepts the ritual game: he so to speak joins in playing it; that is its purpose. Thus the author of Leviticus 16 makes it clear to his readers that God thinks favourably about his people before they try to make him favourable – through rites. What Paul says about reconciliation fits in perfectly there, as we shall see.

7. 'Atonement' as a Christian ritual

I can now sum up in a couple of points what 'atonement' or 'reconciliation' means in a Christian sense.

1. The notion that God has to be reconciled is an expression of an awakened conscience. He must be reconciled = we are his debtors. To say 'God must be reconciled' is to take responsibility for what we do and do not do. Here Jews, Christians and Muslims focus on a personal God before whom human beings are responsible, with all the consequences that that can have. In the development of the doctrine of the

Christian church, for example: God as the wicked king who will not let the sinner go before he has been punished, or as the lord of unfaithful vassals who is content only when satisfaction has been offered for the harm done to him. Metaphors can show sides that lead to strange (and alienating) ideas. Nevertheless, both punishment and satisfaction (the two ways in which according to the classical Christian doctrine God administers the world order) are images for indicating that the world order has been damaged and that if we don't do anything about it, all will inevitably end in catastrophe.

2. We (= we human beings) must do something about it if catastrophe is not to ensue – that is the ritual. It expresses the sense that 'forget it' is not enough, for that doesn't settle the transgressions of the world, and that's where the trouble began: they must be removed from God's sight. Hence the scapegoat, hence the lamb of God that takes away the sin of the world, and such notions. The details of the ritual, the kind of ritual, I mean, don't make much difference. What everything turns on is that human beings are aware of their transgressions and want to be freed from the burden of them. Reconciliation is a ritual aimed at liberation.

3. 'We must do something about it.' The apostle Paul depicts Jesus in the (Jewish) ritual of atonement as the scapegoat which carries away the sins of the world (and not just those of the Jewish people). The special feature here is that in his view God himself is the one who 'does something', who therefore not only joins in the ritual but also as it were takes over our ritual role: he delivers up Jesus as a 'means of sin' (Paul's own words, Romans 3.25). So Paul can say that in the course that Jesus took, God was at work reconciling the world with himself. Here not only any element of changing minds (God first wants to see blood) but also any kind of reparation (we ourselves put it right) is completely ruled out of the procedure. Paul reproduces that perfectly in his 'God was in Christ reconciling the world to himself'.

4. In this way, it should be clear that Paul gives a tremendous twist to the suffering and death of Jesus. What was a murder (as Schillebeeckx rightly remarks, one cannot call it anything else) is turned to good and takes on a kind of world significance: the death on the cross is a ritual that takes away the transgressions of the world, of non-Jews. The Christian tradition of faith hangs on this interpretation of Jesus' death. It does not rule out the possibility that any Christian can happily think about Jesus in a different way from the apostle Paul, or may have objections to 'atonement'. One doesn't need to show (or attempt to show) that it isn't in the Bible, or is different in the Bible, and so on; that is to

lapse into the old Reformed sin of 'it must be in the Bible, otherwise it's no use, and if it isn't there it isn't necessary.' That seems to me to be slavery to the letter. And also self-selected.

5. So reconciliation is not the abolition of our responsibility, a kind of dehumanization that we must undergo. There is nothing of the 'worthless sinner' who is deactivated. Those are caricatures with no basis whatsoever. People who adopt the notion of reconciliation are ready to take themselves seriously as responsible men and women = take responsibility for their actions before the highest authority conceivable, the Creator.

6. What about reconciliation with one another, reconciliation as a social concept? Reconciliation as change, certainly, that concept is included. Those who are aware of the God who was at work reconciling the world to himself are also ready to be active themselves. This means forgiving one another as we are forgiven by a higher hand. Forgiving may be an attitude which also occurs outside Christianity; for Christians it is inspired by God who forgives and is therefore a must. The same Paul (on whom I am so keen) urges Christians to be followers of God.

8. *The atoning blood of Jesus*

There are still a few problems which surround what Protestants call 'atonement' or 'reconciliation' (Roman Catholic Christianity typically uses the term 'redemption'). To begin with, 'the precious blood of our Lord Jesus Christ which has been shed for a complete atonement of all our sins'.

This line is a quotation from the liturgy for the celebration of the Lord's Supper which as a child I heard said hundreds of times in church (although as a child one couldn't take part in the Lord's Supper; one had to sit there in silence through the whole service). Here the words of institution from Matthew were cited, and then bread and wine were distributed. The explanation that we were given as children was that in the Old Covenant (God and Israel), bloody sacrifice had to blot out the sins of the people, and that in the New Covenant (God and the church) the blood of bulls and goats was replaced by 'the precious blood of our Lord Jesus Christ'. 'Rather than leave them [our sins] unpunished, he has punished them in his dear Son Jesus Christ.' Because of his righteousness, God cannot leave sin unpunished. The variant is that God's honour is attacked. He cannot forgive before satisfaction is done for the injury, and in the professional language of the theologians that is atonement through satisfaction. What connects the two is Jesus' blood.

1. It's easy to make a caricature of this: God as the only one who has the ghastly privilege of not being able to forgive without a *quid pro quo* (as Harnack put it). That's where we get when we forget that a ritual is an enterprise from below: people wake up, become aware that they have to do something if they are not to be overwhelmed by God's anger, and turn to God with repentance, with a confession of guilt, a prayer for forgiveness, and a promise to improve their lives. The ritual is 'from below'. That God, as Jews and Christians claim, takes over this rite, makes our role his own ('something must be done'), is not a truth fallen from heaven but a belief, an expectation, a hope, a form of wishful thinking if you like. No one *needs* to believe that, but once one gets involved in the ritual, this is a great insight of the apostle Paul.

2. There is nothing against 'the blood of Jesus' in the sense that Jesus shed blood. A drop of blood that one person has shed for another – I read this in Unamuno – makes that person great, a special person. So why stop at the blood of Jesus? But, first, we aren't talking about blood as a fluid, a substance, with a secret magical power which could emanate from it, but about Jesus who shed his blood. 'The blood of Jesus' is always *shed* blood, and in the ancient Semitic world blood is the vehicle of life (that is why, to the present day, Jews do not eat black pudding).

In an animal sacrifice the life of the animal (the blood) is meant as a substitute for the life (the blood) of a human being. Sacrifices are vicarious rituals. The idea occurs up to and including the ritual in which Paul interprets Jesus' blood as a 'means of atonement' (Romans 3.25): the terminology of blood is the terminology of the sacrificial ritual. To put it more precisely, the sacrificial ritual is a vicarious one. *Made* sin for us, as the apostle says somewhere (II Corinthians 5.21). It can hardly be 'representative'. So does God want to see blood? No, no apostle or evangelist talks like that, and that is no coincidence. According to the Jewish writers God takes over that ritual from below (making him favourable) and puts it in the framework of dealing with him. It doesn't make him benevolent; he *is* benevolent, and therefore there is this ritual. That is also true of Jesus, from A to Z, when Paul (and not only Paul) puts him in the framework of the sacrificial ritual.

3. The vicarious character isn't attached to 'blood'. That's fortunate, because the imagery of the blood is based on sacrificial practices (parts of animals) which are objectionable to us. The symbolism of the scapegoat expresses the same thing, but without blood: the scapegoat isn't

slaughtered. So I'm bringing together all the rituals, the scapegoat which takes away sins, the lamb of God – whether or not it is thought to be slaughtered – that takes away the sins of the world, the way in which Jesus is made sin. The packaging isn't the most important thing: the important thing is that guilt must be covered. The connecting link between the different rituals is that human beings are sinners, and they know it. They also know that they can only have a relationship to God if their sins are covered, are taken away before the eyes of the Most High. That is what we are alluding to in the (variable) rituals of representation, and that is what we call reconciliation.

4. Moreover, forgiveness and reconciliation aren't synonyms which can be played off against each other. Nor can we ask Jews why they observe the Day of Atonement in such a different way. Forgiving doesn't 'just' take place as if it were God's job (as Voltaire remarked); it has firm roots. Those who have difficulty with ritual have little self-awareness, are still too innocent, have little idea of their own misbehaviour. In that respect, too, the theme of reconciliation is a topic from below: we are the subjects, and take the guilt upon ourselves. Grumbling about the circuitous way round is a sign of a misunderstanding, not only about the origin of Christian doctrine, but also about ourselves.

9. *Justification: the Christianized form of the game*

What the apostle Paul calls the justification of the sinner (we might say that this was his speciality) can be understood properly only if we see it as a kind of extension of the ritual of atonement, the game by which human beings can count themselves pure. Playing it means believing that God no longer sees our transgression.

Just read Paul: 'God was in Christ reconciling the world with himself, by *not counting* their transgressions.' Believing means playing that we are righteous before God. We maintain that, and we act as though we are no longer sinners.

Moreover, 'justified by *faith*' is a typical expression of Paul's. That doesn't mean that Christians are righteous people, far less of course that 'believing' here means something like accepting a truth and that's that. That's complete nonsense. But the first alternative isn't on either: the sinner is still a sinner but counts himself righteous.

A risky game? Just remember, as with the Jewish ritual of atonement: it must involve faith, otherwise it's the wrong game. That's the danger attached to rituals: they can degenerate into a ritual dance. To count oneself righteous amounts to believing that God doesn't count one's transgressions. That's incomprehensible language, and superficial into the bargain, unless one thinks of the ritual of atonement (like Paul) and portrays Jesus in that ritual as the scapegoat (as Paul does). I learned from my teacher that 'by faith' meant 'by Jesus Christ'. That brings us back to (or means that we are still concerned with) Jesus as the 'means of atonement', as the scapegoat which, according to the ritual, takes away the transgressions of the world.

'Through Jesus' means the same thing as 'freely', and that again means the same thing as 'not through the works of the law'. Here the apostle Paul clearly indicates the issue. That means that we needn't be Jews to be able to be justified before God. Thus even the *halakhah*, as the symbol of being a Jew, is no longer necessary: the way to Israel's God for non-Jews goes through Jesus as the scapegoat. The doctrine of justification by faith which was forged with such difficulty can therefore simply be read as: you may share in the ritual of atonement even if you aren't a Jew. For God was in Christ reconciling *the world* (and not just the Jewish people) with himself.

10. *He did not spare his own Son. Vestdijk and the cross*

The poet Simon Vestdijk wrote a venomous poem (Ballad of the Fourth Cross) in which he tells God off. The poem is too long to quote in full, so I shall content myself with a few lines. According to Vestdijk, God may have sent his Son, his 'dearly beloved' and 'image', to heal our worst wounds,

> But you never hung on the cross

> It was only your Son; and it may then be
> that you are one with him in other ways
> than seems acceptable to common sense,
> and to the heresy of the Arians.
> You yourself did not suffer the intolerable pain,
> you were not captured in Gethsemane
> and taken away and sent to your death
> hanging between two robbers on the cross.

> But you never hung on the cross

The poem is fierce, emotional. The title makes it sufficiently clear what

Vestdijk is aiming at: a cross is missing, the cross on which God himself should have hung. But God is cowardly, he has evaded the misery and palmed it off on someone else, his son. No father does that, he doesn't let his son suffer, but sacrifices himself for him, says Vestdijk in a subsequent poem. Here are a couple of comments on Vestdijk's view; they may remove one more, last, misunderstanding.

1. To begin with the easiest thing (and something with which I am *not* concerned in this section): what Vestdijk does is to play Father and Son off against each other. But the church's doctrine of the Trinity intended to put a stop at precisely this point. According to the fathers who thought this – Vestdijk knows them, but does he know enough about them? – one must indeed speak of a being existing in three persons, but the unity of the three is again emphasized so bluntly that any theologian could say without thinking: *opera dei ad extra sunt individisa* (God acts outside himself as one). These may be subtleties which we cannot make much of, but Vestdijk could have benefited from the fact that in terms of the doctrine of the Tri-unity of God we can say that God, the Second Person of the Holy Trinity, hung on the cross. That is what makes the doctrine of the Trinity so attractive for many Christians: Vestdijk is refuted; in the Son the Father himself tastes the pains of the cross. The disadvantage is that this makes the suffering, the cross and the death of Jesus one great put-up job, a 'divine comedy', as it then becomes. The suffering is no longer real suffering, as the outcome is established beforehand. Jesus becomes the stylized Christ figure of popular piety, who like Vestdijk makes light of the subtleties of God's Tri-unity.

2. So did God himself never hang on the cross? Vestdijk is right in a different way from what he intended. According to the apostle Paul (whom I am still following), the reverse is even the case:

who did not spare his own son
but delivered him up for us all.

God did not himself hang on the cross; God *made* Jesus hang on the cross. He delivered him up (Romans 8.32). For many Christians that is an indigestible piece of tradition: God delivers no one up to suffering and death. They think it a pity that this stands in the Bible. Is God then a monster? Surely we don't talk like that about God? Other Christians see the 'delivered up' as the height of divine compassion and thank God for it on their knees. Clearly we've reached a point at which Christians today no longer understand one another. Perhaps it's worth investigating what these words say.

3. In any case they say that God didn't himself hang on the cross, under any name or from any perspective. We can read that in only if we assume that Paul already knew the doctrine of the Triune God or prepared the way for it with his terminology. But no one who knows the Jew Paul will want to claim that, and indeed no exegete does. Romans 8.32 – in good Jewish fashion – is about the treasures which from eternity lie with God and in time descend to earth in time. The Torah was one such treasure, once with God, which now has been given as a gift to Israel. So was Jesus, according to the apostle Paul: once with God as the beloved Son, but when the 'fullness of time' had come, born as a woman, as he says specifically in Galatians 4. He did not spare this son, his beloved, but delivered him up for us all.

11. *It was not the Jews . . .*

Vestdijk, Paul's critics and many conservative Christians agree on one point: they stumble over the expression that God delivers up his own son.

1. That happens because they cannot get away from a realist approach and – again – treat the metaphor as a description. That is already quite clear with Vestdijk: the words Father and Son are taken literally rather than metaphorically. I recall a cross father who telephoned me – this was in the 1970s – and told me that I shouldn't be so opposed to war. If God himself murdered his own son (I quote him literally) we mustn't be so afraid to send our sons to death for a good cause. That's just as literal a view as Vestdijk's, and in fact can be developed in all kinds of directions. But God doesn't really have a son, and isn't really a father, as I am a father of a son. All this is 'by way of speaking': in Christian doctrine something is said about God in terms of our relationships. What?

2. Jesus' death is expressed in terms of Jewish symbolism, the symbolism in which the sin of the sinner has to be covered, taken away, by a ritual. According to Paul, God is playing that game; he even accepts it himself to the degree that he himself provides the 'means of atonement'. With the 'delivered up for us all', moreover, the apostle isn't thinking in realistic terms, of the intolerable suffering and death of the son which is imposed on him so cruelly by God. Nor do we read anything of compassion for Jesus, how bad it was and so on; that appears only later in the church. 'Did not spare his son' is metaphorical language; it doesn't describe what happened, but says that what happened is like a ritual of atonement which Paul had got from his religion.

3. But now this is a ritual in which non-Jews can also take part. That's the meaning which Paul gives to Jesus' death. The Christian church followed him here. On Good Friday, the Day of Atonement for the Gentiles, we think of Jesus entirely in accordance with the line by the old Dutch poet Jacob Revius:

It was not the Jews, Lord Jesus, who crucified you.

4. So do we again have a put-up job? Certainly, but not like the Christ figure as stylized by the church, the Second Person of the Holy Trinity, to whom nothing can really happen. According to Paul, God has changed the murder of Jesus of Nazareth to good. Jesus has become the light for the nations (= the Gentiles). What I am saying is that according to Paul God has been intending that for as long as he has been God. How does Paul know that? Good question. Countless of his fellow-believers thought that he was going much too far here. However, Paul is a trump card for the Christians; they sense that their legitimacy in the face of the Jewish community depends on his bold interpretation. If they had no scapegoat, they would be outsiders.

5. Seeing atonement, reconciliation as a ritual, on the same wavelength as the Jewish ritual, has one advantage that I haven't yet mentioned. It certainly presupposes God as creator, but it doesn't need the historical trio of creation/fall/redemption to make it meaningful. We can, in a manner of speaking, even use it under the conditions of a theory of evolution as a very good way of saying what we mean as Christians.

12

The 'religion of Christ' and the
Christian religion

1. Must Christians become Jews again?

Christians aren't Jews, nor can they become Jews; far less must they become Jews. In any case, whatever else history may be, it's a process that no one can reverse, not even God: what has happened has happened. Jews and Christians have gone their own way, and there is no way back.

The Jews have good reason to be cautious of us. They've experienced nothing but misery from Christianity, misery which began with the christology of the early church. Had Jesus not been imagined as God on earth, then the Roman Catechism could not have depicted the Jews century after century as God's murderers. I will not go so far as to make a direct connection between Hitler's anti-Semitism and the teaching of the Christian church, but it was certainly a breeding ground for hatred of the Jews; I would say a reinforcing factor (there was already anti-Semitism before there was a Christian church). So it is time that Christians left Jews in peace, stopped their feelings of reparations; nothing can be made good. The traumas cannot be repaired, the humiliations cannot be swept away, the shame cannot be obliterated. During the 1997 epidemic of swine fever in the Netherlands the papers regularly mentioned the 'extermination' of hundreds of thousands of pigs, the word used of murdering Jews in 'extermination' camps during the Second World War, simply because they were Jews. The word 'holocaust' is used for that, but that's a term which only Jews may use. In the mouth of Christians it's an evasive use of language: it gives a mythical tinge to the annihilation of Jews, makes it an incomprehensible fate that Jews have to overcome, instead of a murder, a mass murder of innocent men, women and children while large groups of Christians passively looked on.

So I am wary of Christians getting too cosy with Judaism. It betrays a bad conscience, certainly, and therefore isn't meant badly, but a question mark needs to be put against it. Once again it makes things difficult for Jews, and can even, though perhaps unintentionally, be an expression of a sense of superiority. Christians are always using the term 'Jewish-Christian'. I regard that with some mistrust, like the endless repetition that without Israel there would be no church. Without *Israel*? That can only mean that the Israel of old, the Israel of the Old Testament, is the nursery of the Christian church. Even if people want to make more of this, for example regard it as an accolade, I still see it as an attempt at a take-over, a continuation of the dominant church. Don't the Jews need us, then?, a lady asked me in a TV programme. To her bewilderment I said, 'No, not at all.' And I would say the same thing today. History has brought only misery, and moreover the misery of the real controversy, the bitter pill that Jews had to swallow when non-Jews could rejoice *en masse* in their access to the God of the Jews, at least according to the apostle Paul, whom I followed. That's another reason, the real reason, why Jews have nothing to look for from Christians.

So to follow Jewish symbolism doesn't mean that we must all become Jews again. I am not at all arguing in that direction, and don't always find such pleas always kosher. What I envisage is the Jewish model: life before God's face as the responsible life of men and women who know of God's mercy and justice, who know of guilt, repentance and reconciliation. In terms of Jesus as what Paul calls a 'means of atonement', non-Jews are imitating the Jewish ritual. Isn't that a take-over, then? No it is a way of adopting Israel's God *without* taking him over. That excludes incorporation; here Jews remain Jewish. Just as Christians needn't become Jews, so there is no reason or need for Jews to become Christians.

2. *Old and New Testament*

The adoption of Israel's God by the Christian church must be openly recognized. I shall demonstrate just what a risky undertaking that has been by means of the annexation (the term is unavoidable here) by the Christian church of the Old Testament, the transformation of the Jewish Bible into Christian scripture. The term 'Old Testament' gives itself away. It only came into being when there was a list of Christian writings, and it demonstrates the dilemma with which the Christian church was wrestling: on the one hand it couldn't do without the Christian writings, but on the other hand it didn't want to give them the same significance as it gave to its own collection. With a show of justification – it may be said in passing – the terminology takes up Paul (II

Corinthians 3); however, Paul doesn't mean by it two sets of writings but two different views of Moses (= Old Testament). We can limit our reading of it to God's covenant with Israel, the Law and the Prophets as the true attachment to one people. But if we do, we are reading Moses with a covering over our eyes: as we would say, blindfold. That blind-fold only disappears, says Paul, when we accept that Jesus represents a new covenant, a covenant in which Israel's God also becomes the God for non-Jews.

We have to recognize the annexation of the Old Testament. It does-n't help to quote the Jewish Scriptures again under their own name, the Tenakh; on the contrary, we can't turn the clock back, and once again this disguises things. To say Tenakh seems to me, despite all the good intentions, to be (again or still) a continuation of the annexation, and in any case it is unpleasant for Jews: it's their book, their terminology, and what are these Christians doing when they make use of them? No, we Christians aren't Jews; we shall not, will not and cannot become Jews. But we can't do without the Jewish Bible; we picked it up when we left home and went to live our own life. It seems to me better to recognize that, and to continue to say 'Old Testament', than to go over to Tenakh.

The real point is not the name but the question whether we allow it its status as a Jewish writing and do not Christianize it in the sense of bringing it into the church, for example through Christian doctrine, in terms of Trinity and christology, and already want to find everything in it or read back everything into it. That is how most Christians are brought up: the Old Testament is a Christian writing; it is legitimated because it contains a hidden testimony to Christ (as Wilhelm Vischer argued). So we can plunder it for 'what presents Christ', as Luther did. Calvin indeed did no less, but the church fathers were already there before him. Or we might think of many forms of (German) 'biblical theology' which try to make the Bible (Old and New Testaments to-gether) one whole, which for Christian theologians can only mean beginning with Jesus Christ as the 'centre of Holy Scripture'. It therefore always ends with the incorporation of the Old Testament into the New, and thus with a form of disqualification of the Old Testament.

I know only two theologians in the Netherlands who are an exception to this rule. Their thought-worlds differ from each other, and so it might seem surprising that they can be mentioned in the same breath, but they can. A. A. van Ruler (died 1970) – I shall limit myself to key phrases – thought that the New Testament could best be called an 'appendix' to the Old Testament: an indispensable appendix, but still an appendix. And K. H. Miskotte (died 1976) coined the term 'the surplus of the Old

Testament'. There is more in it than 'what presents Christ'. Which should be noted.

3. Is the Old Testament outdated knowledge of God?

Christians read the Old Testament, the Jewish holy scriptures, because they keep the same picture of God as that in the Jewish religion. The first followers of Jesus did not depart from this basis because they thought that they had achieved another, viz. better, notion of God than the Jewish one. Old and New doesn't amount to 'sub-standard' versus 'improved'. As far as Christians are concerned, the Old is outdated only in so far as they claim that as non-Jews they too may also share in it.

So the Old Testament does *not need* first to be Christianized in order to be 'of use' to the Christian church. That always goes wrong: history is very instructive on this point. Marcion (first half of the second century) is the great example of a church leader who wanted to keep purely and solely to the New Testament writings, and then only a few of them (especially Paul). In his view one mustn't burden God with creation, as that compromises God. In that case one also has to attribute all the evil in the world to him and that can never be the intention. So we must do away with God as creator. That is a different God from the God of the Christian church. And because the Creator forms the centre of the Old Testament, Marcion writes off the whole of it as an anti-Christian work. The creator is the God of the Jews, a lesser God, the God of vengeance and anger. The real God is the redeemer who appeared in Jesus Christ. It seems to me that no one can ignore the anti-Jewish implications of this kind of theology.

The Christian church rightly condemned Marcion. But did it banish him? Wherever the God of the Old Testament is presented as a God of vengeance and the God of the New Testament as a God of love, the ghost of Marcion still walks (or walks again), fed by ignorance, gossip and above all a sense that Christianity is superior to Judaism, a feeling that does not have a leg to stand on. 'The Lord is merciful and gracious, slow to anger and abounding in steadfast love' – such lines (Psalm 103.8) can bring tears to our eyes, and they are all over the Old Testament. Christians haven't discovered that; they have encountered it in Jewish faith and – here once again their grasp of it is impudent – applied it to non-Jews.

Of course Christianity is free to read the Old Testament as a pointer to the church's Christ: the procedure is quite usual. But the book itself (the Old Testament) doesn't need such an upgrading to be able to have a place in the Christian church. Everything that the New Testament offers we already find in the Old. The image of God that it presents isn't inferior to the Christian image of God. We find all the many faces of God already in the Old Testament, without needing to consider speculations about God's Triunity. The same God, the same atonement, the same mercy, the same promise of life, all is the same. Except for 'God's concern', which in the New Testament also applies to non-Jews.

So there is no need to read Jesus into the Old Testament; that isn't necessary anywhere. Not even 'because Jesus is indeed in it', given the fact that the whole of the Old Testament already has a messianic character. Here Christian exegetes keep falling into the trap. For if the idea of the Messiah was already there, why is a New Testament still needed? What then is the novelty of Jesus' historical appearance? Unless Jesus represents the true messianic explosion and the New Testament spells out more clearly what the Old Testament is already saying. But then Jesus is the revealer of what wasn't yet clear in the Old Testament, and the Old Testament is a light only because it is illuminated by the New. We are back to the subordination of the Old Testament to the New.

4. Breeding ground and foundation

That the roots of the Christian church lie in Judaism says something about our origins. No less, but also no more. It sometimes seems as if modern Christians begin from the fact that when we go back to the sources of Christian faith we end up at the Old Testament as the indubitable foundation of Christianity. That seems to me to be a mistake.

(*a*) The Jewish tradition of faith, the Old Testament, is certainly the breeding ground of Christian faith, but not an anchor for its certainty: a breeding ground isn't a foundation. The Jewish picture of God is like the Christian picture in status, and like all other recognizable patterns of God it comes from below; it is human work. The Old Testament isn't the real revelation of God in the world, Hebrew isn't the language which God spoke, or, if that is too strong, isn't the language of revelation which must not be tampered with (that is not permissible with any language). So we haven't given a successful account of our faith simply if we make it clear how Jewish we really are. The rediscovery of the Old Testament, giving it the status that it deserves, is the rediscovery of a quest, of what Israel thought about God. Here we don't even begin to get it right. That is something that we still have to achieve, Jews and Christians alike. 'Our relationship to God is described in the Old

Testament,' I read somewhere. Certainly, but if it is, it is in the way in which the narrators thought things were. To regard their version of God, human beings and the world as normative because it is in the Bible has no basis: it is left hanging, as all facts of faith (what a term!) are left hanging in the air.

(*b*) The Jewish religious context has quite a different first claim: we can no longer make what we like of Jesus as a member of the Jewish faith, as one who read aloud from the Jewish Bible (read Luke 4). The 'religion of Christ' is fixed and can be discovered. Of course, even then anything can and may be made of it, but not everything is in line with what Jesus was, thought and wanted. In this sense the Jewish context is a dam against 'wild christologies', and all christologies which cannot incorporate the Jewish context are wild christologies. Here I'm putting a question mark against not only the Gnostic but also the church's Christ. They Hellenize (to use an expression of Harnack's) Jesus far too much (although according to Harnack one cannot imagine Jesus as a Jew either).

(*c*) Only against this background does the real question arise. If the Jewish picture and Christian pictures of God aren't essentially different, what wasn't there before Jesus, what stone was moved, what frontier crossed? What makes the New Testament necessary for Christianity – not of course for Jews?

Not a kind of super-revelation: any hint in that direction amounts to a demotion of Judaism. The Christian church has not only taken that path too often and too much, but also quite wrongly. And not only in the past. To my bewilderment I read in a knowledgeable German theologian that God has redefined himself in Jesus Christ. Leaving aside the arrogance of that (can any human being claim to know how God defines himself?), it is offensive that such a statement exalts Christianity at the expense of Judaism. Will they never learn?, one thinks.

So nothing about superiority: Jesus was nothing new by comparison with the Jewish context. He didn't add anything to the content of faith. What happened with him, the new development, was the extension of the covenant (to keep within Paul's view) to non-Jews. That is what according to the New Testament gives Jesus' historical appearance its unique significance and makes the Gospels great news: there is something to tell which wasn't there before Jesus.

5. He preached Jesus to them

A standard expression from the book of Acts points the way for us: he preached Jesus to them. This is reported of Paul or one of the other apostles, and thus is a very brief summary of what Jews who had become Christians (for this is how the Christian church began) thought that they had to report to Jews and Gentiles. Report, yes. From the start the word 'preach' reminds us somewhat of the town crier: raising his voice, and making known an important report, we might say 'great news'. What does this great news consist of?

Briefly, to preach Jesus is to preach God, God as he is experienced by Judaism, but now made known as God for all. Not another God, a new God so to speak, but the same God as ever, now accessible to people who didn't belong to the Jewish people.

I deliberately said 'briefly'. There are a whole lot of perspectives that one can give this turn, but it is the scarlet thread that holds together the series of books that we call the New Testament. Whether we take Paul's doctrine of justification by faith, or Hebrews with its explanation of how the Jewish high priest is no longer necessary, it's all an exposition of God in which he, the God of the Jews, is from now on presented as also the God of the Gentiles. And the writers of the New Testament, each in his own way, show how that can be.

There is much reformulation, reorientation, delight in discovery, in looking. A great deal is said about God, is summed up in the name of Jesus. That doesn't make him a second God, but rather the face of God for non-Jews, for Greeks, Romans and barbarians. How could Paul, as a Jew, preach a second God? He preached the God of Israel, the God of the fathers, but now with the 'new means of atonement' (Jesus) which differed from the old only in scope and extension and not in the need to have a relationship with God and a presupposition of dealing with God. 'Jesus who saves us from the wrath to come' (I Thessalonians 1.10), writes Paul in one of his first letters. What is that, if not bringing the ritual of atonement to bear in his preaching?

Once that process of preaching Jesus as God for the Gentiles began, it started to lead a life of its own. That's natural; that's how things are. In the later books of the New Testament we already meet that distinctive life in all its depth: Colossians, Ephesians, the letter to the Hebrews – by then we are long past Paul. The letter to the Hebrews even sees Jewish faith as superseded by Christian faith: because of its greater scope, but still superseded. We could see these writings as a first step towards an independent worship of Christ, in the context of praise of the depth of God's eternal wisdom: Jesus as the revelation of God's – at least for Jewish concepts – unthought-of and unsuspected way of salvation with human beings and the world. Having begun as God of the Jews, he ends up as God of the whole creation, who sums up 'in Christ' everything, Jew and Gentile, man and woman, barbarian and Greek.

We could understand 'in Christ' as we understand 'in Europe', as a sort of territory in which for God there is no longer a difference between Jews and Gentiles. In reality, of course that is far from always being the case, so 'in Christ' easily becomes a daydream, a project, a vision of a new world, from the New Testament (read first of all the letters to the Ephesians and the Colossians) to the present day. I read that as one reads a sermon: it doesn't say how it was or how it will be, but what we can make of it – as consolation, a lesson and an admonition.

6. 'Believe in the Lord Jesus and you will be saved'

We read in Acts 16 what happened in the city of Philippi. As a result of an earthquake the prison doors had burst open and the prisoners could have immediately got away, among them the apostle Paul and his helper Silas, not villains but nevertheless in prison. For the man in charge of the prison the situation is a disaster: the future seems so dark for him (look at the one who lets villains escape!) that he wants to commit suicide. But the apostle Paul intervenes and cries out to him, 'Do not do any harm to yourself, we are all still here.' The man falls on his knees and asks the apostle what he must do to be saved. It's an ambiguous word, that 'be saved'; it can mean 'What must I do to get out of this pickle?', but we can also read it as a question about eternal salvation. I prefer the latter, given the apostle's answers. That is given in the words at the head of this section: 'Believe in the Lord Jesus and you will be saved, you and your household' (Acts 16.31). I shall go rather more deeply into this, as a contrast to what I have said about 'He preached Jesus to them'. If all is well, the two statements have to correspond.

'Believe in the Lord Jesus.' Believing Christians have heard these words from Sunday School on. But what they summon us to is not as simple as the terminology suggests. What Paul certainly does not mean is that the prison governor will be saved if he accepts that Jesus is the Son of God, the Lord, or whatever other title is preferred. What use would that be to the poor man? The devil can also do as much, by way of speaking, but I don't suppose that he will be saved. The newest translations avoid this misunderstanding: it isn't a matter of assenting to a doctrinal proposition about Jesus but a matter of trust. 'Put your trust in the Lord Jesus,' we now read. That's much better, but it still leaves plenty of room for misunderstanding.

To mention another possibility, we can also make it mean that people are called to believe in God and in addition also to believe in Jesus as a second God. But that would be a serious mistake. When Paul is preaching Jesus, he is preaching God (see v.32); and when people are asked to believe in Jesus, this can hardly be anything other than a call to believe in God.

What other possibilities remain? Here is a proposal that I shall develop step by step, drawing a conclusion at the end. By 'put your trust in the Lord Jesus' Paul in any case and at least means: trust what I have told you (or what I shall tell you) about Jesus. That would fit the whole story well. The second step is: what did Paul then tell? We can fill that in with the help of Paul's preaching of Jesus as the Christ in whom God was reconciling the world with himself. Jesus' death on the cross as a 'means of atonement' for non-Jews, 'Jesus who saves us (the Gentiles) from the wrath to come', or whatever Pauline terms we may want to choose. Paul's preaching about Jesus can hardly have been very different from that. My third step is that this preaching had the sole aim of opening up the way to God for non-Jews: preaching Jesus = preaching God for non-Jews. So – next step – I can read 'put your trust in the Lord Jesus' as a kind of shorthand for something like (if one wanted to write it out in full): trust what I have told about Jesus as a 'means of atonement' and call on God as your God. Last step (and conclusion): we can replace 'Jesus' with 'God who also speaks to non-Jews'. Trust that, says the apostle Paul: trust that God also speaks to the Gentiles. I think that an appropriate outcome, for doesn't the name Jesus from the start mean 'God speaks'?

Of course it can be shorter. Preach Jesus = preach God's mercy to the Gentiles and put your trust in Jesus = put your trust in the fact that God is also the Merciful One for non-Jews. So Jesus is another word for God's mercy. That too is an appropriate outcome.

Why this exhortation to trust Paul's words? That's worth a separate comment. Everyone who listened to Paul and every reader of his letters (and of my interpretation of them) must gradually have developed a burning question: Jesus as the way to God for non-Jews? How can Paul be so certain of that? Is it true?

You must believe it, you must trust Paul's message. There is no other answer. 'Believe me,' says the apostle. Why should we do that, why be so rash as to attach ourselves to such a story without any guarantees?

There is only one sensible answer, and only non-Jews can realize the importance of it, because their entry to God stands or falls by it.

7. *Great news: a faith without ethnic limitations*

Before he died on the cross, Jesus preached the Gospel of God, as Mark reports (1.14), to his own people, the Jews. After his death Jesus himself becomes 'gospel' for the non-Jews. 'Gospel' means 'good report' or, in more popular terms, 'great news'. Strikingly the good news is therefore not the same each time. One could certainly try to put the two together, for example by identifying the kingdom of God with Jesus (he was himself the kingdom, said Origen), but we never hear Jesus say that, no matter what tradition we follow. The imbalance is striking: we could say that as a prophet he *brings* great news; as a 'means of atonement' he *is* great news. But this imbalance is completely in keeping with my story. For the Jews Jesus *had* a 'good report', but he *is* not that good report; they do not have anything extra with him, as I demonstrated in the previous chapter. Why then should they call him 'great news'? Only Gentiles can say that.

Great news wears off. The exclamation seems somewhat exaggerated to us today because we have centuries and centuries of Christianity behind us in which, the more time has gone on, the more obvious it has become that God was not the God of the Jews but 'our God', and not the God of the Jews. The original shine of the message, the emotion, has got lost (inevitably, it seems to me), and cannot be recaptured. But we can certainly imagine why it must once have been 'great news', first of all in the mouth of people like Paul, who truly believed in their mission, but no less in the ears of non-Jews who desired salvation. Not to try to hype the Christian proclamation but to understand better what Christians really believe when they worship Jesus Christ, and why they attach so much importance to him. The great news isn't a new God, isn't the forgiveness of sins, isn't God's mercy: all that had long been taken into the Jewish scheme of God. It isn't the scheme of God and his salvation that changes, but its scope: from now on the Gentiles also belong to this God. And of course the whole scheme of Israel's God was 'great news' for all those who didn't know of forgiveness and mercy. The author of the letter to the Ephesians writes rapturously:

Remember that you were at that time [formerly] without Christ, excluded from the citizenship of Israel, and strangers to the covenants of promise, with no hope and without God in the world. But now in

Christ Jesus you who once were far off have been brought near in the blood of Christ (2.11–13).

So we need no longer become Jews in order to count for Christ, remark Christians to the present day. Indeed we *cannot* become Jews: ethnically speaking we do not belong to the Jewish people and never will. But the ethnic limitations have been removed: that is the great news. The church father Irenaeus (second half of the second century) asked what new element the Lord brought at his coming. In his own words: *Quid novi igitur dominus attulit veniens?* His answer was: himself, in his own person. That's nice, but it doesn't really say what happens if we dare to attach the abolition of ethnic limitations to this person. We can also become descendants of Abraham through faith in Jesus, as the apostle Paul shows us in his letter to the Galatians (3.29). For Gentiles the preaching of Christ is messianic news.

A tricky question: is Jesus then the messiah for whom the Jews were waiting? If we want to put it that way (and I say *if*), then we needn't insult the Jews with it. We do that if we 'de-Judaize' Jesus, but as I have shown, that isn't right in any way. Jesus is a Jew, a member of the Jewish faith; that's the first point. And that he is the messiah, the eschatological bringer of salvation, can be said only by Christians who are glad that through him they have access to Israel's God. Note, however, that this hangs on the thread of faith – they must still be proved right. That's the second point. Jesus opens up the world for God, or better, opens up God for the whole world. For Christianity, that is eschatological salvation. Whether the world becomes better as a result is something that we can believe, but that too has to be proved.

Given this coating – which is of a fundamental kind – and in the description which I gave of it, the belief of Christians in Jesus as the eschatological bringer of salvation remains a bitter pill for Jews to swallow, but it doesn't need also to be loaded with the notion that Christians have something which the Jews are lacking. In the end *both* Jews *and* Christians must still be proved to be right.

8. *Living before God's face. The Christian religion as practice*

Christian faith is a practice, a way of living. You wouldn't say that if you read all the learned and semi-learned arguments about God and human beings and the world which have shaped the face of Christianity for so long. But appearances are deceptive, and moreover doctrinal belief is also a practice, though one which is fought out on paper. I shall not claim here that we could just as well do without it all: on the contrary. Partly the issue is one of responsibility for ourselves and/or for outsiders: it amounts to nothing if we can't explain what we're engaged in. And partly it's a matter of confessing and praising, and yet again it consists in the ritual use of words – all necessary ingredients of a living tradition of faith. But to fix Christianity to that, or even to identify Christianity with it, makes believing a matter of holding to and defending truths, and that isn't enough. Religion is more than an appeal to the understanding.

That goes for the Christian religion, too. It needn't be identical with the 'religion of Christ'; we live in other times and other worlds than Jesus. But what the 'religion of Christ' was must in any case – as practice – be compatible with what we understand by Christian life. What that amounts to I shall sum up under the heading of 'living before the face of God'.

1. 'God is in heaven and you are on earth' (Ecclesiastes 5.1). That's how it is and that is how it must remain. We aren't demigods; we know the distance between God and human beings. Where that is minimized or forgotten, people fool themselves. 'Let your words be few,' adds the preacher in the same breath. Watch what you say; that means that you must always be accountable.

2. We believe in God as our creator. That means not only that we exist through him (human beings as pearls in his crown), but that we are also allowed to exist, have time and space to work independently. Whatever God rules and governs (and he does that) doesn't diminish our freedom. God isn't our rival but the one who inspires us. It's no use looking further for the meaning of our life. We are there and that is that. We can just be there or be there for the glory of God: that is all.

3. Our life is played out before his eyes. We can shape our lives depending on how we see his eyes (as the evil eye or as a glance). We needn't hide anything from him. He is familiar with us and knows us better than we know ourselves. He knows his creature. It is no longer possible to flee, and it isn't necessary either. For 'the Lord is merciful and gracious, and his loving kindness is great', although he by no means regards the guilty as innocent.

4. Living before God's face also means 'seeking his face'. Prayer, fellowship, calling in the night. It can even take the form of intimate conversation. The more you are a friend of God, the more intimate you may be with him, said the rabbis.

5. It is also a matter of dealing responsibly with human beings and the world. Doing good. We have no difficulty over what is good:

He has showed you, O man, what is good; and what does the Lord require of you but to do justice, and to love kindness, and to walk humbly with your God? (Micah 6.8).

That's a perfect description of Christianity as 'life before God's face'. No christology need be added (though of course it may be), nor does Jesus produce any (how could he?) when he sums up his teaching as: 'Whatever you wish that men would do to you, do so to them; for this is the law and the prophets' (Matthew 7.12).

6. Christians don't expect too much; they've learned to be realists and no longer to share a belief in progress. Responsibilities aren't recognized, creatures come damaged from the hand of the Creator, and fellow-creatures now and then make a contribution of their own. Billions of people have come namelessly into our world to leave it again just as namelessly because that is what others wanted; at times the world around us is abominably merciless and we ourselves are no less so. To live before God's face is also to walk in riddles.

7. So there is nothing high-flown about 'living before God's face'; it isn't a matter of storming heaven but more something for ordinary people who do not have or make any more history. It's loving God above all else as the first and greatest commandment and the second that is like it: loving your neighbour as yourself (read Matthew 22.34–40). Just like the Jews (Leviticus 19.18). It's true that Christians don't observe the *halakhah* (the Jewish elaboration of this commandment). They needn't do so to be reckoned the descendants of Abraham (at least according to Paul).

8. Living before God's face is being confident that we will not escape him when the end comes. It is believing that his friendship is eternal friendship, that he will receive us in the hour of our death, to keep us safe for eternity.

IV

What are we to do with . . .

While I could not say that Mark's Gospel is
false, it has much exaggeration. And I would
offer less for Matthew, and for Luke and John,
who gave me words I never uttered and
described me as gentle when I was pale with
rage. Their words were written many years
after I was gone and only repeat what old men
told them. Very old men. Such tales are to be
leaned upon no more than a bush that tears
free from its roots and blows about in the
wind.

(Jesus himself, in Norman Mailer, *The Gospel According to the Son*)

13

The doctrine of two natures revised

1. *We say it ourselves*

After all that I have said in the previous chapter, no one need be surprised that Jesus occupies a major place in Christianity. Christianity turns on Jesus (although it is about God); he wasn't just a prophet like any other, but God was at work in him removing limits.

That sounds assured and convinced, but who says it? Christians say it themselves. How do they come to do so? How do they know? They believe it. Once one has said that, the question inevitably arises: can they prove it? That question is completely misplaced. It is very important to me to explain why.

Whether or not God was in Christ acting in the world in any way has nothing to do with miracles, and therefore nothing to do with proving or not proving. Christians mustn't be led astray and get stuck in that problem (and then come to grief on it). The question is about a belief, certainly, but that belief stands in quite a different context from that in which one speaks of proving or not proving. Nothing at all needs to be proved: Jesus lived, died and was buried, and was raised by God (whatever that may be); he preached – to put it briefly – and is preached. And also? Nothing else, except that through this Jesus (who preached and is preached) Christians have come to knowledge of God. That's a historical fact: people have moved from being worshippers of Wotan or nature to believing in God the creator and preserver of human beings and the world. That simply happened, I would even dare to add. Whether or not Paul was right in his exclamation that in Christ the God of the Jews had reconciled the world with himself (and therefore not just the Jews), at all events through Jesus this world has clearly been acquainted with this God. So what else can Christians say except that God himself was at work in Jesus? People don't thinks in terms of proofs, except for those who believe that a dogma has to be defended. But we aren't defending a dogma; we're simply explaining how everything fits together, how we have come to believe in God and what role Jesus has played here. What in the terminology of doctrine is called christology is simply an indication of the significance of Jesus for Christians by Christians: a value definition, a value judgment about his person.

They (= the Christians) say so themselves. They would be crazy not to; it would make them illegal in the house in which they live; the roof would fall in on them. Nor is there any authority to oppose their belief; what they say can be checked by anyone. The significance of Jesus derives from human beings, indeed just a small number of people, namely Christians. In this sense the value attached to Jesus is subjective. But that doesn't mean that it is arbitrary. Christians give very good reasons why they think the historical person of Jesus so important that they call him Christ: through Jesus (the proclamation of Jesus) they are put on the track of God. Thus God was at work in Christ! That's the least that Christians can say. But is what the doctrine of two natures says also true?

2. *The halo*

In view of Jesus' unprecedented significance, it is no wonder that after the event one begins to ask: what was there in him (Jesus) that wasn't in others? Did he himself say anything in this direction (I'm expressing myself cautiously), anything about a sense that God was at work in him? Could it be seen in him? That's how I imagine the evangelists. They didn't take part in any of it, but historically speaking they still stood quite close and without doubt raised that kind of question when they began to collect the traditions.

What they got from their informants was clear: Jesus had the sense of being a special servant of God or, to put it more pointedly, he was aware that God was active in him, that he had a mission to fulfil. There is no reason to doubt that. Nor do modern scholars do so. Of course we cannot extend that sense of vocation to mean that he was already aware of a mission to the world on which he was engaged. On the contrary, he learned as he went along. A woman had to take him over the ethnic threshold and tell him that he was also called to help non-Jews.

In the production of an account of Jesus' life after the event, what had already been talked of now came to stand in a different light. Jesus was already being preached everywhere; most of Paul's letters had already been written, stories about Jesus were going the rounds, but there was no consecutive narrative about him. What the evangelists do is not only to fill a gap (as I said in Chapter 3) but also to provide continuity from the end backwards. They could survey everything and make it into a life of Jesus in narrative form. And what happens when a story continues to be told many times? It gets embellished, exaggerated: first by the narrators, those who gave information to the evangelists. And later again by the evangelists themselves.

Exaggerated, I said. What does that mean? Deception? Not at all. We do the same thing ourselves. Think of the medieval painters, of Rembrandt with his painting of Jesus blessing the children, of the illustrations in children's Bibles. Who is Jesus in these illustrations? Every child knows that: they only have to look at the halo round his head. That's him. Did he really have such a halo? No, not as a historical person walking around in Palestine, but when we begin to look back from 'God was at work in Christ', we say, yes, he was special, quite different from the rest. That's the halo: by it we're indicating Jesus' significance.

So historically speaking the halo is wrong: it isn't meant as a historical fact, as most believers know very well. Just as there as so many things which aren't historical but which have been written down to indicate the meaning of Jesus. That is the reason why we often no longer know what is historical and what – in our sense – isn't; or, when we are talking about the sayings of Jesus, which are Jesus-authentic and which aren't. Did Jesus really, as the hymn says, descend from highest heaven because he was moved with pity for sinners? 'He wanted to become the Saviour', says Bach's St Matthew Passion. Did he always know that 'on the third day' he would rise from the dead? That would rob his story of any seriousness. As far as I am concerned, that wasn't the case. We do better to see it as part of what I've called the halo. And the same is true with many of the miracle stories: they express warmth for Jesus, trust in his words and deeds, belief in his special vocation and role. Whether they really happened is a different matter. But as I have noted, even the unhistorical lends itself to further telling. It gives meaning; it is preaching, praise, wonderment, worship.

3. The doctrine of two natures as a halo

We don't need much imagination to understand that it is only a small step from 'God was in Christ' to 'Christ is God'. Jesus wasn't only revered, he became the object of worship, of devotion, and devotion means elevation. Jesus becomes God-on-earth. That already begins quite early and in quite an innocent way. In a writing that come down to us, which must date from around AD 150, Justin Martyr engages in dialogue with the Jew Trypho. It's an excellent dialogue, with nothing anti-Jewish about it. But Justin wants to make it clear that the Christians know better than the Jews: Jesus is 'a second God', and in his view that is a correct statement. Is that the case? In any case the doctrine of the two natures became the dogmatic fixation of this view; from 325 the official church doctrine is that Jesus is 'God of God, light of light'. But was he a human being? The Council of Chalcedon (451) put an end to that dispute: he was both God and man. That legitimates the unbridled worship of Jesus: as usual the *lex credendi* is followed by the *lex orandi*. To put it into English, dogma follows piety (as long as it lasts, dogma stands firm and then piety has to adapt to it). From then on Jesus is the church's Christ, stylized, modelled, polished in terms of the doctrine of two natures: born of a virgin, without sin, really God (he may be worshipped), but then as a kind of prince in disguise, God on earth. I regard that as a deviation of devotion, however much we must respect the fathers.

I shall not repeat the objections to it here: a 'double Jesus' is both impossible and unimaginable as a person. Nor of course is he attractive: he departs completely from human nature. What is a human being who knows no sin? In one of the previous chapters I described the construction (for that is what it is) as a time- and culture-conditioned expression of devotion which no longer moves us (if it says anything to us at all) and in addition lands us in insoluble problems (which in their turn issue in heresies).

The first question is: must we drop this doctrine? That's a kind of rigorism in which I cannot share. In any case, culturally it would amount to sheer barbarism. We would be throwing our past away, the images with which we had grown up, the language with which we learned to speak. I have a better suggestion: we can see the doctrine of the two natures as the halo I mentioned in the previous section. This halo wasn't real, and if we take it historically, it causes problems. We can see it as an indication of the meaning that is attached to Jesus. That's also how I see the doctrine of two natures: not of course really two natures, any more than the halo is real, but as a way of imagining things which indicates Jesus' meaning for Christians. Certainly it is an attribution of meaning determined by time and culture. The attempt to establish the meaning of Jesus by raising him above time is totally determined by the philosophy which was most popular at the time of the church fathers: what takes place in time can never be important, therefore the Jesus who appeared in time must really be from eternity God-on-earth.

But if we take that into account as the halo which an earlier time put on his head, the doctrine of two natures is least of all something that has to be banished. Christians can sing and preach about the two natures, use the liturgical formulae which have been forged with them; in short, they can philosophize about the meaning of Jesus in the same way as they can preach about Gospel stories which didn't really happen. What really happened and what didn't is another question. But meaning can also be given through ideas which don't go back how things were, or stories which didn't really happen.

4. *The double certainty*

So the doctrine of two natures doesn't need to be abolished, but we can't adhere to it either. The Christian church has to have a christology, its *raison d'être* depends on it, but the hymn must be transposed a tone lower. The doctrine of two natures cannot be a doctrinal fact that must be subscribed to at the peril of losing the name Christian.

But that is what has happened. When one of the three so-called ecumenical creeds of the Christian church, the Athanasian Creed, which has already been mentioned, sums up everything that Christians must believe to be saved, it includes the doctrine of the two natures of Jesus Christ (which is quite developed). Here there is the misunderstanding that one must accept doctrines in order to be saved. In addition, there is here a notion of the person of Jesus which ends up in a jigsaw puzzle in its attempts to express both the divine and the human nature without damaging either. The religious needs of the first centuries, warm and spontaneous, have been forged into dogma, into the obligation of faith, with Jesus as the victim: he goes cold under the gilding of his divinity.

Of course that isn't necessary. We shall soon see how it happens. First I shall indicate the baneful consequences of this doctrine, beginning with the problem of the double certainty which I already indicated earlier. Here I shall go into it in rather more depth.

How do people come to be certain about what they have heard from God? By encountering God himself; there is no other way to certainty. So there is a good deal of uncertainty, for when do we encounter God? However, we learn to live with that; it's part of believing. According to classical church teaching, too, Jesus was a historical person (as God-man). We gain certainty about a historical person, who he was, what he did and proclaimed, what his fate was, by historical investigation. So what I mean is that believers must take two different ways to arrive at the certainty of faith. To discover the truth about God is a matter of experience, of encounter with God, or however else one wants to put it.

But the truth about Jesus is of a historical nature, and for that we are dependent on scholarly investigation. Thus it proves that the two ways to truth lead to two certainties of different kinds: to the certainty of faith about God, and in the case of Jesus in addition to a historical certainty.

I can illustrate this by a couple of lines from a hymn:

Faith can never expect too much
the saviour's words are sure.

A splendid statement: perhaps a bit too strong for a wavering disposition, but certainly meant to boost that disposition . We are called on to trust in Jesus' promises; his words are 'sure'. 'Trust', 'expect', is the usual meaning that 'believing' has for Christians. But is it also 'sure' that he really said them? Are they 'the Saviour's words'? We also have to believe that! Now belief is rather different from what it was before: it is now holding a historical fact to be true. There must be both kinds of certainty, but they are different, and one comes about in a different way from the other. They can certainly be brought together by requiring people to accept what the church teaches, but that won't do: one can't fill a historical gap with a dogmatic statement.

5. God-on-earth as a double perspective

The real problem with the doctrine of two natures lies in the double perspective with which it saddles faith: we are interested in God, God in heaven, but also in God-on-earth, Jesus. That inevitably becomes a form of rivalry in which God-on-earth wins, as second God.

No doctrine of the Tri-unity of God helps here. The church fathers are to be credited with having seen the problem, and doggedly having made every possible attempt to solve it: how do we combine God-on-earth and God-in-heaven? Theologians can find a solution with Jesus as the incarnate Second Person of the divine Tri-unity, but ordinary believers cannot. Some theologians say that ordinary believers don't even need to believe that doctrine. Nor could they, I would add. Years of study are needed for any grasp of it; it's a theological theory for theologians who talk with theologians. That's certainly worthwhile: why can't there also be a speculative discussion about God? But for ordinary people (non-theologians) it's no more than an incomprehensible holy formula (its holiness lies in its incomprehensibility) with which Christians think that they can indicate their identity as Christians in the midst of other religions.

Back to the point in question: however subtly the doctrine of the Tri-unity of God deals with Jesus' divinity, for believers it doesn't stop the competition. God-on-earth is closer, more comprehensible, more merci-ful, more accessible than God-in-heaven, and can even be depicted and put in holy places. Jesus as a kind of representative God is how many believers see it. So they turn in the first instance to Jesus, invoke him in place of God, until Jesus is so exalted, comes to stand so far away from human beings in his holiness and sinlessness, that there must also be a replacement for him: Mary, as wife and mother even closer to people than her son, and thus in her turn a way to Jesus, who intercedes for the sinner with her divine son. I cannot see that I am distorting this develop-ment, except that – of course – official theology speaks of it in a much more subtle way (for example by drawing a distinction between wor-ship and veneration) than so-called popular piety. But this last is deci-sive: it forms the content of the belief of church people.

Moreover God-on-earth once again forms the pool in which theo-logians of every kind tend to fish for their speculative ideas. I have heard prominent men speaking about Christmas as the celebration of the fact that God came to earth; renowned theologians speaking of Jesus' crucifixion as the death of God which resulted in the death of death; preachers (not the first or best) talking about God who becomes a slave, while the text on which the sermon was based (Philippians 2) speaks of Jesus who humbled himself and took the form of a slave, afterwards to be exalted by God. Everything is possible once one begins to identify Jesus with God, or, as a Roman Catholic woman once assured me: we've always learned that God and Jesus are the same, so why do you make it so difficult?

All that can be sorted out, now that there's no compulsion to follow the doctrine of two natures but rather the reverse: the reception history of the Gospels (with Jesus as the main character) shows that beginning with the evangelists themselves, the notions about Jesus come from the 'users'. This is how they (the evangelists) saw him; this is how they (the readers of the Gospels) could understand him; this is how he has been fitted into ever new horizons of expectation until today he is finally solidified ('fossilized' is even better) in a doctrine of two natures.

6. *God was in Christ/Christ is in God*

Let's begin by saying that there cannot be a double perspective for faith. What then is the alternative? Christianity would do well to revert its worship of Jesus to worship of God. It cannot be that for us – as Islam claims – Jesus has displaced God. That has certainly happened (Justin Martyr's 'second God') and still happens, every day, in so-called popular piety, but in each case that needn't involve the worship of Jesus; to put it more strongly, I think that many believing Christians say Jesus but mean God. Their terminology gets in the way.

To mean God by Jesus is rather different from making him God. It's having God in mind when we say Jesus. Jesus isn't himself God, nor is Mary the mother of God, however much the need for devotion may have contributed to this. In the version of christology which I have prepared for in the previous chapters, Jesus is a further description of God, as 'the Lord is merciful and gracious, and abounding in steadfast love', a Jewish description of God which Christians see underlined, confirmed, perhaps even discover for the first time in Jesus. So Jesus as it were belongs 'in God', in the picture of God by which Christianity ventures to live, only in the picture of God. Jesus 'in God', Jesus as a closer definition of God – that seems to me to reproduce adequately what the apostle Paul meant in II Corinthians (5.19) by 'God was in Christ'.

So Jesus also stands or falls with God (as a scheme which Christianity has taken over from the Jews). Those who aren't interested in God will get nowhere with Jesus. Without God, Jesus is unimportant; his concern is precisely that he is the instrument, the revealer, of God. Take Jesus away and God remains; take God away and there is no longer any Jesus, or rather: a Jesus remains who points nowhere.

So what does this amount to? Jesus stands or falls with the Christian picture of God and not vice versa: God doesn't stand or fall with Jesus. Whether Jesus really was the servant of God, whether he interpreted God well, as Christianity believes – all that remains to be seen. If the Christian quest of God holds, Jesus also holds; and if not, then he gets lost with that quest. In passing I can remove a major misunderstanding: the picture of God doesn't become more certain by introducing Jesus into it. That was certainly part of the secret agenda of the church's christology: to make the certainty of the Christian religion tangible in historical events, Jesus as an anchor for God. But that is to turn things upside down, and the eighteenth century showed up the construction as pseudo-certainty, from which only revelation as revelation of 'what really happened' could rescue it. And even this rescue is sham. We are already presupposing what we want to prove: the Bible must be believed in again (first) as an infallible report.

I shall add three comments. To make Christian theology one enormous concentration on Jesus Christ again seems to me to be a form of devotion which goes beyond the limit. Here I have in mind the project of Karl Barth, who wants only to speak of one Word of God (viz. one revelation of God), namely Jesus Christ. But didn't God also reveal himself in the Israel of the Old Testament? Certainly, so for Barth the people of Israel is a hidden form of Jesus Christ, just as for him the creation in which God reveals himself is a hidden Christ. If one sums up Christ as an idea, for example the idea of the covenant (but also the idea of the Messiah can serve here), such a view of things may perhaps make sense. But the concrete person of Jesus is then volatilized into a theology which is impressive and speculative. Barth had no interest in Jesus as historical person: that fits.

A second point confirms something that I've already said: if Jesus is meaningful only 'in God', then are we not (this is the implication) totally dependent for the certainty of faith on historical questions about the life of Jesus: what did and what did not 'really happen', which are authentic sayings of Jesus and which are not? Of course that's important; we want to know. Suppose that Jesus never existed? But here the investigation is free and Christians can follow it without the anxiety that the outcome could undermine faith.

A third clarification. As a person who lived and worked earlier, Jesus is a further description of God. To put it more strongly; in that status he cannot become a second God to whom believers turn (in place of God himself). As a human being in whom God was active in the past, Jesus is included in the picture of God. It is impossible and unnecessary to transfer him from then to now as a historical person. The Christian church proclaims God, and nothing else, but God with the character of Jesus.

14

Jesus piety

1. Criticism forbidden? Meant genuinely and genuinely true

A problem crops up which is of considerable proportions: I shall call it
Jesus piety. In the previous chapters I came to the conclusion that
Christianity has gone too far in its christology and must take a step
back, but a large part of Christian piety consists in precisely the opposite: one hears believers no longer talking about God but only about
Jesus. What are we to make of this? Dissuade people? That seems
almost a form of robbery. Leave everything as it is? That doesn't help
either. It amounts to not taking other people seriously, and I think that
that's an insult. Is there something in between? For the moment I shall
leave that open, except to say that we mustn't doubt the honesty of
Jesus piety: it is meant genuinely. But that says something about
people's feelings and not about what attracts them and leads them to
worship. A person can in all honesty regard Jesus as the God-man, but
that doesn't answer the question whether Jesus *is* the God-man.

There is a current in theology (and philosophy) which thinks that this
question is an illegitimate one. For this current, what people believe is
simply the truth, and that's that. There's no half-way house. We have
no means of criticism at our disposal (God cannot be tested), and to
take something from people which is dear to them amounts to religious
callousness.

I shall return to these objections in this chapter, and to the whole
problem that is touched on with them, but at this point I want to say
that I don't wholly agree with the solution. Of course what people
believe is truth for them – at least as a rule. But does that really mean
that we must leave things at that and may not discuss or criticize their
truth, and indeed our own? I cannot accept that, and for more than one
reason. Jesus piety corresponds to a particular picture of Jesus; if we
may not touch it, may not approve or criticize that picture, any religious
dialogue becomes superfluous.

For the moment, whether or not it is possible to judge piety, in terms of 'conversing with Jesus', the first precondition is that we must describe it as well as possible. That isn't so easy, given the many different forms of Jesus piety. I shall attempt it by tracing Jesus piety through history, and will do so by selecting three episodes which in my view are sufficiently different to be distinguished: each of them is evocative enough to give us a grip on the phenomenon. First there is the piety attached to the doctrine of the two natures, which is both its origin and its product, piety as the continuation of the halo which is put on the God-man. This form of Jesus piety can be illustrated admirably by the images which are made of Jesus.

After that I go over to another type, marked by a crude transition to Jesus as a subject with whom the individual can converse inwardly. We meet this type in pietism, Methodism and the piety of the Enlightenment. The real difference is that a different world-view underlies it. As a third episode I shall discuss the revival of the icon, Jesus piety which again makes use of the image and thus – though in a different way from before – is a revival of the original piety based on the doctrine of two natures, including the world-view which that implies.

At the end of the chapter I shall give an answer to the question what we must do about Jesus piety.

2. *What is piety?*

Let's begin with some clarifications. By piety I understand devotion, dedication, worship, words which I use more or less as synonyms. In ritual form we know devotion as observance; praying the rosary is an example which will be well known to Roman Catholics. But observance isn't the same thing as piety. One can perform rituals without having any feeling for them, but piety is impossible without feeling, or rather, it *is* an expression of people's feelings about life or, as Van der Leeuw calls it, the subjective side of religion, the experience of religion at the level of emotion. In other words, piety, including Jesus piety, precedes doctrine. Before the existence of the church's dogma of the two natures, in which Jesus was fossilized as a theological construction, there was emotional devotion to Jesus as God-on-earth. We shouldn't be surprised that both dogma and Jesus piety have come down to the present day. Each presupposes the other and evokes the other: devotion evokes dogma, and once the dogma is there, it evokes devotion in its turn. So doctrine isn't everything: faith needs it, but doesn't come about through doctrine and doesn't derive its ongoing existence from it. 'I have a thing about Jesus,' would be the modern jargon. By that people indicate that they have some belief in Jesus, although they can't say precisely what it consists in or how it comes about. Emotion (experience) and rationality (being able to say) are two different things; they don't coincide.

So in this chapter, by Jesus piety I understand the experience of Jesus as reality, as emotional, a reality which is rooted in the feelings. If church doctrine about Jesus is the outside, then Jesus piety is the inside, the inside of christology.

A wish for identification with the person worshipped clings to all piety, and the wish to be like Jesus clings to Jesus piety. Down the centuries this wish keeps returning, in all kinds of crass versions, some of which we can no longer follow – I'm thinking of examples of stigmatization. It would take up too much space (at least a separate chapter) to go into this side of piety. It is enough to quote a children's hymn by way of example:

> I want to be like Jesus, so humble and so lowly,
> his words were always friendly, his voice was kind and holy.
> Alas, I'm not like Jesus in everything I do,
> O saviour, will you help me, and make me just like you.

I had to learn that by heart as a child, in the first class of Bible school, and I still know it. Later I was told that Christians needn't be so 'humble', because that plays into the hands of their oppressors. So we can see that the need for identification will have gone along with Christianity all down the centuries as a form of piety, but the ideal of which Jesus is the vehicle differs from century to century, and will always do so.

However, in terms of emotion and inwardness, not all piety is Jesus piety. I would venture to say that within Reformed Protestantism, Jesus piety is even an outsider. Just as according to the theologian Abraham Kuyper hot chocolate is not the drink of Reformed Christians, so from the start Reformed piety is not Jesus piety or devotion to Jesus but the piety of the psalms. What I mean is mysticism fed by the book of Psalms. The strict discipline about hymns in the Dutch Reformed Church (no songs, but only psalms in church) will have contributed to this, or to put it differently, will be a sure sign of it. The time of the Psalms is now past (to my great sadness), and their place has been taken by hymns to Jesus. How did the shift come about? I shall return to that in due course.

3. A statue of the Good Lord

Piety contributes to the formation of images, literally. That includes Jesus piety. That process can be followed in every book about the history of European art: every age creates its own images, to the present day. I cannot go in pictorial art further, and others are more competent to do so. But I shall begin with an image in the literal sense, because by it I can show that piety is about something.

The significance of Jesus is comparable, at least comparable, with, shall we say that of Alexander the Great, the emperor Augustus or St Augustine. Statues have been erected to all these men, men who have shaped our world. So, one might ask, why not honour Jesus with a statue? He is by no means inferior to William the Conqueror, or Charlemagne, or Winston Churchill. And we owe it to Jesus that we have been freed from the pagan gods: Wotan, Thor, Freya or whatever else we might call them. Now statues of Jesus are everywhere, the world is teeming with them, though we don't call them statues, and they often don't stand in a public place but in churches. So do statues of Mary. Here I'm talking about Roman Catholic church buildings, where century after century the crucified Christ and the Holy Virgin, the cruel and the motherly, have saddled children's souls with conflicting feelings.

We see why we may not call these images statues. People don't pray to Alexander the Great. But they do pray to Mary; at least a large number of Christians do. With Jesus that is even clearer: all Christians invoke Jesus, if not personally, then in hymns and the liturgy:

Christ whose glory fills the skies . . .

Jesus, lover of my soul, let me to thy bosom fly.

Master, they seek you far and wide.

I am mentioning only a few well-known hymns; they could he called spiritual statues, erected by poets and scribes, and daily visited by believers. Why do they do that? What is the function of these images?

There is something ambiguous about them, that's certain. They aren't there only as a focus for reflection, meditation and thought about what has happened in the past. Of course they also serve that purpose; one need only think of the stations of the cross in countless Roman Catholic church buildings, which make it possible for people to follow visually what the gospel has previously put into words. These are images as illustrations. In its zeal for orthodoxy, Reformed Christianity was against even this. The pointed language in which it expressed its objections is too good not to repeat here.

> Should people not tolerate images in the churches as 'books for the laity'? No, for we must not be wiser than God, whose will it is to have his Christians instructed not by dumb images but by the lively proclamation of his word (*Heidelberg Catechism*, Question and Answer 98).

'Books for the laity': the expression comes from the Roman Catholic theologians, who used it to indicate that Roman Catholics did not engage in any worship of images. But practical piety saw far more in them than pictures in a book or images from the past, and still does so. Not only must the past be rethought, but past and present must touch each other, overlap, coincide, if only for a moment. That is what makes Jesus piety (in whatever form) Jesus piety: a picture creates a place, one's own place for Jesus (think of the stations of the cross), where one can come to him. A separate place for Jesus alongside God: that is what Jesus piety results in. It even began there. How big a place this is, we shall see.

4. *Classical Jesus piety. The church's centuries-old treasury of hymns*

'Wicked people have no hymns,' Luther once remarked. That's a good argument for the Christian churches: they have a treasury of hymns which are still sung. In singing, people can show their emotions, and they're taken out of themselves.

The hymns which sing of Jesus have a prominent place in that whole: that's obvious. There are hymns of praise to the stylized Jesus, the church's Christ, which praise him in turn as God who came to earth and/or the Son who was sent to earth by the Father, but in most cases the church's dogma of the two natures is the basis for the hymn of praise, and not the historical person of Jesus. Or rather, the historical person is characterized as the Son of the Father, as God of God and light of light. I call this Jesus piety classical Jesus piety: it should really be called Christ piety.

The church hymns are full of this version. One need only open the index of any well-known Protestant or Anglican hymn book to make a list of them. Here are a couple of examples:

God of God, Light of Light,
Lo, he abhors not the virgin's womb.

Christ whose glory fills the skies,
Christ the one and only light.

Verses like these have made a deep mark on Christians. Believers sing them primarily as homage to the Redeemer, very much in the style of the liturgical 'Praise be to you, O Christ.' But that isn't the whole story. The hymns aim to do more, if we let the texts get through to us: they aim to bring Jesus into the present. Hymns are images, spiritual images, and like all images, they aim not only to illustrate but also to make present. That, it seems to me, is the explanation of the remarkable fact that they create a distinctive, independent point of devotion for Jesus alongside God. To invoke in all needs, as deliverer from distress, the physician of all souls, omnipresent and (this is what I mean by 'remarkable'), yet no one bats an eyelid, so used have we become to it. 'Jesus accepts sinners', a hymn of praise *to* Jesus, becomes, 'O Lord Jesus, accept us,' an invocation *of* Jesus.

The way in which devotion to Jesus has become independent is one side of the matter. The other side is that in these hymns Jesus is assigned the role of God; he is invoked vicariously. To put it crudely, originally we invoked God, but that has become Jesus. I shall leave aside what lies behind that (Jesus closer than God, just as Mary is closer than Jesus?): my concern is with the phenomenon. The hymn – as a spiritual image – makes Jesus present: that's what it's for. And the effect is that Jesus is given the role of God: he is invoked, he speaks, he heals, and so on.

I wouldn't go so far as to claim that of all hymns to Christ. We would do best to keep to 'making present': who knows more than that? But this representative nature, this replacing God by Jesus which is typical of the classical form of Jesus piety, seems me to be one step too far. One cannot pray to Jesus: that is a grave heresy even in terms of classical christology. I know that it can easily be defended with the help of and on the basis of the doctrine of two natures, since in that case, with some good will all that is true of God can also be applied to Jesus (not really, the theologians knew better, but that is how people imagined it). However, I shall leave aside this aspect of the matter here. A personal relationship to Jesus seems to me to be *the* characteristic of what I call Jesus piety. In the classical version of this, the Jesus is the Jesus of the two natures. But things can be different.

5. The Jesus piety of Protestantism

In the sphere of the Reformation a distinctive Jesus piety gradually developed. We could still hesitate over the classical form of piety: was God meant, as the Second Person of the divine Trinity who assumed human nature from the Virgin Mary, or was it about Jesus? In the Protestant Jesus piety which I have in mind here, there is no longer room for this hesitation. Jesus is the explicit subject with whom the believer maintains a personal relationship, and it is authentic Jesus. First I shall give a brief sketch of the two most prominent forms of expression of this.

(a) The pietistic Jesus. Pietism arose as a kind of resistance movement against the rationalistic version of faith, as early as the beginning of the seventeenth century, and it permeated the whole of Protestantism like leaven. It brings with it a distinctive Jesus piety, concerned not to abolish the doctrine of the church but to appropriate it in a personal way by making it inward: Jesus must enter our heart (or we must enter Jesus' heart) and not remain a doctrinal entity. His cross, his suffering and his death are truly believed in only if they are experienced as a personal substitution: it all happened for me = he has thought of me. That is 'personal': an inward relationship with Jesus.

Think of a movement like that of the Herrnhutters, led by Count von Zinzendorf (he died in 1760). The link with the (Lutheran) church (and its doctrine) was maintained, but the inner relationship with Jesus was extended into a Jesus mysticism with an almost sickly intimacy between Jesus and the soul, especially the Jesus of the passion and the cross. Involvement in Jesus' suffering on the cross could go so far that believers desired to have on their hands the stigmata of the nails with which Jesus was nailed to the cross and the scar of the wound which was inflicted on Jesus, on his side, as a sign of union with Christ.

Exaggerated? Certainly, sometimes shamelessly. But we needn't judge. There is more shamelessness under the sun. 'Jesus is OK,' I read in a newspaper, and someone else, 'Jesus is such a nice guy' (it makes one shudder). It's meant well, but it's not for me.

(b) Methodism (conversion must be brought about methodically, hence the name) also knows a Jesus piety, different from that of pietism, but no less prominent. It began its triumphal course from the Anglo-Saxon world. This pietism has many forms, but its fundamental characteristic is that proclamation calls for a decision: now that the call rings in your ears, take the decision to let Jesus into your life today. 'Seize the opportunity given you by God; tomorrow it may be too late.'

Here I have in mind preaching by people like Billy Graham, trained in rhetoric which aims to force people to their knees and decide for Jesus. A pietistic children's hymn speaks of

The Lord who dwells in heaven
and is enthroned in every lowly heart . . .

Jesus wants to dwell in your heart, my children learned at school (that was in 1962). Evangelicals speak of 'letting Jesus into your life', 'accepting him'. That's rather different. In the first place it's an act, a deed, a decision, with all the relief that choices bring to a shaky disposition (Evangelicals are much more cheerful than pietists). The decision means that one accepts Jesus as the master who has the say in one's life. To give a literal quotation (from Beyers Naudé), 'I asked Jesus to become my Lord and Saviour.' That makes this a somewhat risky kind of Jesus piety. There are always representatives or agents of the Lord (in the person of the preacher, the pastor or another spiritual leader) who fill in what the king wants. So along with Jesus one lets people into one's life who decide one's actions, for better or for worse.

What must we understand by 'letting Jesus in' or 'asking Jesus'? Of course that's imagery, but the meaning is the beginning of a personal relationship, this time by an act of will, and not, as with the pietists, by the evocation of feelings. But leaving the differences aside, what connects the two is that Jesus becomes a personal factor, someone with whom one has personal dealings. The believer's essential relationship of faith is not with God but with Jesus – and it's a person-to-person relationship. Jesus piety is the content of faith.

We are in a completely different climate from that of classical Christ piety: one only has to attend a single meeting of a 'full gospel community' for that to become completely clear. Or listen to the Sankey songs, for again the song is the great vehicle of emotion. This completely different climate of piety is bound up with a shift of world-view. I shall try to make that clear in the next section, which is about icons.

6. Jesus as icon: gateway to the other world

Icons are symbols; not, however, as representation ('water' stands for life) but as the appearance, the epiphany of what is presented. Western Christianity knows little or nothing of this. One looks in vain for an entry in encyclopaedias and theological works of reference. These are full of scholastic theology, with ideological subjects, with social and political themes, all interpreted in accordance with the spirit of the time, but 'icon' doesn't appear. So the icon isn't part of the active ideal of the piety of Western Christianity. Only over recent decades has there been some revival of interest.

Jesus as icon is the depiction of Jesus (accepted by the church) which can do what other expressions, words or images, cannot, namely provide a mystical union between human beings and the world in which Jesus belongs, the world of God. In the thought-world of Christians trained by Eastern orthodoxy, the effect of an icon is easiest to clarify with the help of the sacraments. We have also made the sacraments ourselves, in order to help us to experience God's presence. Of course people prefer to experience that directly, without having to construct means for it. But as the poem says,

> the revery alone will do
> if bees are few.

A bit of clover, a few bees, and a little dreaming are enough to make a meadow, says Emily Dickinson. Dreaming is enough. That's how I see the sacraments. If there is little to eat and people sense little of God, there are still always signs: we play at encountering God under the signs. We tell one another that the signs are to be symbols for us in which our world and God's world coincide. So we experience what we put into it. Christians of an earlier age rightly said that the sacraments were only for believers: what they meant was that only people who believe in them (in this convergence) experience an encounter with God in them.

That is also roughly (I am no expert in the piety of the Eastern church) how an icon 'works' for believers. It isn't a matter of seeing God – no human being can do that here on earth; but we can see Christ, or rather the image of Christ. The image itself is earthly reality, made by an artist, but it depicts another reality, that of Christ, just as Christ in turn depicts God. If the icon is successful, believers experience this other reality by looking at it. It lifts up our hearts to God, and in this sense is the gateway to God. Therefore an icon is approached with great reverence, with religious awe; in it people come into the presence of God.

An icon is an image, and according to some artists what is true of an icon is true of all pictorial art: it opens the door to another world, to God. God is beauty. But that's just an incidental comment. Keeping to my subject I can say that the icon presupposes that Jesus has two natures: it is wholly related to that. In that doctrine the two worlds, of

God and of human beings, come close in an exemplary way: exemplary
in the sense that both coincide in his person without being mixed. That
follows the recipe of Chalcedon perfectly: unconfusedly, unchangeably,
indivisibly, inseparably.

7. *The metaphysical longing*

The icon has begun a come-back; in our present-day culture there is
more interest in icons than there used to be. That hasn't just come out
of the blue: it's the manifestation of a metaphysical longing. I haven't
dreamed up the term myself; it comes from the famous Roman Catholic
Dutch Catechism of 1966. At the time it passed unnoticed, and at most
incurred some scorn from the Barthian theology which was prevalent at
the time. Metaphysical longing was 'religion', and religion was thought
reprehensible.

The origin of this longing is formed by the idea that another world
must exist beyond our world, our present world: the world of God. This
idea is as old as religion and forms the framework of all religions. In
philosophy it goes under the name metaphysics (*meta* = beyond, and
physics refers to our existing world), and comprises the view that while
our reality seems to us to be authentic reality, it is not the authentic, true
reality. Plato, *the* philosopher of metaphysics, can speak of it like this.
In his view we must see our world as a manifestation of the authentic
world, or better (for that is already to say too much), as a vague copy
of this invisible, true world. If we knew nothing of this true reality,
never encountered it in any way, it would not penetrate into our world
anywhere; we would sink into chaos. The visible, true reality is the
norm (others later made this into 'the invisible norm is the true reality'),
and manifests itself as the norm of which the visible world forms a
shadow copy. The first theologians of the Christian church accepted
Plato's philosophy most gratefully. He saw that the true reality is reality
as it occurs in God's thoughts, and that our world is a manifestation of
these thoughts. Therefore for them Plato was the first Christian theologian, a Christian before Christ.

Most philosophers dissociated themselves from this static metaphysic,
but not from the idea that another reality is concealed behind the existing reality. We may not be able to say anything about it, but it sometimes shines through what is called a 'clearing of Being' (to use
Heidegger's jargon), a 'clearing' that gives meaning. Some theologians
gladly accept this argument and interpret the illumination of 'Being' as
an experience (viz. revelation) of transcendence. Plato has given way to

Heidegger. But it remains metaphysics, or rather, metaphysics has made a come-back.

I see the revival of metaphysical longing as a new spirituality, aroused and brought about by disappointment at the existing world. It's a long time since people thought that they could remake this world, a long time since the churches emphasized the eschatological aspect and preached the political allure of messianism. But the world has not been renewed, and the price that we have to pay for the failure of Romantic messianism is a return to metaphysics, in terms of an unquenched (and unquenchable) longing for an experience of transcendence.

To return to the icon. So in the strict sense the icon isn't about Jesus but about God's other world, the reality behind our reality, just as in the doctrine of two natures. Here we have the great longing for a depth experience, the experience of God-on-earth. 'O that you would rend the heavens' is a wish of all ages.

The metaphysical background is no longer a factor in pietism and Methodism. Jesus becomes his own subject: personal relations with him, relations with Jesus, become the real experience of faith. Is that possible? Everything is possible, but what I mean is: from the perspective of the Christian tradition can one have an inner communication with Jesus, or does piety – in whatever form – burst its banks here?

8. Omnipresent? An old problem

A bit of theology, a brief intermezzo, for pleasure, but also to show that no problem is new, not even the toing and froing of Jesus between past and present. I want to insert a question, the most normal question possible: how can Jesus, who is someone from the past, be present today? If we think of 'Jesus' as the second person of the holy Trinity, that's always possible; it's no problem. But Jesus isn't the second person of the holy Trinity. The classic doctrine of the church says that the second person of the holy Trinity has appeared in flesh in the human being Jesus without the human nature of Jesus being done away with. So worshipping Jesus as the second person of the Trinity is certainly in conformity with the doctrine (assuming that people know what they are then worshipping), as is communicating with the second person. But here, for the sake of convenience (and for a moment), we have separated the two natures of Jesus. If we reunite them in/as one person, then problems arise. Worshipping then means that we also worship Jesus as a human being, and that is just not on, as Abraham Kuyper said.

Both natures united in one person also means that Jesus is present as a human being today. Surely that isn't on? This is a classic problem in Christian theology, and given the formulation of the doctrine of two natures is unavoidable. Jesus is omnipresent according to his divine nature but not according to his human nature. What are the implications of that? The more one is dealing with God-on-earth, the easier the question becomes to answer: the divine nature finally absorbs the human nature into itself; that's what the divine nature is for. There is no longer a speck of dust on the light – but then one can no longer talk of a real human nature (and – as a reminder – that is called Monophysitism). Those who don't want that (officially, Monophysitism was condemned as a heresy) are left with the problem. To say sometimes that the divine nature is at work and at others that the human nature is at work is impossible, as that breaks the unity of the person. Yet it has to be done if, for example, the divine nature isn't going to go into the grave with the human nature. The unity of the person of Christ is necessarily emphasized again.

In Jesus piety we again stumble over the problem of the two natures. According to the classical doctrine God is omnipresent, but if we begin from Jesus' presence in our life (Jesus in my heart) as crudely as happens in the Jesus piety, there is no alternative to accepting that not only God but also Jesus is omnipresent. Is he?

For the Protestant fathers, the presence of Christ in the bread and the wine of the eucharist was a test case for this question. For Roman Catholic theology, the real presence of Christ (God and man) under the signs of bread and wine was sure. Luther greatly approved of that. On the one hand, he wanted to maintain this real presence which he had learned earlier (in his Roman training), but he was under the impact of 'the new doctrine' which thought that the transformation of bread and wine into the body and blood of Christ (the doctrine of transubstantiation) was idolatry. According to Zwingli, this doctrine even makes people 'cannibals'. Luther found a kind of middle way: no transubstantiation of Jesus, and yet his real presence (in both natures!) in bread and wine. That meant that Jesus could also be omnipresent according to his human nature. Luther accepted this consequence, and devised complicated arguments in support of it, but he had no answer to the objection that the human nature can never have the properties of the divine nature.

This question is of no further importance for us. As far as I know, Protestantism no longer holds the view that Jesus literally accompanies the signs of bread and wine in person. I shall leave that theme (the Lord's Supper and the eucharist) and the differences over it and return to the subject of this excursus: the omnipresence of Jesus as a human person. That cannot be. Quite apart from the impossibility of imagining it – an omnipresent human nature is a phantom, it isn't theologically correct in terms of our time either, at least from the perspective of the doctrine in which Jesus is presented as existing in two natures.

9. *Jesus has to come too. The teddy bear*

Piety is free; it's an emotional expression of devotion. It presupposes the doctrinal structure of the church, but has its own door, the door of the heart. Once within, it feels addressed by a segment, a feature, a bar of the whole bar-code of truth, but about what is it addressed, and by whom? This question has yet to be answered. Why does a person fall for Jesus and cannot let go? I think that psychology can helps us further here. Those who sing

> a faithful friend dwells in heaven
> such as the world does not offer

know the disappointments of life; they certainly aren't in the top social class and experience the world as a world which lets you down and betrays you: even friends do that. A collective experience as a result of which the hymn meets with approval is sung about by people who know it from experience. For them Jesus, and only Jesus, is to be trusted. 'My Jesus is my most faithful friend.'

Jesus can also be a very personal comforter. There was a woman – at the time when I was a preacher – who had one child, a son. His birth caused her life-long paralysis. The young man was called up for military service and sent out to Indonesia to take part in the so-called police action there. This young man, of all young men, died. The mother had no answer to this disaster than endlessly to repeat, as thought it were a mantra, 'Jesus' blood makes all things good.' Was this a real comfort? Did this saying help her? Who can say? In any case, she experienced Jesus as a compensation for her heartbreaking fate, and I didn't in the least need to contradict her.

I see both the first and the second examples in terms of the need to have Jesus near, if one wants to be reassured.

> Do not go alone through life, the burden is too heavy for you.
> Let one give you strength; go to your mediator.

Jesus must be there. Large groups of Christians have song this song endlessly and consoled themselves endlessly with it.

Sail under Jesus' care, with the flag of the cross raised high

ending with

we have the Father's son on board and a safe shore in view.

Jesus has to be there for comfort, just as a child has to take its teddy bear to bed to sleep peacefully. I don't mean this comparison in a disparaging way. I'm trying to extract the psychological factor of this form of Jesus piety. People remain children, or rather: not all children get over their childhood fears. Even better: some people get over them with the help of what they've heard tell of Jesus in their childhood. We can't overestimate the emotional value that their ideas of Jesus represent for them.

Safe in Jesus' arms
Safe in Jesus' heart.

People write this above the death notices of their loved ones. It's their way of expressing their belief in security: to be safe with Jesus is to have landed up safe with God. Granted, this is rather childish, but surely we needn't feel too superior about that? As long as it isn't a universal requirement, children may be children, even in faith, and grown-ups may be grown-ups.

In Jesus piety, Jesus, to be brief, has become the material by which people can express their religious longings, their need for acceptance, for comfort. Jesus is a defence against anxiety about being abandoned: 'Don't leave me.' Jesus is a vehicle for emotions.

Is this neurotic? And superstitious into the bargain? It could be. But it's just as neurotic to make this a doctrinal point. It isn't my concern to extract pure doctrine. On the contrary, my concern is with church people who can't rid themselves of the idea that their piety is really defective. And conversely, not to take away from people who use it to keep their heads above water the feeling of comfort that they derive from this piety and the security that they experience in it. And above all not to allow oneself to be told that piety must be theologically correct.

10. Theologically correct?

Because piety is emotion, in the first instance it makes no sense to try to measure it. Feelings are feelings, and to dispute or deny them is to deny what someone experiences, and that kills any form of communication. To accept that people feel what they feel and to respect it is the necessary basis for any dialogue. How far does that respect go in the case of Jesus piety?

Jesus who fulfils the wishes of all children and grown-ups (it depends on what their hearts are full of) brings us back to the subject of this chapter. In Jesus piety, can we distinguish between the acceptable and the unacceptable, and how do we find a criterion for doing this? May we use such a criterion, or if we do, are we taking from people something which isn't precious to all of them but which they couldn't do without?

I've been aware of the importance of this question throughout this book, and in this chapter I feel it more strongly than ever. But we cannot escape the dilemma with which we are faced: we either think that everything Jesus piety offers is good, or – if we don't want to do that – we try to combine respect for it with a question mark against it.

The phrase 'theologically correct' has already been mentioned as a criterion. By that we could indeed measure Jesus piety of every kind. That happens: theology is full of it. But that isn't the whole story; it's only one side of the matter, that of the official doctrine of the church. If we were to take church dogma strictly (and not overlook all kinds of things that appear in popular piety), then Jesus shouldn't be invoked and Mary shouldn't be called the Mother of God. In other words, there would be a tremendous amount of incorrect piety. There is the further factor that the church's Christ isn't a timeless reality, exalted above history, but a phase in the reception history of the Gospels, and thus itself derives from needs and aspirations, albeit down the centuries. So 'theologically correct' won't do as a criterion. It isn't unusable, forbidden, by definition unfruitful, but it is too unstable to make a foundation for piety.

Is there then no critical perspective? That isn't true either. Jesus piety corresponds with a picture of Jesus, and depressing though it may seem, many pictures of Jesus are no more than religious and/or doctrinal kitsch. It isn't as if we're compelled to respect them because Jesus or Christ is mentioned in them. A good deal of religious nonsense is practised in Jesus' name, or, to put it more strongly: his figure as polished up by the church lends itself readily to this.

So we haven't avoided a criterion, a kind of rule which we can use to establish how far the warmth of veneration of Jesus has blazed up (one might also say burnt out), like the flame of a candle. This surely must be there; it must be used, not to snip off what goes beyond it and thus to teach others a lesson, but to protect us from a false move in piety: where do I want to join in and where don't I?

If that label can't consist in being theologically correct, what does it consist in? We establish what is kitsch and what isn't by means of the criterion of quality. That immediately sparks off a deep discussion about what quality is, but we needn't be deterred by that. On the contrary, such a discussion must use examples, and thus we are precisely where we need to be: where do I want to join in and where don't I? Superficial needs, selfish annexation of Jesus, group annexation (which is even worse than the individual kind) – all that seems to me to be a viable criterion which we can all use by ourselves in order to establish whether as a human beings, with Jesus and all, we fail, and if so where. Self-criticism of our Jesus piety begins here.

The real – critical – question already begins much earlier; I've been facing it throughout this book. Has Christianity always been using Jesus as a substitute for God, and is that expressed even more in Jesus piety? I shall devote the next section to this fundamental question.

11. *Saying Jesus and meaning God. Jesus as metaphor*

In Jesus piety we get inside christology, into the world of the feelings of believers. Dammed up by the emotions, nothing seems to be excessive when people want to name what Jesus is good for. The demonstrations of Jesus piety which are reviewed make that abundantly clear. Nevertheless we can bring it under a single heading. A characteristic of Jesus piety is that Jesus becomes the centre and essence of faith: the believer experiences the relationship of faith in the first instance with Jesus and not with God.

What we have to do is the opposite of this: to reduce this super-devotion and again restore to God the place that he is due in piety. We must trace all mysticism, all devotion, all emotion (without which faith cannot exist) back to where they come from and where they belong (and thus, one can say, where they come home to), namely God. Believing isn't dealing with Jesus as a substitute God, but with God himself.

I would venture to assume immediately that much Jesus piety is also meant in this way. It really speaks in terms of Jesus and strictly speaking isn't about Jesus but about God in terms of Jesus: saying Jesus and meaning God. In any case, that is a plea which I would make here. In making it I am convinced that I am not taking Christianity out of the frying pan into the fire, but doing it a service. See whether it works: you say Jesus but surely you mean God?

I then see Jesus as a metaphor for God, and as I stated earlier, with a metaphor we do not say what something (or someone) is but what he (or it) is like. To say Jesus and mean God liberates us from the strait-jacket of the doctrine of two natures. As a metaphor for God Jesus isn't himself God, but we use his name to talk about God, about God who is merciful and righteous and great in loving-kindness, forgiving the evil but not regarding the guilty as innocent. Jesus as a metaphor for God = Jesus as another word for God's faithfulness to his creation, for God's love, for God who goes along on the journey, for the intimacy of converse with God. Jesus language needn't be rejected, but if by it we mean God, why not say God straightaway? I hope that this gentle hint won't escape any reader. Readers can contribute towards piety getting back on its feet.

15

The Creed

1. 'Reinterpretation'

Jesus was in hell. Earlier church teachers maintained that, in complete accord with the Creed (the so-called Apostles' Creed), which says that 'he descended into hell'. No, said Calvin, that must be thought of in a different way: Jesus went through hell, but he wasn't really in hell. The Heidelberg Catechism (Question and Answer 44) says that he suffered the pains of hell. Now I am not concerned here with the question whether or not hell exists (if I had to say something, I would say that it doesn't). I am not even concerned with interpreting this clause from the Creed. I'm simply using it as an illustration of an approach over which people stumble: interpreting a statement so that it begins to say something different from what it does say. As a theological student I learned that this is called 'reinterpretation'. 'Reinterpretation' is something like giving a different meaning to a statement of faith, but with the connotation of illegitimacy: one can't accept what's written there, but because one can't simply drop a venerable text, one tries to get out of what the words say by making them say something different.

In the past the question became acute in the clause of the Creed which says that Jesus was born of the Virgin Mary. Someone like Emil Brunner, a friend (up to a point) of Karl Barth's had no time for the virgin birth, but didn't want to scrap the clause; instead he read it as an expression of Jesus' sinlessness. 'Reinterpretation', exclaimed a number of theologians, 'and that's evasion: either you accept what is said or you don't.' Karl Barth thought it unimportant as genealogical data about Jesus, but he wanted to keep them as a 'sign': Jesus came from God, from Above. I shall be returning to this at length in the next section.

'Reinterpretation' has a bad name. Rightly so? Yes, if we had to regard the statements of the Creed as having come from Above. However, there are no such statements. Everything that goes the rounds about God comes from below, is human work, with the double implication that not only isn't the human world just the world as people see it, but the language with which they express their experience of the world still bears the stamp of their standpoint and the point in time in which they have their experiences (individual and/or collective). Men and women are historical beings. So 'born of the Virgin Mary' isn't a timeless truth, but an expression of something that people saw in Jesus, then, at that time, and is expressed in terms of that time. So it is itself already an 'interpretation', and what is called 'reinterpretation' is usually a new interpretation, in another time and by other people. That means abandoning the negative connotations; the word interpretation describes a normal way of going about things, even dealing with venerable confessions from the past.

I shall be doing this here in connection with the Creed. This isn't evasion because I can't make anything of what is written there. Rather, what is written there isn't the last word (nor, for that matter, is it the first), but an interpretation which I would no longer understand had not its meaning been explained to me by a new interpretation (by a preacher or pastor). Interpretation, interpretation of interpretation, and so on: we do nothing but interpret! The Creed just as much the Bible; if writings from the past are to function, there's no other way of dealing with them.

But doesn't the Creed give historical facts about Jesus' life? Surely we can't change what's written in it? Indeed that's impossible, but the question is whether these facts that the Creed relates about Jesus relate history bit by bit. 'Suffered under Pontius Pilate, crucified, dead and buried', that's certainly historical. But 'ascended into heaven'? As I've shown, Calvin at any rate wasn't afraid of regarding the 'descended into hell' as imagery and not something that 'really happened'. That's encouraging; we're in good company when we interpret, even when we reinterpret what claims to be a historical fact, for example the ascension of Jesus.

2. *Interpreting the Creed*

Originally the Creed is what candidates for baptism had to learn by heart before they could be baptized on Easter Eve. The central part of it is devoted to Jesus. After belief in God the Father, the almighty Creator of heaven and earth, there follows, attached to the same beginning ('I believe'), what the baptismal candidate confesses about Jesus. The text ends with the Holy Spirit, the church and the so-called last things. Here is the section about Jesus.

and in one Lord Jesus Christ, the only begotten Son of God,
who was conceived by the Holy Spirit,
born of the Virgin Mary,
suffered under Pontius Pilate,
was crucified, dead and buried.
He descended into hell,
the third day he rose again from the dead,
and ascended into heaven,
and sits at the right hand of God,
from where he will come to judge the living and the dead.

What are we to do with a testimony which has so long a tradition behind it and still unites in one confession churches which for centuries have had nothing to do with one another? All right, although it's called the Apostles' Creed, it doesn't come from the apostles (it wasn't so venerable that scholars couldn't already point this out in the sixteenth century), but its credentials do go back to the church under persecution.

Obviously we don't throw it away. Tradition is all that we have; we have to make do with it even in matters of faith and world-view. It is the wisdom, the faith, the experience of God from former generations, as it was handed down in turn to them by their predecessors. No less, but also no more. The Creed has a historical character, and that makes interpreting it unavoidable. What that means I shall go on to explain.

1. Respect for the past, for the tradition of faith from which we come and to which we belong, is sufficient reason not to let go of the Creed. Nor should we drop the Nicene Creed (325) or the Athanasian Creed (though that's not by Athanasius). Their antiquity calls for respect. This is piety towards our predecessors, the church of all ages.

2. The three creeds which I mention here (the Apostles' Creed, the Nicene Creed and the Athanasian Creed) are called ecumenical creeds because they are accepted by all Christian churches as a criterion of truth. To the amazement of some readers, the Chalcedonian Definition (451), with its doctrine of two natures, doesn't stand in the series, although this doctrine as expressed by Chalcedon was similarly accepted by all Christian churches. But Chalcedon also has a paragraph about the Holy Spirit with which even today the Eastern Orthodox Church doesn't agree, and so Chalcedon drops out of the ecumenical boat. Thus the Creed (which is what I am concerned with at this moment) is a bond between the Christian churches, something which is not to be belittled.

3. Should we respect the Creed, even if we cannot possibly subscribe to certain clauses in it? That's certainly a good point. We are moving into the position of having learned to see the relativity of religious formulae – unlike our forefathers. People can express their experiences only in terms of their own time, their own culture; in a word, they are indebted to their own interpretation of their existence. That has caused problems, especially whether this doesn't mean that 'it's all tottering', as Ernst Troeltsch once remarked. But why not snap up the advantages? Think of the emphasis with which the Creed introduces God as Father (this occurs twice). That's problematical for women, say feminist theologians. All right, formulations aren't eternal; they're open to an investigation of the meaning that they had then and the question where they can help us to cope with life today, and how. Nothing need be dropped; we leave everything in, but we can't use it all – at least not today. Perhaps tomorrow?

4. Do outsiders then know where they are with Christianity? I raise this question because we sometimes hear that Christianity mustn't meddle with its own confession, and interpretation is clearly meddling. I can't go along with that. Any view of life, any institution, any faith, deteriorates, and is then renewed so that it can go further; should Christianity just go around in its earlier garb? Of course, having more than one string to its bow makes it that much more difficult for criticism to get at. Tedious for the critics, that's true; they have to make an effort to get the phenomenon of Christianity in their sights. But modification? Every spiritual current modifies. That isn't fiddling, apostasy, a sell-out; it's a sign of vitality.

3. *The virgin birth*

I shall begin with the clause that I've already quoted: 'born of the virgin Mary', in church terminology the so-called virgin birth of Jesus. The evangelist Luke reports (chapter 1) that Mary did not know a man; the fruit of her womb was conceived by the Holy Spirit, and the church fathers interpreted that as a proof of Jesus' divine nature: the child that is born is not only from below (humankind) but also from above (God). Or in a rather cruder form: through the Virgin Mary, the Second Person of the divine Trinity clothed himself with human nature (viz. with a body). In theology that came to be called the doctrine of the incarnation, and in preaching and theology it is presented as God's descent to humankind, but also as an ascent of human beings to a divine level: think what we must be worth if God becomes man for our sake! I shall leave all these developments aside, except to say that Luke doesn't describe the *assumptio carnis* (the second person of the holy Trinity assumes human nature), but the birth of Jesus from the Virgin Mary.

Of course that can be regarded as historical truth. Large parts of the Christian church have done that and still do so, for example the Roman Catholic Church, for which this view is even official church doctrine. And that can hardly be otherwise, since the whole of Marian devotion depends on it, and that is as lively today as ever. Roman Catholic theologians are trying to stem its expansion, or to guide it in another direction by presenting Mary as a symbol of the church which receives her Lord in faith, but they can't do much in the face of popular belief. Moreover they aren't allowed to, since Mary's Immaculate Conception was elevated to the status of official church teaching (dogma) in 1854, and her bodily assumption into heaven was added in 1950. Dogma has followed piety, as so often in the church. We ask ourselves why things keep being added and nothing is taken away, for example when it no longer says anything to believers.

The virgin birth itself isn't a point of dispute between Roman Catholics and Protestants. Even Mary as 'mother of God' (elevated to a dogma by the Council of Ephesus in 431) hasn't always been that. Calvin, Luther and even Karl Barth had nothing against it, provided that it referred to Jesus' divine nature, and thus is treated as a topic of christology and didn't begin to serve as a basis for complete Mariology.

But that's what actually happened. Roman Catholics thought that the status of Mary must match that of the divine Son who produced her. Hence Mary's immaculate conception. If original sin is something (a kind of stain) handed down through birth, Mary too must already have been without original sin. Otherwise she would have infected Jesus. Moreover the official doctrine was that Mary remained preserved from original sin by a preventive divine act; it was reckoned to her so to speak retrospectively, not because of her own worth but because of the merits of her great Son. Conversely, Mary is by nature the one who has the best access to her son; all mothers of the world feel that: she has taken him to her heart. So believers fare well because the Son has his mother close by him.

One cannot deny that this view of things is consistent. The virgin birth (Jesus has no human father) and the immaculate conception (Mary was free of original sin) are indispensable; otherwise not only does Mary lose her place of honour (and believers their extra access), but Jesus loses the genealogical components which make him God from God. But at the same time it's too much of a good thing. Mary as mother of God (Greek *theotokos*) is based from A to Z on the doctrine of God-on-earth, and as I have shown, this doctrine doesn't have much of a foundation. Unless one wants to be a Monophysite, 'Mother of God' will not do, and a Mary free from original sin is an unfounded speculation (quite apart from the question what original sin could be).

Jesus was a human being just like us; he had a father and a mother, and brothers and sisters (the church dogma that Mary remained 'ever virgin' isn't historical fact either). Perhaps like many rabbis Jesus was married and had children. Of course that doesn't fit into the stylized picture that Christianity has painted of him. I'm not arguing for such a view. But we must keep the possibility open if we want to see Jesus remain truly human.

Virgin birth? So no, not really. The story that Luke tells expresses a view about Jesus. Hendrikus Berkhof, in the footsteps of Emil Brunner, pointedly emphasizes that we must take it with 'conceived by the Holy Spirit' and what that means: 'Belief in Jesus as the only son isn't grounded in belief in his virgin birth, but vice versa.'

4. The cross

Jesus did not come for a cross; he was put on one. Had Pilate administered justice, Jesus would have been released and not murdered; in short, had everything gone as it should have done, the history of the world would have taken a different course. We aren't accustomed to speaking about it like that. That's because the cross is embedded in the Christian doctrine of salvation, and has even acquired a central place in it. It has entered history as the symbol of Christianity. I once heard a minister say that the cross is the church's logo.

There is no denying that that means a form of stylizing, and fortunately so, for to imagine a nail going through one's hand is enough to give children nightmares. But its violent character no longer makes an impression; like the violence on TV, it no longer touches the imagination.

But that was the original intention. The cross had to emphasize how much Jesus had to suffer. The Middle Ages are full of it; every church had a crucifix, as realistic as possible: blood flowing from Jesus' side, a crown of thorns on his head, a loincloth round his waist and hung on nails. Suffering. Exemplary suffering, discipleship to be followed by those who wanted to be like Jesus, the cross as the nursery of masochism, as I read in a Roman Catholic author. I can understand it. However horrible iconoclasm may have been, at any rate Protestant

children were rid of it. Although they could of course have been freed
from it in a better way.

How? By making clear that this is a stylizing of Jesus death produced
by faith, a conversion of the crucifixion. From being a disaster, a crime,
a murder, the cross was turned into a blessing, a saving event: the
forgiveness of sins, Jesus as the means of atonement. And talking of
'reinterpretation', making the cross a token of honour is reinterpretation. Had the cross not been reinterpreted, there would probably have
been no churches.

The reinterpretation also has its negative aspects. If everything is as
classical church doctrine would have it, as I have shown, Jesus' suffering and death become a put-up job; he already knew it all. He had come
down from heaven to do something that had been agreed with the
Father; he had dreaded it in his human nature, but as God nothing could
happen to him. Here we find that the story of Jesus is robbed of its ultimate seriousness; another starting point must be chosen, namely the
recognition that it was human beings, the first followers of Jesus, who
explained Jesus' crucifixion, interpreting it as a divine action. He
seemed different, and became saviour of the world. Paul thought this,
and had been preceded by others (for example by intimations of Jesus
himself?), and Christianity all too readily followed him. After all,
Christianity stands or falls by this. For 'the forgiveness of sins' (as the
Christian liturgy says) is and remains an interpretation from below
about what is Above.

Of course the cross has nothing to do with masochism, nor with the
glorification of suffering or propaganda for the killing of victims who
cannot defend themselves. It is rather the reverse: victims can take on a
significance which they themselves couldn't have known about.

5. Risen from the dead

If the virgin birth is a tricky issue more for Roman Catholics, for a very
long time the resurrection of Jesus from the dead has had a grip on
Protestants. I could write about it just as I wrote about the virgin birth:
the resurrection stories are about Jesus' meaning for his followers. The
meaning was there first and the stories came afterwards: they have to be
read as an expression of this meaning.

I am not certain whether it can be so simple, but in any case let's
begin like that. It would get us out of the habit of seeing Jesus' resurrection as a kind of bare fact, which, moreover, must be maintained to
have 'truly happened'. First rescue the bare fact, and then we can talk

about its meaning. I understand what lies behind this, and I can also understand how this argument finds its way into the best circles, but that's not on. We don't know bare facts in the most literal sense of those words. We go on telling bare facts because they mean something. To go on telling them *is* to attach meaning to the events and to go on telling them for that reason. In other words, to hand on the resurrection of Jesus is itself already to hand on an interpretation. Of *what,* of course, is the question. But I shall be coming back to that shortly.

One must have certainty, historical certainty about facts ('what really happened'); that's also necessary, and we can't escape the fact that this can be provided only by expert researchers into the past. If dogmatics can decide the outcome, than anything we like can be declared historical. So that is reason enough not to detach the stories from the meaning they give to Jesus. It protects us from what I read in a religious newspaper as encouragement to go to church at Easter. I quote the minister who wrote it:

'Surprise,' said Jesus after three days. And was followed into the nearest church.

End of quotation. Nice? Yes, but more as a joke, a banana skin that we ourselves have dropped, to slip on later. To see stories as a way of presenting the meaning that people gave to Jesus is always a better way. Isn't that a historical problem? Certainly. But we don't solve it by talking about what 'really happened', outside the significance of that event, in other words in terms of 'the meaning comes later, first the facts'. Quite certainly the historical problem cannot be solved in the way in which the German churches want it to be solved when confronted by someone like Gerd Lüdemann, who in their view denies the resurrection of Jesus. In the church, they say, by Jesus we don't mean the historical Jesus, about whom Lüdemann speaks, but the exalted, risen, preached Jesus. That seems to me to be an evasion rather than a solution, even if it's a quite understandable one.

6. *He is alive*

There is another great advantage in translating the resurrection stories back into the meaning of Jesus. We cannot avoid connecting these stories with Jesus' death; that's precisely what they're about. There is good reason for talking about the 'resurrection of the dead'. Where does this connection get us?

(*a*) 'Jesus is risen' could then mean that his death cannot be the end; it cannot be true that God abandoned him. 'Jesus' cause goes on' is the way in which one German theologian explained Jesus' resurrection. As the Word of God, Jesus goes on after his death, said another (Bultmann). That may not seem much, but the direction in which these theologians are thinking has old credentials. God has turned to good the evil that you did, says the apostle Peter, when he has to explain why he is talking about Jesus. Jesus' life follows the model of Joseph: God turns to good the evil that his brothers did him. God transforms the murder of an innocent man, of Jesus, into a blessing for humankind and the world: the scorned servant of God becomes a light for the nations (the non-Jews). Indeed, that is how the 'cause of Jesus' went on despite his death, and expanded into a world concern.

(*b*) Does he himself also go further? His very first followers were sure of that: he is alive, they said, and believers have echoed them all down the centuries. But what did they mean by it? Not always the same thing, that's quite clear. 'He is alive' is for some the proof that God was behind him, resurrection as a kind of 'permit' from God. For others it is a reward for Jesus' faithfulness to his task, to his ministry or whatever else it is called: resurrection as exaltation after humiliation. Once the resurrection terminology is introduced, then 'he is alive' can even mean the beginning of the new time, the new creation, the great day, the day on which the dead will arise with Jesus as the first of them.

He is alive. But if even the apostle Paul, who defends the resurrection of Jesus against the objections of the Corinthians (Bultmann thought that 'a fatal mistake' on the apostle's part), says that flesh and blood will not inherit the kingdom of God (I Corinthians 15.35–38), then one thing is clear: 'he is alive' is not the resuscitation of a corpse. Before we know it, according to Jan Kal (in his poem 'Superstar') we get to something like

Buddy Holly is alive and well, and rocking in Tijuana, Mexico

and even the most conservative Christians wouldn't want 'resurrection' to end up there.

What then? I don't think that we can form any image of it, any more than we can form an image of ourselves after our death. Of course we have all kinds of pious ideas about it: how we shall see God, or one another, or – in a somewhat pedestrian way – how glorious it will be in heaven. But all that is sheer imagination; in fact we know nothing about it. We must also respect that in the case of Jesus' resurrection. Christians believe that God did not abandon him, especially him. in the hour of his death, so he is alive. And we shall live too, said his followers. To believe in Jesus' resurrection is to believe that friendship with the eternal God is eternal friendship which will not be destroyed by death.

(c) And what about the stories which tell so vividly how people saw him, touched him, ate with him and finally saw him going to heaven?. Don't read them as accounts of the spectacular historical event of the resuscitation of a corpse. Of course they could be. Who could forbid that sort of interpretation? But they needn't be. Nor are the appearances a kind of confirmation. In I Corinthians 15 Paul uses the same word as occurs in Matthew 17, where Enoch, Moses and Elijah appear to Jesus. But surely we don't read any resurrection stories about Enoch, Moses and Elijah? God took them, took them to himself: that is what is told of them. It is there, it seems to me, that the link with the appearances of Jesus lies. Read the stories as visions, and not as evidence of physical resurrection. The resurrection of Jesus doesn't need the stories to be firm; on the contrary, what according to Christians is firm, his meaning for human beings and the world, and his meaning for us personally, now and in the hour of our death, is depicted for us through the stories.

This interpretation will cause fewer problems for Roman Catholic believers than for Protestants. Surely Mary also appears to her worshippers? But Mary didn't rise from the dead. Appearances are no proof of resurrection, and resurrection is not a condition of appearances.

7. *The ascension. Christ the king*

'Ascended into heaven, sits at the right hand of God, the Father Almighty, from whence he shall come to judge the living and the dead.' 'Come,' says the Creed, and in so doing follows the New Testament; it doesn't use the traditional 'come again' terminology. 'Come' implies that he must first have gone up. That's right; that's also how one evangelist describes Jesus' disappearance from the earth: it was an ascension, vividly related by Luke both in his Gospel and in the Acts of the Apostles. It's clear that the story has to fill a gap: someone cannot be above, sitting at the right hand of God, unless he has first ascended to heaven.

Did it really happen? Now that 'sitting at the right hand of God' is figurative language; God is depicted as an ancient ruler who gathers his vassals on his right hand and on his left. The most powerful of them, the one who carries out his will, comes to sit at this right hand. But God has no right hand, or rather, he has one only in the way in which we (sometimes) speak of him. It's a metaphor, really a metaphor within the field of metaphors which express belief in God. Things *aren't* as we say; we say only that what we want to assert is *like* this. And the ascension itself? I think that few people, even few Christians, believe that it 'really happened'.

8. *From whence he shall come. The messianic longing*

Are you the one who is to come? According to Matthew's version (11.2–15), that's a question which John the Baptist put to Jesus. There is an attractive entitled *He That Cometh*, a description of 'Messiah'. Evidently John wasn't certain whether Jesus was the great bringer of salvation for whom the world was waiting. It was right for him to be uncertain: too much was happening that he couldn't place. Perhaps, too, his own fate (he was put in prison by king Herod, where he was later beheaded) played a role here. Jesus' answer isn't either yes or no; he simply points to what he is engaged in doing. John himself must make out what Jesus means by this. Jesus had his reasons for answering in this way: according to the evangelists, it was alien to Jesus to scatter the title Messiah around. Was he himself uncertain about it?

Be that as it may, Christianity was all the more certain: without hesitation it identified Jesus with the one who was to come. The problem of the statement that the son of man will come on the clouds of heaven to judge the living and the dead – as the Creed says – was resolved by reading the 'come' as 'come again'. That isn't misleading once one sees what lies behind it, but it does change the perspective. We live after the coming of the redeemer, still in the uncompleted time to come: we still await the new heaven and the new earth. But in the present God's salvation can already be enjoyed as grace, distributed by the church. The consummation (the stereotyped term for the completion of the future) is still to come; it lies beyond death and the tomb. The future is heaven, where the blessed will be with God, and a longing for the future is the longing to get to heaven.

I have put the verbs in the present tense, since for centuries and centuries this has been the classic Christian view, and it is still what many Christians believe. Theology spoke about it under the heading of 'the last things', down to the middle of the twentieth century. Like an avalanche, since the 1960s there has been a messianic longing for a future here on earth beyond Christianity, at least Western Christianity. 'He who is to come' isn't yet here but must be coming. I remember a service in a church in Amsterdam where I heard the congregation sing

'One day the great summer will come'. The great summer! I can still remember the shivers that ran down my back, so emotional, from the depths of the heart, was the singing of that song by the assembled Christians: faith in the future that the world could depend on. Now the tidal wave has passed by, the messianic storm has begun to subside, the eschatologizing of the Christian tradition is again a thing of the past. To the sorrow of some and to the delight of others, but that's how it is.

That's logical. It can hardly be otherwise. Messianic longing is unfulfilled longing, and must remain unfulfilled, otherwise it's no longer longing. 'Is that kingdom of yours still coming?' isn't a miss but a direct hit. There will be something like an advent expectation until the end of the world.

In other words, messianic expectation is a primal human fact, not typically Christian – the Jewish religion already knew it before Christianity appeared. But the Jews don't have a monopoly of it either: it appears in many cultures, to the present day. That doesn't make it any the less; it simply says that the messianic longing, the longing for a 'whole world', has been one form, one format, one of the many forms of Christian faith. It has made Christianity (also) into a religion of hope, with Jesus as the bringer of eschatological salvation, and the kingdom of God as the great Future. A couple of further notes need to be added.

1. The content given to the great Future is always taken from the present. That includes the Christian content for the kingdom of God; it cannot be otherwise. And how do we get the material for this content? It is contributed by our longings, which betray our preoccupations, our ideas about salvation (= what human beings cannot give themselves). And how are these longings then born? From experiences of the unfulfilled, of emptiness, of misery, of suffering, of burdens with which people cannot bear by themselves.

2. We have lost the world of ideas in which Jesus is fashioned as bringer of salvation, his coming on the clouds of heaven to judge the living and the dead, and thus to make straight all that is crooked on earth. We find it impossible to see this any longer as prediction, as a literal future, as a prognosis of the course of history. This means that the kingdom of God is a utopia, which doesn't become reality, and we mustn't try to make it that if we don't want to claim victims. Utopias are there to be kept alive and to summon us to deal critically with the existing world, and not say that what is crooked is straight.

3. Utopia can be regarded as a promise which will be fulfilled one day. But in my view that's as much a mistake as to want to make it a reality.

It's to show people a future for people in which they will never share, a future which is infinitely distant, as infinite as God is infinite. Just think for a moment about the billions of people who have died before 'the coming of the Lord' and had no other future than death. Isn't Christian faith aware of this? Have the dead missed the boat? Are they sunk, promises and all? However unfortunate the terminology may be (flesh and blood will never inherit the kingdom of God), that is what the Creed was thinking about with the 'resurrection of the body'.

9. To judge the living and the dead

We must also say good-bye to the last judgment, so vividly described in Matthew 25: the sheep on the right hand and the goats on the left. It isn't bad, the idea is the picture and the picture is the packaging of a vision, a faith. We can try to peel that off the idea, and once we've done that, we can see whether we can still do anything with it today. These two steps, peeling off and seeing what we can do, are always necessary.

To begin with, preaching the last judgment is rather different from announcing 'hell and damnation'. On every side one can still hear that this kind of preaching is a trump card. But people who claim that haven't darkened a church door in ages. That time is long past, and no one would want it back.

What is the last judgment, then? That's very easy to say without lapsing into that alien, apocalyptic image of the 'clouds of heaven' on which the judge will appear. In the version of Jesus' speech that Matthew gives, the judge of the universe doesn't even need to come, he's already there. He looks at us in the poor, the oppressed, the prisoners, the sick, the homeless, and we look him straight in the eye. Are the hungry given something to eat, the thirsty something to drink, and strangers a home? 'Inasmuch as you have done this to one of these the least of my brothers you have done it to me' (v.40). We encounter the criterion by which he judges us every day; the judge clothes himself in it. So fortunately we can already know today where we are: no one need wait in anxious tension for what the last judgment will bring.

But there is more to be said. The last judgment, the *Dies Irae* (day of wrath), is a stylization of something that we mustn't want to be rid of; it's the last barrier that we can set up against the belief that injustice always wins in our world. If there is no last judgment, the world's history must be the world's judgment, but it isn't that. To put it more strongly, as the world's judgment, the world's history would be the greatest injustice that we could imagine. 'The spider spins its web to catch the fly, the big ones go through and the little ones die' – that's what the world's history as the world's judgment shows. The executioner gets off scot-free and his victim is left behind for ever. No, it doesn't seem to me – or to anyone else – that justice prevails in the world. 'There is no justice,' complained an old black man when the death of Diana was announced. Whether this was the best occasion to say that is a matter for discussion, but 'no justice' is all too true. So the Last Judgment must remain, simply for that reason.

One more aspect: the idea of judgment belongs with the messianic salvation for which people long. Surely things must be put right? That means that Lazarus must be raised up, the rich man punished, not because he was rich (in the Old Testament, riches are even regarded as a blessing from God) but because he doesn't see the poor man lying on his doorstep. *Dies Irae* is a final settlement, the day of reckoning in the kingdom of God.

Judgment as retribution? Certainly. That's part of putting straight what is crooked. The murderer gets ten years; those close to the victim a life sentence. That conflicts with a sense of justice, and an inability (and a refusal) to accept this is the opposite of primitive. We cannot apply 'an eye for an eye and a tooth for a tooth', because for a long time this hasn't been as clear as we would want. Moreover the principle presupposes malicious action, harming someone 'with a raised hand', and when is that the case? All the same, the death penalty may be unrealistic in practice, be open to abuse, but it mustn't be abolished. Least of all on Christian grounds. It is too foolish for words that one person can kill another with malice aforethought and that we may not then take from the murderer the life that he took from another because we think that a bad thing, or lacking in Christian love of neighbour. Christians aren't soft.

Dies Irae? Even more clearly than in the previous section, here we have a utopia which we ourselves may not and cannot ever cope with. Not a messianic overthrow of the high-ups – in the name of Jesus –, since that becomes murder and killing, of which babies and the poor become the chief victims. *Dies Irae* = 'Vengeance is mine'. That is said in the Old Testament, the Jewish picture of God (Deuteronomy 32.35), and the Christian picture repeats it (Romans 12.19). I can't stop hoping this when I think of my murdered nephew, not one of the six million humiliated and murdered Jews, but still one of the many millions who were killed like flies on the wall.

But we put this beyond the horizon of time; that's what we mean by 'Vengeance is mine!' Like the kingdom of God, which is also beyond the horizon. Like all the other things that we cannot achieve or cannot perform by ourselves. Beyond the horizon: that's what we call the eschaton, beyond everything, no longer our business. Beyond the horizon all our tears will be wiped away. If not there, then nowhere.

16

The Christian festivals

1. *Holy times as festivals of Jesus*

The great festivals of the Christian church, Christmas, Good Friday and Easter, are festivals of Jesus. Pentecost has a different theme, but Christians aren't quite sure what to make of it. There are a few others on the liturgical calendar, but these have never led to festivals with two (sometimes three) days' holiday. In addition, the Roman Catholic Church has its feasts of Mary, which have Mary as a theme but also Jesus, in so far as Mary is venerated as Mother of God. This concentration on Jesus is typically Christian. From the start religious festivals are usually about the observance of pre-Christian holy times, ritual celebrations of the year with its changing seasons. The Christian church made them 'commemorations' and thus gave them a post-pagan attraction. But nature is stronger than doctrine. Whatever efforts conservative Christians may make ('Keep Christ in Christmas'), in practice the festivals are and remain ritually stylized markers in the years.

1. The times at which the festivals of Jesus fall bear no relation to Jesus as a historical person. Christmas is related to the festival of light, the celebration of the solstice, a cyclical feast of nature celebrated by the peoples of northern Europe, though the cultures around the Mediterranean also joined in. Christianity commandeered the festival and domesticated it as Christmas. The other Jesus festivals are parallels to the Jewish days of celebration: the Jews also know the Day of Atonement (Good Friday for Christians), Easter and Pentecost, so the church has also Christianized Jewish festivals.

2. And what about the practices? The festivals of Jesus have recaptured their origin as Christian offshoots, related to their pagan stem; they have become folkloristic offshoots of Christianity. Not that there's anything wrong with that, but we must take note of it and moreover be content with it. We are Christians, but Christianity too is a religion, and can only express itself in religious terms, and for that we need space and time, and also holy times. The festivals are expressions of emotions

which we cannot otherwise express in church, a concession to the ritual needs of believers. Just as candles burn before the Blessed Virgin – I don't believe in the blessed Virgin, but I don't let any opportunity pass of lighting a candle to her.

3. Is the Christian element lost in the folkloristic rituals of holy times (above all Christmas)? Of course not; and I shall come to this shortly. But as festivals of Jesus they too aren't everything, What I would want to do is turn them back a bit towards Jesus as a metaphor of God. That would protect them from getting submerged in folklore.

2. Christmas as a child's festival for adults

'Today we're celebrate the birthday of the Lord Jesus, so let's sing Happy Birthday to You,' said the teacher. 'It's also Walter's birthday, so let's also sing Happy Birthday to him.'

I read that in an American paper and couldn't quite make out whether the paper thought that this was a scoop or a send-up. Be this as it may, teacher is mixing things up: the stories about Jesus are a stylization of Jesus' life to that of the Christ of the scriptures (who in turn developed into the church's Christ). They belong in quite a different sector from what 'really happened'. The penalty for this (the zeal to make it look as if everything really happened) is that Walter and Jesus aren't very different from one another: both get 'Happy birthday to You'. Does that help Walter to understand better who Jesus was?

What the teacher did is in my view an illustration of the way in which we all celebrate Christmas: for a couple of weeks we act as though it really happened like that. Except that as adults we know better. The stories are stories for children, and belief in them is childish belief; Christmas is a children's festival, and if for grown-ups there is more to it than sociability and 'family feeling', that is because they can easily put themselves into the world of children's feelings. And that's a good thing, I would add. But it doesn't alter the fact that this childishness doesn't turn the stories into stories about what 'really happened'. As long as her flock are still small, teacher has to leave that open. Children don't ask about it, and why drive them out of their children's world? The stories are legends, they play their role in giving content to children's faith, though the grown-ups also join in vigorously.

Do I want to get rid of this? Not at all, but I also don't want to make it more than it is: Christmas is Christian folklore. Jesus isn't born every year in the manger, he doesn't descend from heaven every year; the shepherds weren't shepherds; the choir of angels exists in the pious

imagination of the narrator, and the three kings weren't kings but
magicians, who presumably have more to do with pious imagination
than with history. I'm just mentioning a few things off the top of my
head; those who look through the church paper around Christmas, read
the meditations and listen to the sermons, can fill it out as they want.
It's all very nice, and moreover there are a great many good elaborations
and comments in some songs or stories, so what is there against celebrating at Christmas and in this dark time bathing ourselves with
warmth, with piety and with stories which give meaning?

Nothing. There is nothing to be ashamed of in folklore, or in
Christian folklore. A clog dance is a cheerful sight; it's part of our
culture. But we don't wear clogs any more; there's no need to point that
out. It's the same thing with the Christmas stories: they belong with the
festival of Christmas, but they don't say anything, although Christmas
is also regarded as a day of remembrance that we see as historical truth.
The past was very different. If the scholars are right, then Jesus was
probably born in 4 BC, not two thousand years before the new millennium. The date of his birth is completely unknown to us: as I've said,
25 December is related to existing pagan winter festivals. So Christmas
is folklore, or rather, a popular Western European festival. One doesn't
need to be a Christian to take part in it; in fact in the Netherlands many
Muslims join in celebrating it, and it's on the calendar even in Japan and
China.

3. A deeper meaning

As long as one is ashamed of the folklore associated with Christmas,
one cannot talk of a deeper meaning. That always ends up in sermons
against the good food, against the cosy family atmosphere, against
Christmas presents and so on. When I was a minister, I myself preached
against the excesses. I had read a sermon by Kai Munk (a Danish
minister whom I have already quoted) in which he lectured his parish-
ioners fiercely about on the traditional Christmas dish of the region. His
sermon ended: 'I hope that your Christmas goose this evening is taste-
less! Amen.' I thought that splendid, and worth repeating. That was
how it should be. But a quite elderly elder made me see reason: 'you
mustn't use the whip on them', was his comment. I haven't forgotten.
The whip is easy moralism, but it doesn't help anyone. No whip at
Christmas; that isn't the deeper meaning that Christianity has in mind.
So what is it?

For an answer let's take up the symbolism of light, which in the end is the ground on which Christmas came to blossom. At the darkest time of the year we have a hunger for light; people are ready for, say, festive lights on the Christmas tree, candles on the table. I don't see how one could have a better moment for talking about why Christians represent Jesus as the light of the world. Why him and not, for example, Muhammad? What is light, then? It is said that believers have seen the light. Can they explain to one another what they've seen? If 'believing' isn't to be idle chatter, a Christian must be able to explain that to a Muslim. And also practise it.

A second way in is Advent, assigned by Christianity to the four Sundays before Christmas. Advent touches on the theme of the messianic longing, the hope of another world (advent means both the expectation and the coming of . . .). Christianity deals ambiguously with this hope. It keeps it alive – as hope – through the four Sundays of Advent, but it celebrates the fulfilment at Christmas. First we have to behave for four weeks as though Jesus hadn't yet come, and we hear sermons on Isaiah 9.1: 'The people that walked in darkness shall see a great light.' And then suddenly with Christmas the great light comes and we needn't wait any longer: God has visited his people (Luke 1.68).

We can play at that, but in that case we need a couple of explanations. First, the people whom God visits is the Jewish people: read carefully what is there, and God is the God of the Jewish picture. Christianity very easily goes too far, and in no time commandeers God and his promises for the Christian church; it dissolves Advent into Christmas (what is there still to be expected if the long-awaited one has already come?) and pays the penalty by losing the messianic longing. We should celebrate Christmas far more in the style of Advent, as an unleashing of the Advent feeling, instead of as its fulfilment.

One gain here would be that our Christianity would become rather less triumphalist. Christians aren't sufficiently aware of how much they offend Jews with their Christmas fanfares, and how little reason they have for them. Our world seems very much unredeemed. That must be a painful experience for Christians, given their triumphalist faith. Don't they ever secretly think, 'Are you he who is to come, or should we look for another?'

Light and messianic longing determine the deeper significance. It isn't my intention – in keeping with the tenor of this book – to lay down what can and cannot be done here. Let a thousand Christmas candles blossom, but know that Christmas thoughts and lights on the tree, good food and company form an complex mixture of nostalgia, of illusion, of longing for another world, a concern to transcend the sense of 'is that all there is?' That we also see all these longings and needs once again clothed with motifs from the Christian tradition means that in the folk-lore of Christmas a fundamental problem of human existence – or one of them – and of the Christian faith tradition make contact.

We can't just tell one another that God is the light that lightens us, far less that Jesus is the bearer of light. But we could perform these roles ourselves. All Christian festivals are stimuli for the doing of 'good works'. For example, the celebration of Christmas gives us more scope for doing something for those for whom there is no room at the inn. If grown-ups don't forget that, they can happily leave the rest to the children and their own childlike feelings.

4. *How do I tell it to my children? Childlike faith and adults*

The traditional Christmas celebration brings the temptation of present-ing children's belief as true faith. But that would be a mistake. Children grow up, they grow out of their childhood, perhaps to their sorrow; sadly they don't believe as they used to. Sadly? Grown-ups are more complicated; adult faith moves in the frontier territory between truth and illusion, between faith and doubt. But that's not fortuitous, far less something to be ashamed of; on the contrary, it's a sign that faith functions. Faith is exposed to life as a roll of film is exposed to the light: if there is something on it, what then? Parents, in my experience, don't think that it's anything that they can present to their children. But it could be that these children are better off with somewhat shaky cer-tainties than with the cast-iron assurances of pure doctrine.

Doesn't it then prove difficult to present to one's children things about which one is uncertain oneself? As long as fathers and mothers think that they're wrong, that they really should know better, and that uncertainty must be counted as a failing in faith, they will find any con-versation with children difficult or evasive. But things can be different.

Now that we're talking about it, let me try to make this clear in con-nection with the telling of the biblical Christmas stories. Of course we tell these. Think of your own experiences when you were small. A touch of imagination (there are some very good children's stories) makes it possible to be vivid. For children a crib is tremendous, only surpassed by the chance to have a role in the nativity play: Mary, a shepherd or if need be the donkey. So tell them, freely.

1. But the Christmas stories should be told in such a way that the children can drop them again; they shouldn't be dotted with doctrinal statements, and shouldn't suggest that all this really happened (to assert

the opposite is of course just as dogmatic). Just wait until the children begin to ask questions themselves. Then the time of 'enlightenment' begins. Without that, things won't work and Jesus will share the fate of Santa Claus. If he doesn't exist – and every child hears this at some time – at least for a moment the child's world collapses. I wouldn't want to disenchant all Christian children who ask in an anxious voice, 'Then didn't Jesus exist either?' Of course the opposite can just as well happen. At college I had a student who would have nothing of 'enlightenment'. She had come to the conclusion that Jesus belonged with the Santa Claus of her childhood, and when I tried to make it clear to her that this was stepping outside the Christian faith, she was deeply disappointed and even cross: 'You're destroying my faith.'

2. Parents mustn't be afraid of giving enlightenment. Growing children ask precisely the questions that we had always wanted to ask but hadn't dared to, either of ourselves or of others. The stories exalt Jesus because he was so important for the story-tellers. That's something that adolescents understand very well (at least if they're interested). To exalt means that not everything needs to have happened in the way that the stories would have us believe; some things didn't happen at all, but in a manner of speaking they could have. That often occurs when we want to emphasize what we see in someone. I can't imagine that the best growing adolescent wouldn't then ask, 'But what do you see in him then?' Then the conversation starts rolling and the only person who is afraid is the mother (or father), because they haven't learned to talk about doctrine like this.

3. So 'How to I tell my children?' isn't 'How do I teach them church doctrine or Christian dogmatics?'. Children get that at school or at catechesis. What they want to hear is: what do my father and mother believe? And they don't expect the triumphant, firm language of faith that parents think that they must offer (which of course doesn't work); they're more curious about what an adult approach to the tradition of faith implies.

They should hear that. Adult faith teaches us to drop some traditional ideas and to keep others, and sometimes there is no answer as why one keeps some and not others. That's all right: not everything has an answer and I'm always suspicious of those who have an answer to everything.

4. Children unlearn what we've first taught them. With care and wisdom, but they still do. The whole mass of children's belief – Jesus can do everything; when we die we go to heaven; safe in Jesus' arms – all that is part of childhood. 'Safe in Jesus' arms' becomes meaningless;

'Jesus can do anything' is quickly devoured by the tooth of time, and the feeling that nothing can happen to us melts like snow in the sun. An adult faith has learned differently. It's adhered to for other reasons than considerations of security.

5. What children keep of this must sink in of its own accord; otherwise it becomes indoctrination, and parents shouldn't want that. Of course it's an evil which brings its own punishment.

5. 'Weep not for me.' Good Friday and Easter

No festival is without festivity, which usually consists of good food and drink, inviting the family, friends and acquaintances. Not Good Friday. As I see it, that's a Christian festival without all the eating and drinking. It's a day of reflection, penitence, remembering that 'he must stand there for me'. The whole of the *St Matthew Passion* can be performed and listened to, one of the best ways of showing what the day means: commemorating the suffering and death of Jesus.

But we usually do that in the wrong way: we bewail Jesus, sit at his tomb with tears and weep over the saviour. However, Jesus says something different. He says, 'Weep not for me, but for yourselves and your children' (Luke 23.28). 'O man, bewail thy grievous sin.' Christians must do that on this day, not try to play how bad it was for Jesus (he failed, was crucified and went through hell), but bewail their own sins. Moreover that is only half the ritual; the other half is celebrating liberation, the taking away of all that has clung inside us like dirt. The two elements belong together, as do Good Friday and Easter – but we shall be coming to that.

On Good Friday in the Netherlands Christians used to go to church in the evening to celebrate the eucharist. That was an old Protestant custom which was abolished in the course of this century. A pity. Just as it's a pity to celebrate the eucharist every Sunday. It's an imitation of the Roman Catholic sacramental tradition, including the doctrinal background to it, adopted by Catholicizing Protestant theologians and introduced into their churches as an attempt to liven them up: we too have symbols and rituals. But what Rome can do, Protestants cannot. It waters down our special characteristic: a festival celebrated every day is no longer a festival.

So we celebrate Good Friday once a year, to confess our sins and celebrate their covering by the Most High: he covers them by putting his hand in front of his eyes. The celebration needs to be modelled on Judaism: three days (at least) holiday. In some Protestant countries

(Scandinavia), Good Friday is a quiet day, not a working day. I like that, not because I want imitation, a kind of Good Week in which we re-enact Jesus' life and death, but because there must be one moment in the year, one day, when time stands still, when we bow before God, confess our sins and ask him for forgiveness. That day is Good Friday.

And Easter is the second part of the festival, the rebirth, the day of joy, to celebrate as 'it can't be true that it's all up with us'. That's what we mean by 'believing' at Easter.

Easter, I think, will be the only Christian festival to withstand becoming folk-lore or disappearing. Folklore doesn't succeed here: there's no game with a tomb here, but greenery is brought, spring is enjoyed and there is good eating: all to taste that the Lord is good.

6. Pentecost

Most Christians can't make much of the feast of Pentecost, the feast of the outpouring of the Holy Spirit. That's because although the holy Trinity is celebrated as the deepest mystery of the Christian faith, they can't understand it. Pentecost is a feast of the Trinity, and the Sunday after Pentecost is with good reason called Trinity Sunday. Pentecost made the image of God complete. Is that true?

On the day that the Holy Spirit is poured out (Acts 2 describes the event at length), all were filled with the Holy Spirit, tongues as of fire appeared above their heads, and when they began to speak, each of the bystanders heard them speak in their own tongue. I say that somewhat cautiously, since long disputes arose over the question whether this was a speaking miracle or a healing miracle. However it's meant, the outpouring of the holy Spirit is described to us as a religious event with spectacular features. The charismatic movements, of earlier times and of today, refer back to it and think that the church always needs to look like that; the church is where the Spirit is, and Spirit = gifts of the Spirit, charisma. Whether that is the case is something we shall return to in due course. First the question what Acts 2 is really about.

(a) The Holy Spirit is a representative of Jesus. The evangelist John (who wrote so much later than the three Synoptic Gospels) already talks about that with a clear view of the future. Jesus will not always be there. He is returning to the Father, so the direct relationship with him is broken, but the Father will send someone else, a comforter, a representative, or whatever one wants to call him (this is all described at length in John 14.15–31). This other is the Holy Spirit whom the Father will send in Jesus' name; he will instruct the disciples in what Jesus said and did. And the early church said that the Holy Spirit is God, completely God: the third person of the holy Trinity.

(*b*) That was going a long way. John makes the Spirit a gift of the Father (14.26); he doesn't go further. Acts 2 doesn't even go that far; we learn that according to Peter the Spirit is a gift of Jesus (vv.2,33). That's how Pentecost has entered history, as the festival on which Christianity remembers that the promise of the Spirit ('what you now see and hear') was fulfilled by Jesus. So indirectly it is to be called a festival of Jesus, in so far as the Spirit occupies the empty place of Jesus; one could almost say that it's a manifestation of Jesus. When the dove descended on him, Jesus is taken over by the Spirit; with Pentecost it is the other way round: Jesus takes over the Spirit.

(*c*) A small discrepancy: in Paul we find an identification of Jesus with the Spirit: Jesus = the Spirit, he says in the second letter to the Corinthians (3.17). In John the Spirit has become rather more independent over against Jesus. He is Jesus' advocate. But that difference needn't cause any problems. Both see Jesus in heaven with God, and both see the Spirit on earth. It is the doctrine of the early church which first makes the Spirit the Third Person of the Trinity: no longer a representative sent by the Father (John), nor Jesus become Spirit (Paul), but the Spirit proceeding from the Father *and* the Son and therefore completely from God. That was going too far, and not only for the Eastern Church (which found the procession from the Father enough); even within the Western Church the carefully developed parallel between Father, Son and Holy Spirit came up against protests. Read Berkhof's *The Christian Faith*.

(*d*) What then? This is how I see it. In the picture that we have of God the creator (taken over from the Jews), God is also presented as Spirit, as creative Spirit. He is already that 'from the beginning', says the picture. In other words, we encounter the Creator not only as fate, as disposer, as maintainer and ruler of our world, with all the riddles, the extremely painful riddles, that go with this, but also as Spirit. That is: God as we *experience* him in our spirit, are *aware* of him as Creator, as the God who gives and creates life. From this perspective the Spirit isn't something new. He doesn't need to be poured out on Pentecost; he was already there as 'the life-giving Spirit'. Also with special gifts. All artists know that every day they experience every day his grace, which comes over them and keeps their creativity alive.

(*e*) My explanation of the Pentecost story is that there is also this creativity in the preaching of Jesus. To proclaim Jesus is to proclaim that God is there not just for the Jews but also for the Gentiles (there is good reason why each person heard Peter speak in his own language). God's creativity nestles in the preaching of Jesus. 'The Lord *is* the Spirit' or 'the Lord *sends* the Spirit'; there isn't much difference. The outpouring of the Holy Spirit on the (Jewish) feast of Pentecost is to be read as a kind of legitimation of what the apostles began: preaching the God of Israel to the Gentiles, and thus a legitimation of the Christian faith.

(*f*) *If* it is, does that legitimate the Christian faith. That remains to be seen. The charismatic movements say, 'Surely; that's clear? Look at us, at the gifts of the Spirit which burst out among us like buds in the spring! Speaking in tongues, healings through prayer, trances – if that isn't a proof of Spirit and power, what is?' Lessing could have put it like that. I don't want to do down the joy which charismatic Christians experience in their expressions of faith. But they still have to be proved right. Celebrate trust in your own faith: we can't go further than that at Pentecost.

V

The Legacy

'Now the Lord is the Spirit, and where the Spirit of the Lord is, there is freedom'

(Paul, in I Corinthians 3.17)

17

A coatstand christology for whoever wants to put on God

1. *The threefold ministry*

What Jesus can the Christian church present today? That cannot be established by decree, not even by church decree, in terms of a doctrinal precept. There must be doctrine in some form, the tradition of faith, what we 'hear said'. But what we do with it is a matter for 'us'. Without people who do something with it, the tradition itself is written off as dead. So I prefer a more or less empirical answer. What do people see in Jesus today, what influence do they say that he has on their lives and why? So it is not so much what we *must* believe (we know that very well) but what he says to us: that kind of christology, a functional christology. To make it quite clear, that isn't the same thing as the actual meaning of Jesus in someone's life. People can confess with their lips that Jesus rules their life and meanwhile allow themselves to be led by other powers: that can happen even without there being bad faith. But that is an ambiguity which is part of our public statements, and isn't confined to religion and morality. So I shall leave that aside.

I shall not be completely empirical; if I were, I would have to make a sociological investigation of the role of Jesus in human consciousness. I can't do that, and indeed it seems to me to be impossible, Moreover it would get us no further than a sum total of roles which Jesus plays in people's lives (in other words their views), and there are too many of these to mention. I need only recall the wild christologies, and rather closer to home the different practices of Jesus piety which I evaluated in a previous chapter, including forms of christology, views of Jesus. Counting heads gets us nowhere, or at best to a christology which is so varied as to be out of control. So there is a need for some kind of norm; however, this must be something which (*a*) remains as close as possible to the tradition of faith, and (*b*) at the same time has such wide boundaries that none of those who 'have a thing about Jesus' need feel excluded.

I find such a christology in the doctrine of the threefold ministry of Jesus, 'ministry' being regarded as appointment by God. That seems to me to be an appropriate garment for christology as I mean it, full enough to cover a good deal, but still a garment. Here I'm making a choice in a well-known dilemma, namely that between the person and the work of Jesus. In all the books of dogmatics there is an detailed account of this double approach, and it usually ends with the statement that the two cannot be separated. Jesus' work is the main thing, but what makes his work so important is that he was *this* person, the Son of God, who performed it. And in addition, this unity of person and work is very carefully separated, first by an extended account of the constitution of Jesus Christ, his make-up of two natures in one person, and then a discussion of his saving work. So I'm not going to adopt this approach. This extensive interest in the person is necessary to safeguard God-on-earth, but I've rejected that dogma as an exaggerated form of worship. I see the work of Jesus as the motive force of christology. To summarize this under the heading of three ministries has old credentials. We already find references to it in the church fathers. But it was the Reformation theologians, especially Calvin, who first made a point of it, made it a motive force, as I called it. They didn't do away with the dogma of God-on-earth, but alongside it – to a greater degree than previous theologians – they set an extensive account of the work of Jesus. As if they had their suspicions.

This approach has the enormous advantage of leaving Jesus – as a person – in the past: it takes him up as the special servant of God who lived at a particular time. The speculations about God on earth can be left behind. In this christology Jesus cannot vie with God or cast him from the throne. God doesn't get a rival in Jesus, while the key position which Jesus occupies in Christianity isn't made any the less.

By 'prophet' I think of Jesus as preacher, as guru, as leader in life and faith. What he did or didn't say – see the section on Jesus-authentic sayings – remains a troublesome but ultimately historical question. With 'priest' we no longer stand before the preacher but before the Jesus who is preached or – if one thinks in more Roman Catholic terms – the Jesus of the sacrament. And king? The title is derived from the kingdom of God which is preached by Jesus. The church father Origen said that Jesus himself is the kingdom. Wrongly, as we have already seen. I shall be interpreting 'king' as Jesus-for-the-whole-of-humankind, and not as ruler (or as obtrusive servant, which is the same thing), but as the one who unites humankind by abolishing ethnic limitations: Jesus as a multicultural promise.

2. *Jesus as our prophet (i) Leader in living and dying*

Before Jesus was venerated as priest, king, Son of God, God-on-earth, Lord, or whatever, people saw him as a prophet. That is his first and oldest honorific title, as Edward Schillebeeckx rightly points out. We must remember here that these first hearers (and worshippers) were Jews, brought up with Jesus in the Jewish faith. What Jesus had to say, his wisdom, his criticism of the perception of religious obligations, of people's dealings with one another, of their lack of faith and mercy, his perspectives on the morrow, his ideas about God – all that is utterly Jewish, Jewish wisdom: he taught the people like a rabbi. That we also think today that this is Christian wisdom has partly to do with the way in which his words have been Christianized, and it partly means that the Christian truth is seasoned with Jewish religion to a greater degree than the church would have liked.

Let me give two examples of this religion ('the religion of Christ' that I was speaking of earlier) before I begin on the doctrinal wisdom, the prophetic attraction of Jesus. First of all the way in which Jesus prays. Also *what* he prays, though we really know nothing of that. Except that we may assume that with the so-called Our Father, Jesus didn't hand on to his disciples words which he himself never said or in fact never used. But leaving aside *what* Jesus prayed, he also says *how* one must pray. Rather differently from what happens in the church. As a small boy I had to go to church, and one already knew in advance that somewhere in the middle (that's how it was) there was what was called 'the long prayer', an hour (or so it seemed). During it, one kept one's eyes closed while the minister, once he had got going, seemed as if he would never stop. That long prayer in church was a punishment for children. And not much of an invitation to join in oneself.

According to Jesus you must go into an inner room; that means that others have no place there. This is something which takes place between God and you; this isn't coming in front of the footlights, giving oneself airs, a demonstrative gesture to outsiders.

According to the Gospels, Jesus himself practises what he preaches: he goes apart to pray, as we read, for example, in Matthew 14.23. He does that even when he is in great distress and no longer knows whether to flee or to contemplate death (Matthew 26.36–46).

My second example comes from Jesus' death. In Luke's Gospel, hanging on the cross in his last moments, he calls on the name of the Lord (I love that expression). He does so – as Jews were taught to do in the hour of their death – with the prayer from Psalm 31.6, 'Into your hands I commend my spirit'. In this way the moving, disconcerting drama of the betrayal, the crucifixion, the abandonment by God comes to rest. Jesus lives before God's face and he dies before God's face. That is the 'religion of Christ'. He prays in a manner which shows us the way; he dies as I would want to die, commending my spirit into God's hands.

3. *Jesus as our prophet (ii) The Sermon on the Mount*

Love God above all and your neighbour as yourself: if you ask people what Jesus commanded, that's the answer you get. It's all right; for the precise formulation see Matthew 23.34–40 (see also Luke 10.27). Most people don't know that Jesus is quoting the Old Testament (as we call it) here; in Leviticus 19.18 we read precisely the same thing.

But where Jesus' wisdom has also become famous is the so-called Sermon on the Mount, which is to be found in Matthew 5–7 (there is a somewhat weaker version in Luke 6). One needn't be a Christian to be impressed by it. A person like Gandhi (who didn't himself want to be a Christian) couldn't fail to pay Jesus his respects for the Sermon on the Mount; he even used it as an element in the non-violent resistance with which India undermined the colonial (English) authority.

> You have heard that it was said, 'An eye for an eye and a tooth for a tooth.' But I say to you, do not resist one who is evil. But if any one strikes you on the right cheek, turn to him the other also; and if any one would sue you and take your coat, let him have your cloak as well; and if any one forces you to go one mile, go with him two miles. Give to him who begs from you, and do not refuse him who would borrow from you (Matthew 5.38–42).

Christianity has never completely been able to escape the force of this kind of statement (the Sermon on the Mount links a whole series of them together), although in practice it doesn't know what to do with them. It wouldn't be the best thing if one couldn't offer any opposition to someone taking one's clothes. Or if one could no longer swear an oath (see vv.33–37), to bear witness before God that one has spoken the truth. Our fathers (and not only our fathers) were wise enough to say that the Sermon on the Mount wasn't intended for the state but for the church. Law must prevail in the state; the lamb must be protected against the wolf, and as far as possible deceit must be banished. So should the Sermon on the Mount be limited to the church? But even that doesn't seem to work. 'Anyone who looks on a woman to covet her has already committed adultery with her in his heart' (v.28). What are we to do with that? It's all very well to say that Jesus' words betray quite a 'masculine' world: why is only the man addressed and not the woman? But leaving that aside, must we understand that saying as Tolstoy did, and read into it that the best thing for us to do is to avoid sex completely?

Of course Jesus is using figures of speech here. No one need cut off a hand or pluck out an eye (read vv.29–30) to enter the kingdom of God. Why then only the right hand and the right eye? These are figures of speech which are meant to give emphasis to the demand. Albert Schweitzer said that this was an interim ethic. These were such strong demands, incapable of being fulfilled, because Jesus thought in terms of only a brief span of time: the kingdom of God would still come during his lifetime, so how important was this world? Schweitzer may well have been right, but what is impossible to fulfil remains just as impossible to fulfil. Schweitzer's advice was in any case to note the unconditional seriousness which marks the life of a Christian.

Thus this Sermon on the Mount remains enigmatic. It mustn't drive people mad, it mustn't frustrate ordinary life, prevent men looking at women and women looking at men, oaths being sworn where they are necessary and violence being used where the weak have to be protected. But more than that? With his Sermon on the Mount Jesus must for all times remain a disturbing figure. Don't be too pleased with yourself, as if that were the whole story.

4. Jesus as our prophet (iii) The guru

As a prophet Jesus attracts people; it is the ministry with which he inspires, creates a new spirit, wakes people up. Hence all kinds of other names are also good, and sometimes express even better what has made people see him as inspired: master, pioneer, guide, teacher, leader in life, and such like. I shall single out one title which can clarify an aspect which so far hasn't been sufficiently indicated: Jesus as guru.

The word 'guru' simply means teacher, but there is something ambiguous about it in any case. I'm using it as an ambiguous term: a teacher with something extra. Its rise in Western culture is connected with this. Teachers in India are called gurus; the term is really an import. The time when it was introduced can be identified: the end of the 1960s and the beginning of the 1970s, the years when a world of young people developed, rebelling against their own European twice-two-makes-four culture and wanting to replace it with the broad perspective of the imagination.

So the years are dawning in which the gurus are presenting themselves as new authorities, disguised of course as liberators from all that is stuck in a rut, but nevertheless new authorities. They have such a great impact because freedom brings insecurity; for the first time one has a personal say in what must or mustn't happen. By no means everyone dares to accept this personal responsibility, and many people, weary of searching and sighing, fling themselves into the arms of someone who is ready to take over, a guru.

That defines the length and breadth of Jesus as a guru. People can never surrender their own responsibility without losing their own humanity. Not even to Jesus? Certainly not to Jesus. That would rest on a colossal misunderstanding, the misunderstanding that Christian faith takes away people's responsibility. Of course that happens, and people even look for it: 'Let Jesus decide'. But when that happens, the Jesus freaks already have *what* Jesus has decided up their sleeves; there are the small gurus who make use of the authority of the great guru. To use Jesus to deprive people of their responsibility seems to me, to put it bluntly, a misuse of Jesus. In any case it doesn't fit what I understand by Christian faith, or *Jesus* as a leader and teacher. For Jesus' teaching, Jesus as a prophet, makes people more human and not less.

So what? Jesus as our guru – it sounds splendid, at least as enthusiastic as 'Jesus our prophet'; it can serve as a new name for discipleship of Christ. I would even go a stage further: under this name Jesus can be accepted as master without all the by-products which Christian teaching usually associates with discipleship. You needn't be a Christian to follow Jesus as the guru in your life. But a test question remains: am I occupied in throwing away my own responsibility or am I learning from this teacher precisely how I must use it?

5. The priestly character of Jesus

Prophets have been stoned, their death is a vocational death. That's also how Jesus' death can be explained. He even explains it in this way himself when, looking into the future, he speaks of Jerusalem as 'killing the prophets and stoning those who are sent to you' (Matthew 23.37). With Jesus as priest we also come up against Jesus' death, but now not in the sense that he has died as a *victim* of his vocation, as a victim of others, but as a sacrifice *for* others.

If we may believe Albert Schweitzer, the notion that Jesus sacrificed himself, or more strongly that he saw his approaching death as a voluntary sacrifice, is part of the oldest traditions. Even if that cannot (yet) be interpreted in Pauline fashion, it doesn't alter the idea that Jesus died on behalf of others. He offered himself as a sacrifice.

The priestly role of Jesus, his offering of himself as a sacrifice, first of all takes us into the past, to the only thing that we don't ourselves contribute as Christians: the atonement. The inspiration that Jesus evokes as prophet is included, but we've already talked about that topic; he only needs to arouse what is already there. What he has become indispensable for, what we didn't have, is access as non-Jews to the God of the Jews. We wouldn't be Christians had there been no Jesus whom we could put forward as our ritual scapegoat.

Today we see Jesus' priestly function developed widely in sermons and depicted just as widely in the sacrament of the eucharist. There are differences between the traditions in ritual, in presentation, in theological expression, but they unite in referring back to Jesus as the priest who has sacrificed himself, Modern Protestants even tell us that the terminology of the sacrifice that is offered to God is black-stockinged Reformed church terminology, but that's a misunderstanding. The celebration of the eucharist as established by Roman Catholic doctrine at the Fourth Lateran Council (1215), and repeated at Trent (1545–1563), concentrates entirely on the sacrifice. Not only does consecration change bread and wine into the body and blood of Christ, although they preserve their outward appearance (the council called that 'transubstantiation'), but it is equally emphasized that the holy mass must be regarded as a sacrifice made to God. That sacrifice is Jesus.

Thus with Jesus as priest, thoughts unavoidably go back to the past, to his death, which is seen by the Christian church as a sacrifice for sin. But the priestly character of Jesus need not end there. Whatever religion one looks at, a priest is a mediator between God above and the ordinary people dependent on him here below. The priest is the one who is initiated into the rituals that must be performed if there is to be contact between Above and below. Seen in that light, the eucharist can be interpreted without any difficulty as an instrument of the priest, the only one which priests are authorized (by themselves or their cast) to master and control.

A priest is there as a mediator: that brings me to Jesus as 'our priest' in the present, the intercessor who intercedes for us with the Father. What we are to understand by that 'intercession' can be read in detail in the letter to the Hebrews. This is one of the most remarkable books in the New Testament, a kind of sermon, in which there is a constant switch from the priesthood of the Old Testament to Jesus as the real priest, from the sacrifices of Israel to the real sacrifice, Jesus, and all in a very artistic literary form. The readers must have been very erudite, familiar both with Jewish religious customs and the preaching of Christ, to understand what it is sometimes about. Here is a key sentence:

> For Christ has entered, not into a sanctuary made with hands, a copy of the true one, but into heaven itself, now to appear in the presence of God on our behalf (Hebrews 9.24).

The learned author returns to this later and confirms that Christ 'after offering for all times a single sacrifice for sin, sat down at the right hand of God' (10.12). The statement recalls the apostle Paul, who begins from the same image in Romans 8.34:

> It is Christ Jesus who died, yes, who was raised from the dead, who is at the right hand of God, who indeed makes intercession for us.

'Sitting at the right hand of God' clearly includes interceding on our behalf, and must therefore be read as presenting the sinner's plea to God. That is the priestly ministry of Jesus today; with good reason the old Reformed Christians spoke of Jesus as mediator.

We have lost a vivid idea of all this, as of the priest who is the mediator. Just imagine, God on his throne and Jesus standing before it making a plea for sinners as a kind of advocate. That needn't be turned into dogmatics, nor can it be. Hebrews is a long sermon for people who can understand it properly; we don't always grasp what the author says, and we don't know who he wants to convince. From such a letter we learn how people used to describe Jesus' significance; where they were at, what problems they wanted to solve when they set to work. No more than this. Paul makes use of the same metaphor, which is really a metaphor in a metaphor. Jesus isn't exerting pressure on God by interceding for all sinners, as if that were necessary, indeed indispensable. But we below know that we are dependent on mediation, on a mediator. I read that as another name for a communication with God which cannot be taken for granted, a communication by the grace of Christ. Christians remind one another of this when they bring in Jesus as 'their priest'.

Children in Protestant families learned that every prayer has to end with 'for Jesus' sake'. That seems to me to be too much of a good thing. As if otherwise God wouldn't listen to prayers. I'm more in favour of the customary way of ending public prayer in the churches, 'in Jesus' name'. That reminds God of Jesus. Is that necessary? No, but we are reminding ourselves of our weak position before God. Hence our introduction of Jesus as priest.

6. Our king too?

I have difficulty with king, the last office, at least if it is interpreted in the sense of Jesus as ruler. That's not on, however much sympathy and care is used here. In our hymnbooks there are splendid hymns about Jesus' power, about the cross which goes over the world as his banner: 'Jesus shall reign where'er the sun', a hymn which people still sing enthusiastically. But what about that reigning? We've learned to recognize it as triumphalism. It returns in all kinds of familiar ideas.

(*a*) By his own confession, Abraham Kuyper, the Reformed Church leader whom I have already cited frequently, was guided by the saying: 'There is not an inch of our human life over which Christ, who is sovereign of all, does not proclaim "Mine".' Fortunately he didn't put this into practice: for him Christian politics wasn't politics on the basis of the gospel, but politics on Christian principles.

(*b*) In the course of time, Dietrich Bonhoeffer replaced his 'mandates' (guidelines for life which emerge from creation) with what he thought a better idea, the 'rule of Christ'. This is a much more cautious introduction of Jesus into politics and society than Christ the king, but still, to the 'lordless powers' the 'lordship of Christ' is not very different from what the gospel is to the revolution. The claim that underlies this, namely that the Christian church – viz. the church leaders – is better at unmasking the 'lordless powers' than the secular guardians of the constitutional state, cannot be established empirically and theoretically is too much of a good thing.

(*c*) Karl Barth speaks rather more modestly about the 'lordship of Christ' in his *Christian Community and Civil Community*. The Christian community (the church) is held up as a model for the civil community. This isn't a matter of ruling – that much is clear – but Barth does mean that in the church and its structure (and thus in Jesus Christ as its Lord), there is a solution for world politics, indeed a blueprint. Barth was less pretentious in his so-called Tambach Lecture in 1919 (for the experts). Politics must be practised without being 'hyphenated with Christ' (i.e. without the predicate 'Christian) – in other words pragmatically. We would say that we get the criteria from moral principles and not from faith in Jesus.

There are three examples, and the question is: is that what we mean by the kingly office of Christ? I see things rather differently. This name is derived from the vision of the kingdom of God, the Christian utopia of a healed world. The kingly office of Jesus takes this up. The Christian church preaches him as the way to God for non-Jews, for all men and women without differentiation. The healed world is the world without ethnic limitations; everyone belongs to it and no one is excluded. Where that happens, or where things begin to look a bit like that, Jesus is exercising his kingly ministry. This gets its real chance in a multicultural society (ours or any other): what Lucas Grollenberg called Jesus as the way to a peaceable society. Jesus will reign from sunrise to sunset? That can only mean that Christians don't make any distinctions: all people are God's people.

7. *A coatstand with many coats. Norm and variation*

The classical doctrine of the threefold ministry of Jesus Christ seems to me to express a particular happy understanding of the practical significance of Jesus. It keeps Jesus in his historical place – he performs a ministry – but at the same time doesn't shut him up in the past. Ministries are ways of functioning, but that functioning isn't always tied to time and place; it can also happen today. Today is also a reality in which people can see Jesus as their prophet (guru), priest or king.

Moreover there is something liberating about there being three ministries: Christians needn't get at odds with one another if they have a preference. Why shouldn't that be possible? A christology of prophet, priest and king is a doctrine – I don't deny that, but it is a doctrine in which everyone can have their due because it involves minimal regulation without giving up regulation altogether. So it's a coatstand christology, on which many coats can hang. It takes account of the historical investigation of the Gospels, the layers of tradition which are laid bare by the researcher's scalpel. If careful reading of the Gospels demonstrates that the tradition isn't as clear as we imagine, what is there against allowing a variety of conceptions to stand side by side today? Not everything in the Gospels is the same. Why does it have to be in the church?

I see all those Christians for whom Jesus as a historical person is the great personal inspiration latching on to the word 'prophet': from Schleiermacher, for whom Christianity manifests itself a religious awareness but is then filled with the person of Jesus Christ (as I said earlier, he had this from the Herrnhutters), through Albrecht Ritschl, who promised that Jesus would realize the brotherhood of humankind, and Albert Schweitzer, who maintained only the unconditional character of the moral demand, up to and including what in the nineteenth century was called freethinking. In the Reformed circles in which I grew up as a young man people talked about 'Sermon on the Mount Christianity', and I understood that to be sub-standard. But it isn't; the time of judgment is not only past, it needn't be like this. I don't see what is wrong with experiencing Jesus as a leader for personal life.

Conservative Christians are primarily taken with Jesus as priest. They can give their hearts completely to this. Protestants take strength from the proclamation of what has happened: the death of Jesus on the cross, the celebration of Good Friday as the Day of Atonement, Jesus as priest and victim. And also the intercession of Jesus in the present, 'who also prays for us': to be read as 'us poor sinners'. Roman Catholic Christians are devoted to the eucharist. Of course they will experience all kinds of things in it in which Protestants do not share or do not even think of, but what is there against seeing the celebration of the eucharist as the experience of Jesus' priestly ministry?

Above all Christians who are interested in society and politics will feel at home with the Jesus who preached the kingdom of God. No more divisions, no more poor against rich, no more man against woman, slave against free, white against black, no discrimination, no more ethnic restrictions, but righteousness which sweeps down like a flood. Jesus as the hope for the society of human beings and peoples.

Must these three ministries of Jesus all attract a person to the same degree? No, I see that as the great advantage, if the christology of the church continues along these lines. People needn't become judgmental if Jesus doesn't function in other people's lives as he does in theirs. We may choose and share, combine and drop. This is a christology of 'not getting in each other's way'.

I once came across a nice biblical text in a so-called old writer: 'Ephraim shall not envy Judah and Judah shall not be jealous of Ephraim.' The names refer to the two halves into which the kingdom of Israel had split. They shall no longer be rivals, runs the prophecy of salvation (Isaiah 11.13). The official Dutch translation adds a note that this means that the community of Christ shall be united in holy peace. Indeed this is a prophecy of salvation, an almost unbelievable one.

8. 'Why have you been called a Christian?' Discipleship of Christ

Luke reports that in Antioch Jesus' followers were called Christians for the first time (Acts 11.26). Not Jesusites, just as we don't call Muslims Muhammadans. The name Christian has a significance; there's something in it: pledged to nobility. That's clear to friend and enemy. There is a good reason why Christians are so often shown up by outsiders: people had expected something different, just as, on the other hand, Christians sometimes think that they are different from (viz. better than) others. Nevertheless, there must be some sense in using the name, being Christians, wanting to be Christians, and that must have something to do with Jesus Christ.

One can render that 'something' as believing in Jesus Christ, and of course there's nothing wrong with that. But that still makes it possible to limit being a Christian to an intellectual exercise, like this book. But will this book make anyone a Christian? The Heidelberg Catechism, which I quoted in the heading of this section, thinks differently, and I approve. Being a Christian is a way of living; granted, it comes from what we hear said, from a knowledge of Jesus' words and actions, but this knowledge means something if it also motivates a person. I once had an eye-opener in reading Wittgenstein:

> The bicycle is not one of those machines which one can turn without the rest of it moving.

When one wheel moves on this machine, so do the rest. A faith that doesn't move me isn't really part of myself. Paul impresses on us that faith that moves things isn't the whole story. Even if I could move mountains, if I didn't have love, I would be clanging metal, a tinkling cymbal, a ringing bell. And by love he doesn't mean something silky – read I Corinthians 13, from which I'm quoting Paul here. Love bears all things, thinks no evil, doesn't recompense evil with evil; it's something that you can get your teeth into, and not a hazy cloud. Why are you called a Christian? I understand better why some church members sometimes hesitate to call themselves Christians. It involves a way of living which makes more demands than usual (Matthew 5.47).

I sum this up under the heading of discipleship. That isn't imitation, as Thomas à Kempis thought, although he wrote a profound book under this title. It's more inspiration, a flame that begins to burn. The Heidelberg Catechism divides that life into three, parallel to the three ways in which Jesus functions, as prophet, priest and king. Being a

Christian is corresponding to the picture of Christ, the democratization of his functions. It isn't as if Christians could be little Christs, little messiahs who take the suffering of the world on their shoulders (although we do occasionally meet such Christians); it's more something like the glory of the Lord seeping through to his servants.

I shall leave aside how that is described further in the Catechism. It has little basis, and still presupposes a society in which everyone is thought of as Christian. I prefer a style of life in which Christians have something prophetic, priestly and kingly about them, some attraction. Let me give as examples three modern saints in whom I think one can find this style.

I see Martin Luther King as a prophet, as a Christian who had the courage to stand up for justice in an unjust society. Not long after King's death, I had to give a lecture on some subject or another to the preachers of the Christian Reformed church gathered in Grand Rapids. There were questions afterwards. The group was (then) politically very conservative, and one of the questions was about Martin Luther King. 'Was he a messiah?' 'No,' I said, since I knew the gathering. There was loud clapping. When it had finished, I ended my sentence, 'but he followed in his footsteps'. There was a deathly silence. The death of Martin Luther King is a model for the vocational death of a prophet.

I see Bishop Romero as a model of the priestly ministry, interceding with God for human beings, and with the powerful for the weak. Above all a mediator, a mediator between disputing, irreconcilable parties. He paid for this with his death: a priestly man made the sacrifice, the bloody sacrifice of his life.

I know no better example of a royal life than Dietrich Bonhoeffer, whom Rothuizen described as the representative of an aristocratic Christianity. Christians may take over something royal from Jesus; they may live royally and die royally. Those who are not afraid of eternity live like a 'great lord' who even today is above the vicissitudes of fortune: married as if unmarried, possessing as if not possessing, they live in an eschatological style.

The three examples I have mentioned had to pay for their discipleship with death, victims of their lifestyle, of the discipleship of Christ. Modern saints. One has to be murdered (which isn't the same thing as having to be dead) to achieve this status. We know no saints who are without spot or stain. Moreover there are many more whose names we have forgotten or do not even know. But there are people who combine the prophetic, the priestly and the kingly in their lives.

18

The church as the legacy of Jesus

1. Did Jesus want the church?

The Christian church is named after Jesus Christ, but did Jesus really want the church? That's a tricky question. There's a famous saying of Alfred Loisy, 'Jesus preached the kingdom of God and what came was the church,' or words to that effect. Loisy clearly didn't like the church, and one can understand why: his church (the Roman Catholic Church) was busy defending itself against freethinkers like himself (he was excommunicated in 1908) with all the power that it could deploy. Of course the church today isn't the same as the church then; its secular power is less. It has even more self-critical figures within its walls, but they are down in the lower ranks: the higher one gets, the more power there is and a sense that this power needs to be exercised. And at the top, there is the Curia, which won't budge an inch when it comes to institutions like hierarchy and celibacy.

If Jesus wanted a church, did he want this church? Harnack once called it 'the most extreme perversion of the essence of the church' and in my view one cannot deny that he was to some extent right. The mysticism, the symbols of faith, the dedication and the self-sacrifice within the church, are all frustrated, if not nullified, by the institutional scaffolding.

I find it difficult to believe in a church which maintains palaces in Rome, a Vatican City, a pope as representative of Jesus, a court, and cardinals who have themselves addressed and treated as princes. As far as I'm concerned, they needn't live in a stable with a manger as a bed, but they could be a little less ostentatious. 'The king too rich,' Mönnich once wrote. When I think of Rome I can understand the anger of Pablo Neruda about the religion which he encountered in the East:

It was all there, the whole earth
stank to heaven and heavenly
merchandise.

'You make it a robbers' den,' said Jesus after he had overturned the tables of the moneychangers (Matthew 21.12–13). The poor wouldn't need to steal any bread any longer if some Catholic bishops persuaded their church that it should share a little bit, just a little bit, of its wealth with the poor. An address to this effect to the church by them would seem to me more appropriate than a call to the authorities to do something about it.

If I may go even further, I find it difficult to believe in a church which wants power like the power of the lords of this world, as they are called by Jesus; a church which has to have pomp when it wants to demonstrate its importance to the simple; a church whose greatest anxiety is to maintain its status a church which cannot be open to discussion and is always right, since it possesses the presence of the Spirit of God. One can certainly ask people to overlook all these shadow sides by pointing out that the church is a mystery, but I regard that as an evasive manoeuvre by means of which they can leave things as they are.

Must we then believe in it? Of course not. 'This is not a pipe,' wrote Magritte under his drawing of a pipe. Under the picture of the church which I am painting here I write, 'This is not the church, this is not the body of Christ' (which according to its interpretation of itself it should be able to be). But it isn't another form of organization for the Christian faith, so we mustn't go along with it. Moreover not all churches – thank God – have such a stubborn sense of themselves as the church of Rome, so who knows, here and there is still an underground address for the body of Christ.

2. Jesus of Nazareth and the European Jesus

The Christian church is the institutionalized form of religion in Europe. It bears the stamp of Europe; it is the religion of Europe. It isn't the only religion; the mosque is already there and the synagogue is still there (hardly thanks to Europe), but I shall be coming back to that later. The Christian church – and here is the difference – is indigenous to Europe as a religious formation and has had a hand in shaping Europe. Just as the opposite is also true. The church isn't a pure Christianity, above culture, still original; the church is what Europe has made of it, the European version of Christianity, modelled on the government apparatus of the Roman empire, as one power among others. The church (also) made Europe just as Europe made the church.

The protests against this church didn't come out of the blue. Take the mendicant orders in the Middle Ages: their rise speaks volumes. But they offered no solace, or only temporary solace. The Reformation under Luther, Calvin and Zwingli was a similar protest: it produced independent, mature Christians, and forms of being the church which could do without excessive pomp and a demonstration of power. These could replace monarchical leadership with a more democratic church order. A note must be added here: because of the need to be important and not to fall short of the Roman Catholic church in honour, at present Protestantism is keeping an eye on the way in which Rome is a church; it too is trying to play the political game, albeit awkwardly and clumsily, because it overestimates its power. In this way it is trying to compensate for the loss of respect that came with secularization. What no Reformation Christians ever thought possible has even become the order of the day: the Protestant churches are talking about church leaders and grass roots, as if this is right.

The newest form of protest is apparently definitive: a day of reckoning in the form of people staying away, turning their back on the church. It began with Jesus of Nazareth (thus the title of a book which tries to lead people to faith), and where is it ending? With a European Jesus, his cross stylized as a crucifix, and the crucifix in a modern design. The pope goes round the world with such a crucifix, as the TV shows us. Isn't that all right? After all, for the blacks Jesus is black, for the Chinese, Jesus is a saviour with Mongolian features. Surely every culture makes him in its image and likeness? Certainly, that is now his fate. But does he himself still have a contribution to make, and by 'he' I don't mean the church's Christ, the Christ of the council of Chalcedon and afterwards, but Jesus of Nazareth. Not all that much of him is left in the European Jesus.

Back to the subject of this section: the protest against a church which has become a business, the business that controls Jesus. Not only must Jesus have failed to foresee such a church (no one will argue with that); it seems to me certain that he didn't even want it (had he been able to foresee it). That excuses the most radical protest against it, the young who turn their backs on it.

3. *Secularization and a food shortage. Religious 'shopping'*

Travelling in the wake of Europe, the church has landed up in so-called secularization, the growing worldliness of culture, where worldliness implies that people wriggle out of the control of the church. Now and then those who hand on culture rub their eyes: is it possible that they have to be responsible for the way that human beings and the world have to take without the leading strings of the church? As far as the church is concerned, of course not. For the churches, secularization in terms of a loss of influence on public and personal life is tantamount to rampant autonomy, the degeneration of society, and must be changed, come what may. This notion is so deeply rooted in church officials that they pay hardly any attention to the question what underlies this process of secularization. Self-defence comes first.

There is no better guide to what underlies it than practice. The fences weren't yet down, believing was only dimly recognized as a completely voluntary act, or the sheep went in every direction. That means that there was little to eat, no grassy pastures, no surplus, no great bale of hay. In a very short time half of it disappeared, and more than that; it was impossible to get any. Or – another possibility – was the food so pre-digested that many people no longer saw it as food, or at any rate weren't attracted by it? Perhaps one could make something different of this, but I can't. When they finally dared to come to themselves, all too many people didn't find themselves back in church, they couldn't make their own contribution there, and no one took any notice of them as people any longer.

Strangely enough, that's still most true of the Roman Catholic church, which still has a good deal to attract the senses, all the senses and not just the ears, as is the case with the Protestants. The only explanation for this – and I shall be coming back to it – is the hierarchy in office there, the clergy who know it all and thus are allowed to say it; the laity (the word tells the whole story) have to listen.

That's deadly. it produces people who think that the pastor will be able to answer all the difficult questions and then stop thinking for themselves, or put their questions on the back burner. And as soon as the scales fall from their eyes, that's the end of their obedience: I know of no more damaged ex-believers than some of my Roman Catholic friends. They are not only out in the cold but also thought odd; that's the feeling that they're left with.

That's how I explain the paradoxical situation. The churches are empty, church attendance is declining, church buildings are closing and sometimes are being rebuilt as shops and stores, and church people, first disconcerted and anxious about the course of things, are putting their heads in their hands, stunned by the noises that the church has made. Yet at the same time society is teeming with religion and religious entrepreneurs. This seems to me to be a sign of unsatisfied (and perhaps even insatiable) hunger. To put it more precisely: there is a hunger which isn't satisfied by the churches. People don't go shopping for no reason, and the 'marketing' of religion which is so reviled doesn't drop out of thin air. Moreover the charge (made by the churches) that people want a warehouse rather than a church, a supermarket in which the client is king (rather than the clergy), is far removed from the truth.

Wouldn't people stop all this of their own accord if there were no longer any lack of food (see above), space (see above) and quality (see above) in the churches? Why do they go anywhere except for what they find useful? Those who think that improper should ask themselves whether they would go back to a church which ruled rather than served and offered opportunities.

Jürgen Moltmann, a well-known Protestant theologian, regards the marketing, the church as supermarket, as a consequence of the tendency to see faith as a private concern, something for one's personal salvation. If that is legitimate, he argues, everyone chooses from what is on offer and the result is a consumer church. His advice is to make faith political again: Jesus wasn't concerned with something like the church but with the kingdom of God (here we note a faint echo of Loisy), a grasp on the world, the society of all men and women. Moltmann means that well: we don't believe in Jesus in order to go to heaven or to secure salvation in another way. If consumerism means living as if there is no other existence, then whatever else it may be, it isn't Christian. But to make faith in Jesus political isn't a good defence against that; it isn't the end of thinking in terms of the religious market. On the contrary, if you aren't careful, the idea of the market comes out on top: increasing market share by demanding a monopoly for one's message. In my view the only way of having customers and keeping them is to make sure that there are good products in your shop.

4. *The social value of the church*

The European churches are tough, but they can be swept away, brushed aside, absorbed, as a cloud is absorbed in the stratosphere, never to return. 'The gates of hell shall not prevail against it,' says Jesus according to the evangelist Matthew (16.18). That may be true, or one may hope that it's true, but here Jesus wasn't thinking particularly of the European churches (if, as I said, he ever thought about the churches at all). At all events we have to reckon that a Europe without churches is possible. For centuries there was a flourishing Christian church in Asia Minor, a breeding ground of theology and learning and of mystical church fathers. It no longer exists. The churches of North Africa even produced someone like Augustine, but there's no longer a Christian church in North Africa either. Is it now Europe's turn? That would be a great loss, also because the institutional church as a product of the European spirit represents a value which can't just be crossed through with a stroke of the pen.

I shall begin at as low a level as possible, and say that the most obvious value is the social significance of the church. According to some, that's the highest, but I don't believe it. It cannot be disputed that the church's social aspect is an essential part of it, even on the basis of its own interpretation of itself, but that isn't everything, at any rate in terms of what I call 'social' here. Here I have a practical question in view.

It isn't about the church as the conscience of society or – even more – of Europe. The church may once have felt this to be its role, but society has grown up, and has a conscience of its own (or rather consciences in the plural, it should be noted). And the churches have so much egg on their faces, have so often blessed weapons (usually the wrong ones), have enslaved so many souls and broken so many lives, that I don't think that they deserve the honorary title of conscience of the nation. The scant commitment to humanity that we find in the churches – welfare work in poor districts and so on – is the minimum that they could do for their credibility. Thus we must maintain that – at best – they are the useless servant from the Gospel of whom it is said that he did only what he had to do. So there is no place for pretensions, and certainly not for self-congratulation.

By social significance I mean what emigrants experience of the church abroad and countryfolk in the big cities. It represents somewhere to belong, a place of knowing people and being known in a place where only strangers cross your: a village in the big city. The Christian church isn't the only authority that seeks to provide a place for these people to be, but it does that too, and is even well equipped to perform this role. So I'm talking about social contacts: the church as a body that facilitates social contacts.

However many times that may be a subsidiary function of the church, in practice I would venture to say that the more time goes on, the more it becomes a practical main function, the most attractive factor of being the church. Those who don't want to be lost in a sea of strangers, in a world that they can't comprehend, seek the security of a group, usually a little group, since this can be coped with, and people count in it. Hence the flourishing of what so lovelessly are called the sects. They're a home for the homeless. The gates of hell certainly will not prevail against them.

Accordingly – I'm drawing the consequences – if the churches are wise and loving, they will give priority to pastoral care. The individual mustn't just die as an individual but must still believe that among countless millions God still keeps an eye on this one sparrow. The same problem, the same solution: people want to be known by name. Church or pub, they go where they're known.

5. *The symbolic value of the church. Human beings as religious animals*

Why still the church, if one has so many criticisms of it? I'm giving answers, in an ascending series. After the social value of the church I'm moving on to what I would call its symbolic value.

1. There is no town or village in Europe in which one doesn't come upon a church building. The Christian church has a visible side; everyone can see that it exists. Its sheer existence is a 'reminder' that there is something more than what can be counted, measured and weighed. Technology tends to regard all problems technically. So the suggestion is that we have to go there for the solutions to our problems of living. This is a sequel to the time when we thought that all problems were political or social, and enthusiastic politicians were greeted as saviours. But neither technology nor politics turned out as we would have wanted. There are problems which technology does not foresee: one can't spend one's whole life swallowing pills to suppress anxiety about his; one doesn't regain joy by getting an artificial limb; and one doesn't find anything like all one needs to know from digital channels. And while dying may be a universal human phenomenon, it cannot be banished from the world by social or political measures. Much can be done if one tackles it well, but not everything. People sooner or later come up against a blank wall in their experience because people are people and not machines. We have at least to master thinking in terms of twice two is four if we want to survive culturally, but that isn't enough. There's more, and the church building is the first and best reminder of that.

2. The more technical our culture proves, the greater need people seem to have for that 'more', for something that transcends digital thinking. I interpret this need as a need for religion, a religious hunger. Human beings are religious creatures; they can't leave it alone, and guess at this 'more'. But what does it consist of, where do we find the Exalted = what transcends the flatness and uplifts us?

Culturally that's a very important question. What uplifts people, what gives them dignity, raises them out of the mire, is the authority to which they dedicate themselves unconditionally. In my definition that's the hallmark of religion. There is that 'unconditional' element in it. We're all dedicated to the 'good cause', to the beloved, to the club of which we are members, and so on. But unconditional dedication, unconditional trust, is something cannot be surpassed. That makes it a god, and the result can be catastrophe. Think of former Yugoslavia. Here people unconditionally dedicate themselves to nationalism; to the present day that is costing ethnic minorities their lives. Where people have a Christian faith, that cannot happen: the party cannot become a god, nor can the Führer, sex, capital or the economy, nor the church or doctrine, nor even the milieu or the maltreated animal, and so on. God as 'that than which there is nothing greater' preserves a society from unconditional dedication to what is not God, to gods which swallow up human beings.

So it isn't backward to occupy oneself with religion; religion isn't a dispute over 'foolish abstractions'. On the contrary, it's backward to think that it doesn't matter what God people follow.

3. With the word 'God' I'm thinking of what the churches have: a tested picture of God, God's salvation and God's promise which has matured through history: God as the one to whom all human beings are responsible for what they do. I understand the verve with which the churches hurl themselves into social questions; it's because of a weariness about the religious clichés in which God must put in an appearance. But surely this isn't altered by successful slogans from the left wing or the right?

6. *The church and the tradition of faith*

Europe is much indebted to the existing churches (I shall be discussing this at length in the next chapter); it is suffused with Christianity to the smallest capillaries in its circulation system. It may do something in return: see that the churches continue to exist. But of course the churches must first of all see to this themselves by doing what they're there for: handing down the Christian tradition of faith to subsequent generations.

(*a*) To proclaim is to hand down the *meaning* of Jesus for faith in God. This rather solemn word comes from the time when the churches thought that God himself spoke in the Bible and thus also spoke in the words of the preacher when he kept to the Bible. The Second Helvetic Confession of 1566 stated that proclamation of the word of God is the word of God. Some preachers have cheerfully begun from there: it's a great honour to be allowed to be called a servant of the word. But some have also found this a strain. Is preaching the same thing as introducing God speaking? No, said Karl Barth, we have to say that preachers speak the Word of God only 'wherever and whenever it pleases God'. That's nice, but even that's too much; it's still always related to preaching = announcing. We would do better to drop that exaggerated concept of preaching and, in so doing, in the same breath say goodbye to ortho- doxy and magisterium (not doctrine). The church is better as a rainbow church, characterized by the fact that it is the place, gradually the only place, where God is spoken of in so many words. When we all kept talk- ing at once over meals, my mother used to say, 'It's like a Jewish church here.' In my view the church is beginning to look more like such a Jewish church.

(*b*) In the rituals we *play out* Jesus' significance for our faith in God. There is a multitude of rituals – I'm talking about church rituals. Everything that we repeat, from morning prayer up to and including 'a mass of thanksgiving', is a ritual. Rituals are extremely functional; they have something of an advantage over the sermon in that one doesn't need to prick up one's ears each time; one can take part in them with- out overly personal participation. Faith is set free, allowed to freewheel and yet to remain faith. Rituals engage us in role play: we move in them without getting completely caught up in them, since we never coincide one hundred per cent with our role.

Just as the Protestants are better at sermons, so the Roman Catholics are better at rituals. It would therefore be best if we could get the pre- scription for the one from the former and the other from the latter, without synods or bishops putting a stop to it. But that's a detour.

(*c*) Both sermons and rituals can go off course. A sermon can become a ritual, and a ritual can become a jingle. Then it no longer has any significance; there's no longer any sense of the viability of the tradi- tion: people simply hear the well-known sounds and are content. And rituals? Their strength – repetition – is at the same time their weakness. The game goes on, can go on, eternally, like a carousel which continues to go round, even if inward participation has been reduced to zero. Though we shouldn't be surprised that taking part in this can unex- pectedly bring people back to the underlying belief. For that's naturally how things are: behind the rite lies the myth, and behind church rituals is faith.

(*d*) Replacing worn out rituals with new rituals doesn't work. I read somewhere of a preacher who had bits of a tangerine shared among the churchgoers, an action which was meant to illustrate how believers belong together; each one was encouraged to see himself or herself as part of the whole. But this doesn't become a ritual: it doesn't work and people get sticky fingers; they praise the good intention with some embarrassment and a smile, but think, 'Not again, please.' They're right. One doesn't go to church to be submerged in the awkwardnesses of a previous generation, in today's catchwords, or in specialities of the preacher or priest who happens to be passing through, but for an exposition of the meaning of Jesus for belief in God, for the sermon. And for participation in it through rituals.

7. *Church and government. Church asylum as a test case*

In Europe, or at least in what I regard as Europe, church and state are separate: Europe is (also) a normative concept. That's an achievement of modern culture. It has done away with theocracy – God rules, and does so through the clergy as his representatives on earth. Islam is still sighing under the theocratic yoke, but when secularization also becomes established there, certainly in countries with a Western tendency, it will have had its day.

This division doesn't go unchallenged even today. The church of Rome cannot forget the time of the two swords and the underlying theology: the pope bears the spiritual sword and the emperor the worldly sword, but since the spiritual is higher in rank than the worldly, the pope has the last word. That means that the church is above the state.

Not only does the Roman Catholic Church find it difficult to give up this idea; it's still always a temptation for the churches of the Reformation. Luther had a strong doctrine of two kingdoms which stand side by side, each with its own responsibility: the church the spiritual kingdom and the government the worldly kingdom. Calvin was his equal, as we can read in the *Institutes*. Here they do not give secular life *carte blanche* for lawless action, as was once asserted. Both envisage an authority which is Christian at least in name, which can read the Bible independently and can learn from it what the authorities must and must not do. Society still existed in undivided form as the Christian *corpus christianum*.

Since the separation of church and state, the state as Luther and Calvin knew it has been transformed into a constitutional state. That isn't a neutral state: law is based on moral starting points or it isn't law. All members of the state submit to the legal rules which hold there. In a democracy they've even collaborated in making them, even if they interpret them differently from what they had hoped or wanted as voters.

Those who don't want to go back to the time of theocracy (mullahs, priests or preachers regulating affairs on earth) must therefore accept more or less a secular doctrine of two kingdoms. Since Karl Barth, the doctrine of two kingdoms has seemed unfashionable to many Christians. There is only one Word of God, Jesus Christ, in whom all that needs to be said is said. That's an enormous boost for the church (with good reason Barth's view has been given a tremendous reception by church people), since in the last instance it is necessary to go to the church if one wants to know what must be done in the state. Even Christians who don't agree with Karl Barth can hardly get this thought out of their heads. So-called church asylum is a good test case for this.

There are no problems where this issue is a humanitarian one. Everyone must protest against unjust laws, laws made by whites about blacks, to mention one instance, or by men about women; that's necessary. If the implementation of these laws amounts to a grave infringement of human beings, we can appeal to human rights: internationally recognized, but not implemented. If even that doesn't help, then all human beings are personally responsible for deciding whether they want to sabotage the laws which have been made, democratically or not, and accept the punishment imposed for transgressing the law. Your law isn't ours; people can choose, and put themselves outside the law and outside the protection that the law offers. So anything is possible: illegal immigrants can be hidden and even candidates for the death penalty concealed (to mention two instances); above all one can have reasons which sometimes deserve approval and sometimes do not.

What applies to individuals applies just as much to groups, communities or churches. In all conscience they observe the demands that the constitutional state imposes on them, or they do not – again in all conscience. The consequences are precisely as I have described them: the sanctions which the constitutional state imposes on disobedience to the law are accepted. No trouble so far.

But things go awry in the question of church asylum. Why don't the churches break the law and stand up for it, if it's so important for them? Because they don't feel that they're a group or a community but *churches*, and associate with this the privilege of a special position in the constitutional state. They don't have this position. Their longing for it is a relic from the time of the theocratic idea, the state which is led by the church, and this fogs the discussion.

The Christian church may give the government as much social and political advice as it wants. So may the synagogue, the humanist alliance and the mosque. So may the Association of Neonomous Workers of Salvation (if such an organization exists). Any government knows the difference between the bodies which give it advice; they will treat a venerable institution with respect, but that's where it stops. The government doesn't prefer one religious group above the others. For it – apart from what I said about being venerable – all such groups are the same. Churches in their turn don't sit in the seat of government, even if they are all agreed and one no longer needs to ask 'Which church?' Nor must they want to sit there, to seek or maintain such a privileged place.

So? If giving refuge to asylum seekers is a humanitarian demand, every individual, every club, every association, must observe this demand. It isn't the prerogative of the churches to do this. If laws are transgressed here, then no one is exempt from sanctions, not even churches: they sin just as grievously as everyone else, and mustn't ask for exemption or count on it because they are the church.

Does the church (viz. the churches in the plural) then mean anything in society? As far as usefulness to state or society is concerned, its importance is almost nil. That must continue to be the case if the Christian religion isn't once again and for the umpteenth time to get caught up in the tug-of-war between left-wing and right-wing politics. One can score successes with religion, but church leaders mustn't want to. Religion is a separate province in the human heart, as Schleiermacher pointed out: not morality, not philosophy, not a means of social or political power, and therefore it falls outside any utilitarian reckoning.

Whether faith and politics are related is quite a different question. Of course they are; to deny that would not only be nonsense, but would also fail to reflect what faith means. Believing as a Christian (to stick to that) involves an attitude towards human beings, the world and culture; it involves rules of humanity, a sense (however one has arrived at it) that God wants some things and not others.

8. The Christian church in 2000 and beyond

It's like moving house: you suddenly see how much rubbish you've accumulated over the course of years, sometimes hidden away in a remote corner and consequently forgotten. And now all at once there it is, a mountain of unused and unusable junk, which you don't want to take to your new home. Despite all the misery it brings, moving house is revealing: you see what is ballast and what isn't.

That's roughly how I see the situation of churches, not necessarily because soon they will be entering a new millennium (we are hyping the year 2000 into something special) but because culture is changing and the churches are engaged in following this change, though at a distance and as slowly as they can. A good deal is going overboard and there is yet more to follow. That's a good thing, although one hears both conservative Christians and intellectual outsiders who want to tie the church to its untenable theories. Those who understand, know that even churches move house, leave aside what is worn out and keep what they don't want to get rid of.

The churches should be more naked, less churches of the clergy, and more churches of men and women. The less the churches can leave behind, the more they will become an institution intent on self-preservation. Here the Roman Catholic Church has already gone a long way, but there is a temptation to every church community which draws on its past reputation and authority. Indeed the dilemma is heart-rending: lose oneself and the world loses the church; save yourself and you lose yourself as a church. Certainly the Christian faith will not survive without being institutionalized. But if there is one institution that mustn't end up in compulsion, that's the church. Why isn't that clearer?

Will churches survive? Although I have no prophetic gifts, I don't doubt that they will be there down the years. However, that isn't the most important question. Nor do I doubt that faith, hope and love will remain, these three. But will we find them in the churches as we know them today, or must we look for them outside? That seems to me to be the issue. The more those in office in the churches are interested in this, the less they can be intent on self-preservation, and the more easily they will fit in with what people accept of the tradition and what they leave out. I am not claiming that people always make a good choice – the *vox populi* is not the *vox dei* – but that an insistence on doctrine will make the churches even emptier than they already are. A new dilemma: no church without doctrine (the tradition of faith), but no church with a doctrine in terms of a magisterium either.

So for both officials and volunteers, to keep alive the church 'where you go on Sunday' is a chore, a difficult chore, that has to be accepted and done. There may be quirks and whims in sermon and ritual; the minister is also an entertainer (the first thing that you mustn't do in church is to be boring) and the priest also performs an act. But they do so as aids to preserve faith: ministers must have something to say, otherwise they may as well pack it in – and priests must have something to share. That is, if church services are to continue! There too I am not certain, or rather, I think that they will remain, that the buildings will prove indispensable for celebrations in which people get out of themselves, but they will be accompanied by other forms of handing on faith. In the 1960s the German sociologist Schelsky coined the term 'ongoing reflection', reflecting on things without making direct choices. We've given far too great a place to the element of choice in the church, in our model of believing. It presupposes an iron certainty and we don't have that. 'Ongoing reflection' can be translated simply as continuing to talk with one another. Forms will develop for that, indeed they already exist. This picks up what Paul Ricoeur says about dogma: it makes one think (which is rather different from saying that it tells us what we must think).

People will continue to believe, but will do so more as an act which is constantly resorted to. Believe, not that God exists – what can you do with such bare faith? – but that God supports, rules, forgives human beings and the world, reconciles them to himself, does not regard the guilty as innocent but offers a new opportunity after each shipwreck, welcomes the little ones, gives strength to the weary, looks after the fearful, welcomes the dying on distant shores: in short, is a hiding place for those who turn to him, now and in the hour of their death.

19

Jesus as the legacy of the church.
Cultural Christianity

1. The church outside the walls

There is more Christianity than what we encounter in the churches. Abraham Kuyper, the father of the present-day Reformed Churches, whom I have quoted often, already thought it necessary to point this out. Alongside the church as an institution, say the church on Sunday with its rituals of preaching and celebration, its disciplines and its limits, he also saw a church which he described as an organism (his term): church people who stand in the midst of culture and take part in this culture as Christians, without having any fuss with their church. This put Kuyper in bad odour with some Christians (the formation of the Christian Reformed Churches is one consequence of this): he was said to attach too much importance to 'the world'. And indeed he did (he coined the expression 'the world also counts'; he meant it well but nevertheless it sounds very arrogant); for him culture too was a gift of God, a sign of what he called God's universal grace.

I shall leave aside here the terminology, the background and the context in which all this can be found in Kuyper, especially the fact that for him the organic church consisted of believers. What I am interested in his evaluation of culture and the notion that this is connected with the Christian church, just as the Christian church is connected with culture. The point that he wants to make is that Christianity isn't exhausted by its ecclesiastical form, and in this chapter I agree with him here, whatever else his vision may prove to contain.

I even want to go a step further than Kuyper and see our Western culture as a unique form of Christianity. Just as the church was (also) formed by European culture (see the previous chapter), so culture in turn developed through the Christian church. It bears the stamp of Christianity, just as – to draw a comparison – the Arab countries bear the stamp of Islam. I myself see the distance between church and culture, between church and 'world', as the churches themselves like to say, as being much less than people usually imagine. To make it a gulf shows a lack of perspective. To indicate the subject of this chapter briefly: in addition to church Christianity I shall also speak of Christianity as a culture or, rather more briefly, of cultural Christianity. That's quite a vague term, but I'm choosing it deliberately. It's a broad heading, which can encompass a great deal.

2. Richard Rothe

Abraham Kuyper's intentions didn't go further than making his own church members less shy of engaging in social and cultural life. Richard Rothe, an extremely interesting theologian from the last century (he died in 1867), went a great deal further. In his view the Christian church has to be seen as a transitional phase in the process of humanization. Human beings appear on earth as natural beings, but they must become cultural beings, and that is possible only through a victory of the spirit over nature. People are predestined for that, and they can perform this task, but on the way they would still go astray under the burden of their natural inclinations if they had no help from Above, in the form of Jesus Christ as the Redeemer. The church as the fellowship of believers which allows itself to be raised up by its faith in Jesus Christ is therefore necessary, but only for a time. History is moving towards a time when the stage of the 'church' is past, and the 'church' is no longer needed: humanization reaches its consummation, and the church is transformed into culture.

I am putting this into my own words, and popularizing Rothe's views somewhat, to avoid his nineteenth-century jargon. The remarkable thing is that he advanced his argument at a time when there were not yet lamentations about the state of the church in Germany. Intentionally or unintentionally one is getting involved in this if one says that the church is only a phase and not the goal of God's ways, not an end in itself. Rothe thought that the Reformation had already seen this clearly by withdrawing a great deal of public life from the power of the church (in other words 'secularizing'). Real life is not so-called church life (as many conservative Protestants still think today), but secular life, culture, one's career, one's work, one's loves and one's fellow human beings. Withdrawing from the church is not the same thing as withdrawing from Christianity; on the contrary, it is only by withdrawing from the church that the emancipation of human beings from nature is accomplished.

Rothe is an exciting, a forgotten and a neglected theologian, but two things spoil the story. First, his idea that the humanization of human beings must be regarded as a history in which human beings conquer their own nature. I don't believe that, or rather I believe that there is a demonstrable split between what we want and what we realize of it. *The God of Little Things* is about that, and the author, Arundati Roy, sums up this split in a nutshell when she describes the downfall of the Communist party in India:

Another building erected by the human spirit and brought down by human nature.

That's rather different from the conflict between natural and spiritual. It's about human nature.

Rothe's view of the kingdom of God also puts us on a false trail. He turns it into belief in progress: human beings will steadily get better, as individuals, as human beings. That was a popular idea in the nineteenth century, just as in the twentieth century it was popular for Christians to believe that the more time went on, the better society would become, both socially and politically. Neither of these two ideas will hold, as we are slowly realizing. As I have already said, the kingdom of God is the Christian utopia. 'There will be no temple there' (the vision of John on Patmos, Revelation 21.22) needn't be taken literally, as a fact realizing itself (or to be realized) in history. What I would retain from Rothe's views is the thought that withdrawing from the church needn't mean withdrawing from Christianity. Christianity also exists as culture, or, as I say in this chapter, as cultural Christianity. In terms of the topic of this book, christology, Jesus, is not only of the church but also of the world. But he is of the world in a different way, transformed into a praxis, a way of life, which is constitutive of what we call Europe. Who can say whether that will end up in a total transformation, in something like a defeat in which the church is incorporated into culture? In any case it isn't what I have in view here. Alongside church Christianity, Jesus in the church, I also see cultural Christianity: Jesus outside, the church's Christ outside, I should really say, dropped on the soil of culture, left behind. And does he do anything there?

3. Church leavers as school leavers

Does the emptying of the churches pose a threat to humankind in general and Western culture in particular? It certainly does to the on-going existence of the churches themselves. Every new statistic about people leaving the churches strikes fear into the heart of many believers. According to Cardinal Simonis, the best remain, but that seems to me rather like making a virtue out of necessity. In any case it unsettles believers. And as for 'the best' who remain, do they remain and are they the best?

No one knows, nor will I venture a prediction in any direction. It would of course be extremely sad if church Christianity, the guardian of a tradition of faith which derives its existence from the appearance of Jesus, should go under: a tragic end to a history which began so hopefully. But would it be a disaster for the world, a kind of sinking of the *Titanic*, with only a few rescued? No, not if there is also Christianity outside the church, for in that case the one around whom the church revolves, Jesus, is not only inside but also outside, not only outside the church but also – as a legacy of the church – outside culture.

If it is right that leaving the church doesn't mean leaving Christianity, to begin with we cannot regard the emptying of the churches as sheer catastrophe, which is what usually happens. For whom is it a catastrophe? For those who leave the church? In any case this isn't something to get worked up about, as many parents do when they see their children dropping out. What do they drop out of and what don't they do any more? The criterion by which this exodus is assessed is far too much the church as the real place where people live. That thought is mediaeval, the idea that there are two spheres (like the 'two swords' in politics), the worldly sphere and that of the church, and that the church sphere is the real sphere. That's how Augustine thought, and Karl Barth couldn't help following that model: for him the church was the main thing and culture incidental. I must also add that for him it was the consequence of there being only one 'Word of God', Jesus Christ, which the church can know (in faith), and thus no alternative than for culture to circle round the church. Or to *become* the church, a view which someone like Van Ruler strongly opposed – and rightly so.

In other words, the church as an institution must dissociate itself from any suggestion that things began with it. Years ago I wrote an article about the church as a kind of bellows: what goes out at the front has come in at the back. That seems to me more than ever to be a truth: people who get cold in our world, who become terrified when they no longer feel any ground under their feet, go into the church (also for their feelings), while just as many people leave the church again because they find that the church regime stifles them.

So does one keep going? Indeed, that's how the church keeps going. It can claim success: it functions, at least for part of society, as a school in which life with God is learned. But we don't spend our lives sitting at desks. After a while we've seen enough, learned enough, and we go into the world to try out what we've learned and to learn new things. The school never replaces life, nor the church culture.

So one can look at what is seen as the wretched situation of the church from a much happier perspective. Church leavers are school leavers. The Christian church need no longer be what it has been and has very much wanted to remain: a guardian of life. Enough remains for it, what Han Adriaanse calls the substance of religion, but people have outgrown the church as a guardian. The Christian church should be much more pleased about that; it should be proud that it has succeeded in leading people to live independent lives. Long ago we learned reading and writing there. When we could read and write, the pastor didn't need to do any more for us. People have done science independently, without the church; science has even become a separate activity, a necessary (which is not the same thing as sufficient) ingredient of our orientation on life. In the long run it also proved that morality could stand on its own feet, and it's a long time since we needed the church for politics. The church is no longer indispensable even for Christian faith: we can also believe outside its walls. Through the church without the church: that is the European spirit of today.

4. Cultural Christianity

Jesus bequeathed the church; at least so tradition has it. In their turn the churches bequeathed Jesus to Europe as the church's Christ. As the Christ figure, Jesus in our Western culture is no stranger: for centuries, in pictures and in words he has kept children company in school; in the museums he appears on the canvases of the great painters; and in Roman Catholic countries he stands, or rather he hangs, as the crucified one at crossroads and by the wayside. Those who know nothing of the church's Christ know nothing of their own history, and those who do not know their own history cannot interpret their existence.

A legacy is completely free, and those into whose hands it falls may do what they will with it. That also happens with the church's Christ. That is how in previous chapters I have explained the wild christologies:

Jesus (as the church's Christ) is taken over by outsiders who do what they think good with him. He plays new roles, must satisfy new religious needs outside the official religion, go new ways as guide and guru. In that case we're talking about the church's Christ as a *religious* legacy.

One could also call this cultural Christianity. Just like the Christian era which the Christian church has imposed on all the world: this book is appearing in the year of our Lord 1999. But I still regard all this as an effect of the Christian churches, a side-effect of their preaching of Christ. Jesus enters Europe riding on an ass (compare Matthew 21.1–11), the ass becomes a horse, or rather a war horse which subjects the peoples to the church's Christ, to the cross as a new law, as it is called in the documents of the early Middle Ages. And then? Then the new religion (the church's Christ instead of Wotan and Freya) once again leaves a culture behind, a culture which in turn we can again call a legacy of the church's Christ. So the term 'cultural Christianity' is no longer about the church's Christ in person, about the legacy of the churches *to* Europe, but about a phenomenon which is one step further down the road: Europe itself *as* a legacy, the church's Christ transformed into culture. That's what I mean by cultural Christianity: the point lies in the 'transformed'.

So what do we mean by culture? There are a great many descriptions of that in circulation, too many (and often too technical) to be useful. I use the word as a designation for a way of life which people share with one another, and in so doing I am thinking of both their spiritual and their material aspirations. To the degree that people share such a way of life, one can speak of a particular culture. How this came about, the role of tradition in it (no culture without tradition), I shall leave on one side here; what I have said in this chapter is sufficient.

Back to cultural Christianity, the church's Christ, changed, transformed into culture, to a recognizable unity of life. How do we make that true? Here I shall single out two cultural facts, the morality that we hold and the language that we speak (morality is also a kind of language), and by this indicate whether and to what degree one can talk of a cultural Christianity. And of course also what we are talking about in connection with it.

5. Morality as cultural Christianity (i) What is morality?

The morality of Europe is Christian: of course there are arguments over that, but in my view it can hardly be disputed. However, Christianity didn't think it up, nor invent it, but is its guardian. As for an inventor, there are as many – and as many different – group moralities as there are churches. This state of things is given with the phenomenon of morality.

There is morality as long as there are people: in fact morality is the most important factor in what is called the process of human socialization. By definition people have both parallel and conflicting interests. Take sexuality: almost all human beings have a need for a partner; in that respect they are alike, but very soon they become rivals if they want the same partner. Put positively, morality helps society to run as smoothly as possible; put negatively, it helps to avoid or reduce conflicts as far as possible. It develops along with humankind, a kind of growing light, a system of habit-forming on the basis of practical utility, guided and changed by the situation of the community (for example the climate) on the one hand and the predominant ideals of humanity on the other.

In this wide context, there was morality long before there was Christianity. The apostle Paul could therefore take over the household codes from the Stoa, an ethical philosophy from before the beginning of our era (read only Ephesians 5 and 6, assuming that Paul is the author), not to mention the Ten Commandments and the double commandment, which Christianity took over from the Jews – and they aren't the first among whom we encounter that kind of rules. So moral instructions for action do not come from above; morality is not revealed, as some Christian communities like to maintain. We (we human beings) came up with these instructions ourselves, and what religions do is to take moral requirements under their protection. The Christian church did just the same thing.

Did it also make its own contribution to morality? Unmistakably, I think. It furthered the process of socialization by its own ideal of humanity: human beings may by nature be wolves to their fellow human beings, but those who follow Jesus also love their enemies. The Christians were a peaceful folk, not aggressive; they harmed no one, says Gerd Theissen in his sociological investigation of the first generations of Christians. Their mutual concern, their commitment to one another, also made them popular with outsiders: in part it even explains their missionary power. Down the ages loving care has remained an

important ingredient of the Christian church. But in other circumstances
and under other conditions. It makes a great deal of difference whether
people help one another in a group of underdogs or in a feudal society,
like that of the Middle Ages. And while it may have been natural to love
one another, at least as a commandment, loving unbelievers is excluded,
as is shown by the Crusades (undertaken in Jesus' name) and the
Inquisition (to the greater glory of God). So the Christian church
undoubtedly contributed to the morality of Europe, but 1. we mustn't
think of this in too exclusive terms: we also encounter the idea of
loving one's enemy in the Stoa. And 2. we mustn't exaggerate. This
contribution has been inserted, down the centuries, into a social infrastructure with its classes and roles, which in turn have contributed their
own moral instructions for action. As much of what we regard as indispensable for morality has developed against the will of the Christian
church as has developed with it. So-called human rights may recogniz-
ably go back to Christian starting points (all men and women equal
before God), but they are not the product of a church concern; rather,
they came about in spite of the Christian church. The same thing applies
to freedom of religion; the church had to be fought for it. And as for
respect for the environment: the church is smartly following the prevailing morality (if we do not have to see the environment as a religion).
Of course there is nothing against terming that Christian; I'm mentioning it as an illustration of what I call demands. The church always
comes afterwards.

6. Is Christianity Christian only if it takes a Christian form? Morality as cultural Christianity (ii)

Why does traditional morality go wrong? As Marx already knew (and
he got it from Hegel), the prevailing ideals are the ideals of the rulers.
As old as Europe, morality is a network spun over human society, and
so maintaining it has always been the concern of the state: How do I
keep a grip on morality?, and of the church: How can the sheep remain
Christian? The Enlightenment wanted to get away from that: it wanted
neither the state nor the church as master. 'Ni Dieu, ni maître' is what
we owe to it. According to the Enlightenment, in place of church and
state there was only one authority which can tell people what is good
and what isn't, human beings themselves. The only thing that they
didn't mean by this was: you do it. On the contrary, provided that it is
used well, human reason as a master preserves us from immoral behaviour and arbitrariness. Immanuel Kant thought in exactly the same

way, so Kant's Reason too is a master (with good cause he wrote it with a capital letter), and a very strict one at that. Hegel could go a step further and recognize that morality precedes us; society is expressed in it, but this society consists of human beings and human beings are rational, so rational people will never have difficulties with morality.

That was extremely optimistic thinking, but with Hegel social roles were still fixed: a housewife is a housewife, a baker a baker, a father a father and a soldier a soldier. So what had to be done was clear to each of them. For 'role', think of a line by Eva Gerlachs about her father in the nursing home:

The corridor tells him how he must walk.

The corridor has gone, and therefore the walk has gone. That is the situation today: once we knew what had to be done, but the infrastructure in which we move is so changed that old customs are no longer practical and useful for the development of humanity. People feel hampered, if not enslaved, by them (think of the sexual morality of the Roman Catholic Church, which has devastated so many lives), drop them and choose their own way. Human beings aren't there for morality; morality is there for human beings. The network must make sense, otherwise it's no use; and we must be able to see the sense of it ourselves.

The churches don't talk so much about that; they talk about a bankruptcy of morality and unbridled autonomy. They mean that people cannot and may not decide for themselves what is permissible and what isn't. Not only Karl Barth, but also conservative Christians, both Protestant and Catholic, think that 'ethics is a bad idea'. The bishops then refer to the church for regulation, and orthodox Protestants to the Bible.

If this interpretation rests on a mistake, a kind of optical illusion on the part of the churches, then the summons to return to Christian norms and values completely misses the point. It is more an attempt on the part of the churches to rescue what they can from the estate and to confirm their identity by claiming their specialities as Christian or, like the Roman Catholic Church, as natural – here we have to note that Rome may say the last word about what may pass for 'natural' and what may not. Moreover, what the churches call 'Christian' must be read as 'church Christian'. As soon as one begins to supply any content, that becomes clear: different church communities prove to understand different things by it.

So it is by no means the case that only what is labelled Christian is Christian. That's certainly how it began, with the church ordering life, establishing roles, classes and status, and everyone knew what they had to do. But Christianity has become cultural: the current morality and the (inevitable) opposition to it together form a cultural Christianity. Can this be recognized over against other cultures? Certainly. We need only take the conscience, the never-resting sense of responsibility that Europeans have. That exists only in a culture of guilt like Western culture: a culture of shame isn't burdened by it. And take the content of the conscience, where the conscience is aware, say, of the infinite value of the individual (thus Harnack). That too isn't to be found in all cultures. Whether people listen to their consciences and whether they do so sufficiently is another matter. But trifling with one's conscience doesn't do away with it, far less the possibility of appealing to it.

Morality as cultural Christianity has good credentials, as I can read in a saying of Jesus in Matthew (7.12): 'Whatever you wish people to do to you, do to them', or in the negative formulation: 'Whatever you wouldn't want to happen to you, don't do to others.' 'For that is the law and the prophets,' Jesus goes on to say; in his view that is the whole of them. The good thing is that this saying (it is called the Golden Rule) can be found in many other cultures. Jesus' morality isn't exclusively Christian. He uses the rule of reciprocity, and reciprocity is the logic of morality. Nor is it too pious, as if the other should be everything, or too egotistic, as if I myself am everything. There's a balance: doing good is defined by what I myself experience as good, and doing evil by what I hope people will spare me. No principles, no values as a guideline, yet one could hardly have a better divining rod for making out where we must speak of good and where of evil.

7. *Cultural Christianity as language*

A European conscience is one manifestation of cultural Christianity. Language is a good second: I'm using 'language' as a blanket term for all the forms of expression which people use, i.e. everything where there is interpretation. Take the etching of Rembrandt which depicts Jesus before the Sanhedrin. We say that the picture speaks; the picture is an expression which says something, does something, makes people curious, perhaps moves them. For me that comes under the heading of language as speech, language which is put into speech. The madonnas are language, as are the paintings of Giotto, Grünewald's Christ; the whole of graphic art falls under language.

Europe has lived with and experienced Christian language for centuries, whether it uses words or images. It has communicated in it,
handed down what it wanted to go on telling, discussed, fought, sung
and so on: people couldn't get by without this language; it has pene-
trated all relationships, and even provided the secular communication of
images taken from the church and the Bible. Everyone knows what the
'Benjamin of the family' means and what is meant by a 'Judas kiss'; the
linguistic expressions of the Christian church were at the same time
cultural expressions. Language has been a legacy and the Christian
church the testator.

Up to the present day. People who have long ceased to be church
members use fragments of this language, with dissent or unostenta-
tiously. A doctor who doesn't go to church tells me that his spine
tingles when he switches on the BBC TV Songs of Praise. Roman
Catholic friends who have long ceased to have anything to do with their
church get a lump in their throats when they see above a death notice
'in paradisum deducant te angeli' (may the angels bear you to paradise).
We call that nostalgia, to mask our emotions. It's a colourless way of
describing what is happening: words have power to arouse a past.

So that we don't imagine it in rosier terms than it is: the same words
are exposed to wear and tear. Think of a word like sin: it dies in our
mouths. Or think of hell, heaven, atonement, damnation and so on – all
key words from the Christian tradition of faith. They haven't gone, disappeared from the vocabulary; people use them every day. But what
do they mean by them? Do they still have power to say something to
people or have they become empty words?

8. *The semantic potential*

Empty words don't do anything. Hence the poets, who preserve us from
a language of empty words, from the noise that we cannot do without
(noise means good people) but with which we cannot live. Poets confront us with the power of words; through their work we rediscover that
words do something.

Therefore poems can speak to us, even if we don't understand them.
So one could call the poem a fight against empty words.

There are still the words of the Christian tradition of faith, as I
remarked at the end of the last section, but they no longer do anything
for many people; they no longer speak to them. In our Western culture
it seems that they are increasingly empty words. Is that the end of what
I called cultural Christianity?

It will emerge that we cannot say either yes or no to this. That isn't meant to be sceptical but rather to be encouraging. Language (speech) can do something; it has a special potential. Ricoeur calls that the 'semantic potential' which clings to the Christian tradition: its words have the capacity to become meaningful again. That's another of the wonders of language (as speech); one doesn't need to be a poet to be able to experience it. We can sometimes talk about, say, heaven, and heaven can immediately roll in on us. From words we step into reality, just as formerly reality stepped into the words. I found this suggestion in Han Adriaanse, whom I quoted earlier. It opens up perspectives. Talk about something, however hackneyed it sounds, and however hackneyed the things may be that we talk about, is evidently more than just talk. Putting things into words can, miracle of miracles, bring them alive: things, people, events, as if they were slumbering in our language. But for that to happen these words must be there. That brings me to two conditions for the liberation of what we could call the 'semantic potential' of Christian words.

The first is (as I have already said) that the language which the Christian church has left as a legacy to Europe must still be present. Cultural Christianity has little future if the words of this language are simply no longer used by anyone any more. That's a good reason for the Christian church to exist, and an attractive description of its task: keeping culture alive by not killing off God. It may continue to provide the words and stories.

The second condition is that words aren't just spoken; something must happen, something that makes an impact. Anyone who sees a child killed by a truck exclaims 'O God', whether he or she is a believer or not. People always say God, heaven, hell, Jesus for some reason. When we first realized that the environmental policy could end in a catastrophe (around 1967), I read on a big poster in an Amsterdam park, 'Jesus, the world is going to pieces.' The language is, as it were, already clear; it becomes speech again by what comes over people or what they experience, and it puts the words into their mouths again. In this way they can become 'meaningful again'. I had good reasons for saying 'can'. The question is, will they?

9. *The Spirit in Europe*

In my view, the power of words, the 'semantic potential' of language, is the same thing as what the Reformed fathers called the Spirit. They connected it with the word, they could even write the word with a capital letter when they meant the power of words, 'Word and Spirit'. In classical Reformed theology they belong together.

Where words are, there is the Spirit: the Spirit shows itself in the power of words. I find that perspective in the apostle Paul when he reminds the Corinthians that the Lord is the Spirit (II Corinthians 3.17). Spirit has an element of action in it, just as when we say of someone who exudes something that he or she has spirit. That's what Paul seems to mean. When he is talking about Jesus he always (I'm thinking back to Chapter 12) has in mind the Jesus whom he preaches, the Jesus who is expressed in words and stories. These words and stories do something. How can that be? They not only have spirit but according to Paul they *are* spirit; they are the Lord transformed into Spirit. Jesus is present in the words and stories as the Spirit, as its power. 'And where the Spirit of the Lord is, there is freedom.' In passing I might also mention that we recognize the Spirit by its freedom.

Is that a bit long-winded? Not at all. Even the apostle Paul has to have an answer to the question how the Jesus of those days could have power in the present. This happens through a metamorphosis: Jesus' aggregate state changes; he turns into Spirit, into the 'semantic potential' of the language of faith.

So the 'state of the union' message about our culture needn't prove as sombre as it is often presented as being in our lamentations. The language of the Christian tradition is a power, there is an opportunity in it for the Spirit. Where there is language, there is Spirit. Not automatically, of course. Christian language (speech) is an inheritance, a legacy of the church, and, as I have said, the heirs can (and may) do what they like with the legacy: the testator no longer has any say in it. The spirit blows where it wills.

So no one can predict whether and how long the language of tradition will last, and whether the words will again become inhabited words; who the new inhabitants will be and what meanings they will attach to them. All that one can say is that we are open to this possibility from Above as long as the language of the Christian religion still has a home in Europe.

To avoid any misunderstanding: I'm far from claiming that Europe is Christian or, even more crudely, that it is a creation of Jesus Christ, as Bonhoeffer could still write in all innocence. If we still begin from Jesus as the only authentic true revelation of God, then only one conclusion is possible: the West is God's special creation in comparison with the rest of the world and its secularization is apostasy from God. That's what Bonhoeffer thought in his *Ethics* (in his *Letters and Papers* he

knew better). A Christian Europe is too much of a good thing. There is
Christianity in Europe, and we encounter that Christianity as church
and as cultural Christianity. If the church may give the spirit, there is
still the legacy of the church, the spirit of Christianity.

10. *The defence of the inheritance*

In 1529 the Turks stood at the gates of Vienna, the capital of the Holy
Roman Empire: what one might call the Europe of the time. That was
a shocking and quite terrifying event. Would Europe, Christian Europe,
be trampled under foot by Islam? Not only did the Turks have a bad
name (they employed scorched earth tactics in their campaigns of con-
quest), but they also represented a faith from which the Christian religion could expect little good. Didn't Christianity have to defend itself
against Islam and engage in a war of religion?

Luther, the German Reformer, gave serious thought to this question.
It was clearly so important to him that he dedicated at least three robust
treatises to it. I shall not go into the ins and outs of his argument
here, but only extract his solution, for reasons which will soon become
apparent. For Luther, Christianity *as faith* is a spiritual matter which
can only be defended spiritually and not with violence (with the sword,
as 'violence' could be described in those days). In his view, church and
state each form separate spheres, separate kingdoms, as he calls them,
and the two mustn't be brought together, because that causes *confusion*
(his term), and a confusion of the two kingdoms is the worst thing that
can happen to the church. Worldly rulers may not rule spiritually, nor
spiritual rulers in a worldly way. This leads to degeneration in the
church: it begins to behave like the world, and the state begins to
embellish its worldly power with power over souls. So no confusion and
therefore two kingdoms. Luther has been criticized for this down the
centuries: he was said to be a quietist, a lackey of princes, an arch-
conservative and so on.

But that isn't right. The Luther who says that faith is spiritual and
may only be defended spiritually could summon the worldly rulers to
take up the sword against the Turks, precisely on the basis of his doctrine of the two kingdoms. Provided that they didn't do it to defend the
church. The emperor has to fight against the Turks, he says somewhere:
not, however, as head of Christendom, as the guardian of Christianity,
but as the head of the worldly authority which has received from God
the duty to protect its subjects against any attacks from third parties,

including the Turks. The authority not only may do this but must do it; that is its obligation under God.

I should make it quite clear that the Turks that Luther is talking about aren't present-day Turks: that was the current term for Islam in his time. And we can leave aside the rest of his argument. What remains is the question whether there is something to defend when we are talking about Europe and cultural Christianity. The time is past for defending the church. Not only can that no longer be done with the sword, but it is far less simple to do than we thought earlier. What religious right does the church have which, for example, Islam doesn't?

But Christianity as a culture – Mozart, the St Matthew Passion, the value of the individual (especially the woman), freedom of expression through the gift of freedom, respect for civil rights by not making a Muslim a second-rate citizen? These are just a few examples, and one can think of more problematic ones. But they have to be defended. I think that we can (and may) learn from Luther that there is something to defend, that it cannot be the Christian faith but the legacy that it has left behind, the deposit in terms of Western culture.

11. *Christianity and the religions*

'Multicultural' also implies religious pluralism. Those who visit, for example, south-east Amsterdam will see that this pluralism is no longer limited to Islam and Hinduism, but includes expressions of faiths for which we do not even have a name. Christianity still prevails in the midst of them as the dominant religion, from time immemorial organized into the institutional church. What has church Christianity to do with these other religions, the rivals?

First of all, it must give up the idea that Christian faith (still) must dominate, and indeed can dominate, because it is the true faith. To be brief, that idea is fundamentalism of the first order. This fundamentalism needn't express itself in the way in which we encounter it in other religions (with the oppression of others, favouring of its own position and so on) to live from its roots. These roots lie in the claim that it is right, on the basis of whatever theory of revelation, and in the presentation of its truths as revealed truths. It's beyond recovery. Those who begin from their own truths as truths revealed by God are always right, and how far fundamentalism extends into practice depends on whether these truths involve the forced conversion of others.

Take mission. I'm not saying that Christianity mustn't be exported. One can export everything of value, including religion. Moreover, the

Christian religion has a universal dimension, in so far as the Christian picture of God doesn't see God as a specific saviour from all need (to make just one point) but as creator and sustainer of human beings and the world, a feature which it shares with Judaism and Islam. But the story immediately stops there. Those who read church history, especially the history of the Christianization of Europe (for example in the readable book by Peter Brown) will look with bewilderment at the tricks, the manipulations, the regular extortions and marauding expeditions by means of which Christian rulers extended their territory, and in passing Christianized the territories that they had conquered (sometimes, conversely, Christianizing them in order to conquer them). Whatever blessings Christianity brought to Europe, it got a firm footing by means which were in conflict with its own preaching. The only justification advanced for that was the revealed character of the Christian truth. Should mission still have that as its foundation, then we could hardly see this as anything other than a continuation of fundamentalism.

At this point, too, it seems to me that theology must become somewhat clearer. I can understand the wrestling with tradition, with the question how true truth is, but this question must be resolved without the thought that the exclusivity of Christian truth is indispensable. If people continue to start from that, all the space that they give to other religions proves illusory. In a German paper I read that this question could be solved by speaking of an 'inclusive exclusivity'. That was meant to be a formulation by means of which justice was done to both sides: the right of the other religions to exist and the truth of Christianity. I see that as a last attempt to maintain the exclusivity of Christian truth through a fudging of terms: the others may share provided that they fit in with Christianity.

No, in that case Peter Bishop's question is much better: can Christianity be true in a way which doesn't involve the other religions being untrue? That seems to me to be the only good question. Is there an answer?

Certainly. In principle it amounts to the fact that people speak about Above from below and that everything that we can contribute to religious knowledge is knowledge in terms of a picture which awaits confirmation, the only confirmation that is possible, from Above. In other words, pictures are expressions of quests. Believing as living with pictures of God and his salvation involves: 1. Being aware of the existence of others, each with their own pictures of God (whether they themselves see it like that is another matter), and taking their honesty as seriously as our own. 2. Adhering to our own picture because it feeds us, has brought us the experience of that discovery. The relativity of religious notions can go along with believing, just as seeking can go along with finding.

That doesn't imply that all religions are right, by any means. Nor does it imply that we need immediately accept anything, from whatever religion. It implies that we must let go of the claim to exclusiveness without letting go of the fact that we are completely caught up in the picture of our own religion: it is our picture.

20

By way of a summary

1. *What this christology is arguing for*

The changes in christology which I argue for in this book are drastic. The question remains what there is to be said for this christological scheme. I shall formulate my answer as a summary, in the form of theses, first of all in terms of the conditions for a Christian christology.

1. A christology has Jesus of Nazareth as its subject, in the sense that it seeks to express his significance. A first condition for this is that he himself appears in it as a historical figure. It's a question of *his* significance. That distinguishes christology from a myth, a story about the gods. Human beings can also benefit from this, but that isn't the 'benefit' that Christian faith is talking about. We know one thing for certain about the historical Jesus: his faith. He was a member of the Jewish religion. A christology into which the faith of Jesus will not fit is a christology without Jesus himself.

2. Jesus' God was God according to the Jewish picture, the God of the Jewish religion. Jesus saw himself as God's servant, as an instrument, as the one who carries out God's will. Jesus can be important to people only in so far as they think God (from now on the God of the Jewish picture) important. Who is God? That proves to be the only really central question in the christology which I present.

3. That Jesus followed the Jewish picture of God means that he never saw himself as God-on-earth. To see Jesus as other than a further description of God is to do him violence. He isn't a second God, or the second person of the Holy Trinity, who took flesh from the Virgin Mary. The purpose behind these doctrines is clear: worship of Jesus as God-man raises a problem. The solution is unnecessarily complicated, a theological theory, good for theologians who talk with theologians and so by no means invalid: why not speculative discussion about God? But for ordinary people (non-theologians), it is simply an incomprehensible sacred formula (its holiness lies in its incomprehensibility), by which some Christians seek to indicate their identity as Christians in the midst of other religions.

4. The doctrine of the two natures (the divine and the human nature are united in one person unconfusedly, unchangeably, indivisibly, inseparably) is a phase in coping with the problem that was created with Jesus as God-on-earth, and is utterly dependent on this notion. It has as little claim to eternity as the Gnostic Jesus or the Jesus of the Enlightenment. If Christians don't want to have a different religion from Jesus, then they must dissociate themselves from the two natures as a Hellenistic form of worship, and see no more in it than the halo that we find in children's Bibles.

5. The idea of Jesus as a Second God, as God-on-earth, is responsible for a form of piety in which Jesus is made the centre of the believer's experience: the believer lives with Jesus instead of with God. That's moving in the case of children ('Mummy is with Jesus'), but in this way adults make Jesus a substitute for God, like Mary, who in turn came to replace Jesus. God himself is shifted to the periphery.

6. In the christology which I propose, something happens, something indispensable, a 'saving fact', to use the classical terminology. It is not that God is born as a child (Jesus isn't God) or that God is led to think otherwise by the cross of Jesus. God doesn't first begin to be merciful and gracious, righteous and great in loving-kindness, when Jesus appears on the scene. He was already that; that is how Jesus preached him. According to Christianity the great event is that from now on God's mercy can also be preached to non-Jews: in Jesus they have their scapegoat, and in Good Friday their Day of Atonement.

7. In this christology, doom is the same for all human beings, Jews or Gentiles: the failure of human beings to stand before Creator and creation, God and fellow human being. Human responsibility is the presupposition of this shortcoming. Reconciliation with God, in the sense of taking away the guilt that human beings load on themselves, is a precondition for dealing with the Creator.

8. Since Jesus, non-Jews may relate to God in the same way as Jews. Through the ritual of the atonement they play at being righteous before God; they belong to the God of Abraham and Jesus, and can begin a new life.

9. The controversy between Jews and Christians is not over Jesus as the God-man ('Christians believe that, and Jews don't'), but over the proclamation of Jesus as the opening of the way to Israel's God for non-Jews. The Jewish and Christian pictures of God do not differ in content; at least they needn't. The difference lies in their scope; all people are God's people.

10. This christology simplifies Christian faith, and helps it to escape

a crust of doctrine which has grown over it historically. It lets people live before God's face, doesn't compel them to accept eccentric notions on pain of ceasing to be Christian, and in addition also allows relations with other religions.

2. *Jesus cannot replace God*

Why a revision? In order to restore to God his place in Christian belief. To a considerable degree God has surrendered this place to Jesus as second God. What I want to do in this book is to put a brake on this development, which is going too far. Jesus is of vital importance for Christians; they wouldn't be there as a Christian community had there been no Jesus. But the worship of Jesus has gone beyond the bounds of faith, and the Christian church has lost the power (and the right) to change that. 'It did not please the deity to pour itself out in one instance,' said David Friedrich Strauss. The Christian church maintained that it indeed pleased the deity (God) to do this, and as long as its authority was unbroken, there was only this one 'instance', Jesus Christ as the only manifestation of God on earth. But the Christian church has lost its authority, the floodgates have opened, and manifestations of God are cropping up everywhere, sometimes in the garb of Christ figures. I think that these wild christologies are an unintentional but nevertheless real consequence of the church's christology; they undermine 'God is in heaven and you are on earth'. My plea is to go back to believing as a relationship with God.

The other side of the coin is to liberate christology from being overloaded. It isn't possible to fill the God-shaped gap with Jesus; that's a reversal of the relationship between Jesus and God. As an instrument of God, as the one who carries out God's purposes, Jesus derives his importance from God and not vice versa. God doesn't derive his importance from Jesus. Those who have no interest in God and his ways also have no interest in Jesus, at least in the Jesus who lived at the beginning of our era. Jesus stands or falls with the scheme of God. If that fails, there is no more Jesus, at least no more Christian Jesus.

So the appearance of Jesus doesn't make the Christian religion more certain. That was the intention: God-on-earth, what more could you want? But this idea is itself a view of faith and not a safeguard for Christian faith, an extra hook on which we can hang our faith. Like the picture of God that Christians have, their christology, too, is 'from below'. Theologians who say 'revelation' when they mean Christian faith and 'the centre of revelation' when they bring Jesus on the scene forget that. They argue from the idea that the Christian faith is a universally accepted truth, even if it hasn't been proved, rather than one faith among others.

But all religions must prove themselves. That's also true of Christian faith. It isn't better off or safer provided that it can legitimate itself from Judaism, since the Jewish religion too has the status of a picture. So 'God has revealed himself in Jesus Christ' doesn't solve the riddles of the world; on the contrary, it is one of the riddles of the world. How can the Christian picture of God be 'the end' now that there prove to be other pictures?

3. Christology isn't everything

That Jesus cannot replace God also means that Jesus isn't the solution to all the questions of life. For this the Christian religion points to God. Jesus becomes 'meaningful' as a bridge to God, so he is recalled, preached and worshipped: as the Jesus of the atonement, of the ritual to which non-Jews owe their access to God. In so far as non-Jews encountered God (merciful and gracious is the Lord) for the first time in the preaching of Jesus, Jesus has become the face of God for them. However, he is not God himself, the one to whom Christians address their prayers. Jesus is called 'the way', and the way isn't where you want to be; the way takes you there.

When it comes to the questions of life, the load-bearing capacity of christology is limited. What it leaves out is no less important; it simply says that Jesus cannot become 'meaningful' in every connection. Some existential questions are exposed in christology, or really only one. If we overlook that, then that a whole host of tortuous constructions come rushing in that lay all human needs and aspirations at Jesus' feet: will he please fulfil them or at least take them under his protection? He doesn't do that; as Jesus Christ he isn't equipped to do so. According to him you must go to God for that.

Selection = which sinew of human existence is exposed in christology? Even if we ourselves have become insensitive to it, christology draws our attention to its presence. For christology read the preaching of Jesus and we are where the church has to be when Jesus becomes the theme. From my perspective this open sinew of human existence is and remains the problem of 'guilt and penitence', the roots of which lie in human responsibility and having knowledge of them (= the conscience). It is a mistake to think that only the Jews know about this. The classic tragedies of the Greeks present the topic in a way which catches us by the throat when they show us how guilt pursues people, down the generations, and how heavy is the burden, the jumble of burdens, which people have to bear once they have become guilty. Even if that happens involuntarily, guilt remains guilt. King Oedipus is married to his mother without knowing it, has become guilty through no fault of his own. Nevertheless he accepts what he has done, leaves the throne and goes into exile. Such a tragedy endures over the centuries; it bears witness to a deep insight into the human situation, a deeper insight than that of some Christians today, who would much prefer 'guilt and penitence' to disappear from Christian christology.

Death is another problem which constantly returns: the frustration at dying, sorrow over the great separation, and uncertainty about what comes next. The apostle Paul links (sin,) guilt and death together. We needn't follow him here in making sin an explanation of the origin of death. That's outdated wisdom. Nevertheless we can sympathize with the link: death destroys what is dear to us. It's part of human existence, but according to the apostle the sinner can do nothing about it. Suffering belongs in the same cluster: it's an announcement of death, a foretaste.

There is no mistaking the fact that the 'eternal problems' of humankind also include survival, procreation, the political ordering of society and the social ordering of the desire for possession. There too we need answers, but we needn't go to christology for them. Jesus cannot be 'meaningful' for all problems of life, not even all the problems of action (think of politics in the sense of the formation of political power, of violence and war) without Jesus being made a monster and christology a panacea.

4. Back to God

Why is Jesus so necessary? Who needs him? It is Christians themselves who – following the apostle Paul – interpret Jesus as their scapegoat, the lamb of God who takes away the sins of the world (or whatever ritual people prefer), because their legitimation in the face of the Jews, from whom they have detached themselves, depends on it. They walk on the thin ice of Paul's interpretation, but are all too happy to believe him: this interpretation is the branch on which they sit. Moreover they share in the course of history: Jesus *has* become the gate to God for non-Jews, though he seemed rather different. In passing, people believe only if they think it important to have a way to God.

We have to go to the God of Jesus. That is what Jesus himself proclaimed. Since he has been preached as a scapegoat, non-Jews have also been called. That is the preaching of Christ: Jesus-preaching as back-to-God preaching. God is the important one. So I see Christian christology as a back-to-God movement, and Christian preaching as a preaching of God. 'He preached Jesus = he preached access to God for non-Jews.' 'Put your trust in the Lord Jesus = believe that God has an ear that also listens to non-Jews, and an eye that also sees non-Jews.' This is the God for whom Jesus also spent himself.

Back to God – here I am not arguing for the abolition of Jesus piety, but for a shift in it. Jesus as a metaphor of God: we say Jesus but mean God by it. That doesn't make Jesus God; on the contrary, it brings Jesus back where he belongs, to God, a further definition of God, an extra clarification of God, a characteristic of God, meaning that he is also there for non-Jews.

Acknowledgments

This book is the result of decades of dealing with the Christian tradition of faith and what has been written about it, as a trained practitioner of theology. For that reason alone it is impossible for me to provide the reader with a detailed apparatus of notes which would show where I have got everything from. Now and then authors are mentioned in the text whose remarks are engraved on my memory. However, I am indebted not only to them but to all my predecessors and contemporaries for what I have taken from them. I have reread some authors, especially Albert Schweitzer, David Friedrich Strauss and Gotthold Ephraim Lessing. I also steeped myself in, or read for the first time, T. Baarda, Peter Bishop, Peter Brown, Maarten van Buuren, Theo L. Hettema, Franz Mussner, Edward Schillebeeckx, Reinhard Slenczka and Ellen van Wolde, who here stand for many other newcomers from whom I have learned much.

Some of the authors of Jesus books which I have read are mentioned in the text. There are others that I have read and even more that I have not read, and more still of the existence of which I am not even aware.

A short list of books referred to in the text has been added to the English edition.

For further reading

Hendrikus Berkhof, *Christian Faith*, Eerdmans and T.&.T.Clark 1980

Marcus Borg, *Jesus. A New Vision*, Harper and Row 1987

Lucas Grollenberg, *Jesus,* SCM Press 1978

C.J.den Heyer, *Jesus Matters*, SCM Press and Trinity Press International 1996

David Flusser, *Jesus*, Herder and Herder 1969

H.M.Kuitert, *I Have My Doubts*, SCM Press 1993

Reimarus, Fragments, edited by C.H.Talbert, Fortress Press 1970 and SCM Press 1971

E.P.Sanders, *Jesus and Judaism*, SCM Press and Trinity Press International 1984

Edward Schillebeeckx, *Jesus. An Experiment in Christology*, Collins 1979

Albert Schweitzer, *The Quest of the Historical Jesus*, SCM Press 1983

D.F.Strauss, *Life of Jesus*, reissued by SCM Press and Fortress Press 1973

Nico ter Linden, *The Story Goes: 1. The Stories of the Torah*, SCM Press 1999

Nico ter Linden, *The Story Goes: 2. Matthew's Story and Mark's Story*, SCM Press 1999

Gerd Theissen and Annette Merz, *The Historical Jesus*, SCM Press and Fortress Press 1998

Ellen van Wolde, *Stories of the Beginning*, SCM Press 1996

Index

To make passages easier to find, here is an index of names.